T0301992

The Private Sector's Role in Disasters

Leveraging the Private Sector in
Emergency Management

The Private Sector's Role in Disasters

Leveraging the Private Sector in Emergency Management

Alessandra Jerolleman
John J. Kiefer

CRC Press
Taylor & Francis Group
Boca Raton London New York

CRC Press is an imprint of the
Taylor & Francis Group, an **informa** business

CRC Press
Taylor & Francis Group
6000 Broken Sound Parkway NW, Suite 300
Boca Raton, FL 33487-2742

First issued in paperback 2021

ISBN 13: 978-1-03-224267-5 (pbk)
ISBN 13: 978-1-4822-4408-3 (hbk)

Visit the Taylor & Francis Web site at
http://www.taylorandfrancis.com

and the CRC Press Web site at
http://www.crcpress.com

CONTENTS

CONTENTS

EDITORS

Alessandra Jerolleman, PhD, CFM, is a senior emergency management and hazard mitigation planner for JEO Consulting Group Inc., as well as the executive director of the Natural Hazard Mitigation Association. Dr. Jerolleman's experience includes the following: serving as a program specialist in the Gulf Coast with Save the Children USA; working on a resilience initiative around children's needs in emergencies; hazard mitigation planning at the local, state, and campus levels; community education and outreach regarding mitigation measures and preparedness; development of collaborative networks and information-sharing avenues among practitioners; and delivery of training and education to various stakeholders. Dr. Jerolleman is one of the founders of the Natural Hazard Mitigation Association (NHMA) and has served as executive director since its inception. She is involved in various aspects of planning and policy at the national and local levels, including participation in several workshops each year. Dr. Jerolleman speaks on many topics, including hazard mitigation and climate change; campus planning; threat, hazard, and vulnerability assessments; hazard mitigation planning; protecting children in disasters; and public–private partnerships.

John J. Kiefer, PhD, is professor and director of the MPA program at the Department of Political Science at the University of New Orleans (UNO). He is also a faculty associate at the Center for Hazards Assessment, Response and Technology (CHART), UNO's applied hazards social science research center. In his applied research, Dr. Kiefer specializes in the development of outcome-focused collaborative networks to create disaster resilience, especially focused on vulnerable populations. He is currently either principal investigator or a research team member for several projects that include elderly evacuation, technology initiatives for vulnerable populations, repetitive flood loss mitigation, and a disaster-resilient university project. John has been principal evaluator for a broad range of programs funded by the U.S. Department of Education, State of Louisiana, and several cities. He has delivered numerous papers and chaired panels at professional meetings in the United States and Canada. John serves on the Executive Board of the Southeastern Conference for Public Administration. His current research interests include hazard policy, emergency management, and program evaluation.

CONTRIBUTORS

Jacqueline Brubaker
University of New Orleans
New Orleans, Louisiana

Monica Farris
University of New Orleans
New Orleans, Louisiana

Sabrina Freeman
University of New Orleans
New Orleans, Louisiana

Susan Lenore Garner
University of New Orleans
New Orleans, Louisiana

Race A. Hodges
University of New Orleans
New Orleans, Louisiana

Jeremiah Jones
University of New Orleans
New Orleans, Louisiana

Tara Lambeth
University of New Orleans
New Orleans, Louisiana

Lawrence Mason III
University of New Orleans
New Orleans, Louisiana

Maggie Louise Olivier
Jefferson Parish
New Orleans, Louisiana

Kimberly VanWagner
University of New Orleans
New Orleans, Louisiana

Sarah Wild
University of New Orleans
New Orleans, Louisiana

Melissa Wilkins
University of New Orleans
New Orleans, Louisiana

INTRODUCTION

This text explores the role of the private sector, including the intersection of the private sector with government in all phases of emergency management. The private sector plays a tremendous role in the creation of policies related to emergency management, as well as their implementation at the federal, state, and local levels. At times, public–private partnerships allow for greater leveraging of resources. At other times, the private sector simply provides services for a fee—with varying results. The intergovernmental transactions required for emergency management are further complicated when contractors interact with each other on behalf of the government agencies by which they have been hired. This creates a situation in which employees of firms that compete for similar work are in the position of essentially regulating one another.

The chapters in this book examine the role of the private sector in emergency management, and how that role is changing over time. They cover some of the policy and implementation challenges posed by the current contracting model, while comparing emergency management to other government services that have been privatized. This book looks at the areas where government regulation and guidelines promote or encourage private sector involvement. It also looks at best practices for public–private partnerships and some common pitfalls of the contracting model. Although there has been a recent focus by the federal government on the value of public–private partnerships in local emergency management, as shown within several recently published documents, these documents have largely ignored the use of the private sector as contractors.

The characteristics of private sector involvement in emergency management heavily influence the outcomes, and can be quite complex. There are a wide range of private sector entities involved, ranging from individuals who work as consultants, usually involved in small local efforts such as mitigation planning, to the national and global firms that work at the state or federal levels. In between these two extremes are small- to medium-sized firms that become active in in the industry through the natural course of business expansion and are able to develop a professional reputation for themselves locally. These firms may be primarily engineering, planning, or geographic information system (GIS) firms that have developed a disaster response/recovery specialization and have added specialists in the other areas as needed.

Just as the range of private firms is complex, interactions between various private sector entities and various levels of government are also quite varied. There are a number of possible scenarios, ranging from a small firm working one-on-one with a local government, to a large firm under contract to the federal government to administer grants at the state level, to a medium-sized firm under hire, to a large firm contracted to coordinate Public Assistance (a federal program that provides funds for repairing damaged public facilities) efforts at the local level. For example, large national firms are far more likely to be involved with federal mitigation efforts and far less likely to pursue the much smaller contracts available for local planning in small jurisdictions.

Emergency management has never been formally nor completely privatized* (i.e., the entire service has not been sold to a corporate entity†), yet there is much in the literature on privatization that can be used to explore the pros and cons of privatization in other areas of service delivery. There is an extensive body of literature in the fields of public administration and political science that has looked at the privatization of government services in general and that has focused on particular contexts such as those that involve schools and prisons. This literature, which serves as a starting point for this analysis, includes works by Calhoun (2006), Chamberlin (1987), Denhart & Grubbs (2003), Feigenbaum & Henig (1994), Franklin (1998), Giddens (1998), Gormley & Balla (2004), Healy & Malhorta (2008), Heclo (1978), Lipsky (1980), Moe (1987), O'Toole (1999), Trebilcock & Iacobucci (2003), among others. These works, while not specifically focused on emergency management, provide a historical context for the time period when privatization advanced within the realm of hazard mitigation and disaster recovery. The literature has focused heavily on the *make-or-buy decision*, more specifically on the decision of whether to perform a service or to purchase

---

* Savas (1987) defined privatization as: "… the act of reducing the role of government, or increasing the role of the private sector, in an activity." Under this definition, hazard mitigation could be said to be privatized.

† In hazard mitigation planning, just one component of hazard mitigation, the vast majority of local and state plans are written with the use of a consultant (Respondent 25).

it. This includes extensive discussion of the strengths, weaknesses, and dangers of increasing private involvement in activities that are under the cognizance and responsibilities of local, state, regional, and/or national governments.

HISTORY AND EVOLUTION
OF GOVERNMENT–PRIVATE RELATIONSHIPS

The discussion of privatization has a long history within the fields of political science and public administration. In fact, the field of public administration was born out of a desire to understand how the business of governing differed from that of private business. The earliest literature deals with the question of whether some government services ought to be provided by the private sector and with the question of how to determine which sector—public or private—is best suited to serve the public. The federal government itself has provided guidance on when it is appropriate to use the private sector. As an example, Budget Bulletin No. 55-4 (BB 1995) indicates that federal policy is to not produce products or to provide services that are available from the private sector. This guidance, from 1995, indicates the existence of a political and government climate favorable to private provision of services. However, Part 7.5 of the Federal Acquisition Regulations indicates that activities that "significantly affect the life, liberty, or property of private persons" ought not to be contracted out. This guidance provides a clear test for the make-or-buy decision, but it does not appear to have been applied to the creation and implementation of emergency management programs. Outside of emergency management (which certainly influences life, safety, and property), this is mirrored in the privatization of prisons, police departments, and national security, all of which would appear to go against this guidance.

In the case of many emergency management programs, it appears there was an assumption (as evidenced by the lack of attention to the make-or-buy decision) that privatization would be the best, or possibly the only, option. Several things led to the decision to use the private sector: (1) the strong, ideological preference for privatization at that time period (Cohen & Eimicke, 2008); (2) the existence of firms that had relationships with the Federal Emergency Management Agency (FEMA) and that were well positioned to add another product line; and (3) in the case of hazard mitigation, the concern that risk assessments were too complicated for most communities. Considering the existing climate, primarily the New Public Management (NPM)* movement that was emerging in the United States at the time of the creation of hazard mitigation policy and activities, it is not surprising that the private sector played such a key role. Furthermore, once private firms were hired to draft the programmatic guidance, they operated from the assumption that the local implementation would involve similar (or sometimes the same) firms. This reliance on private sector expertise and on labor by bureaucrats is currently seen at both the federal and local levels (Cohen & Eimicke, 2008), with the federal government currently using more contractors than at any other time in history (Breul, 2010). It is therefore not surprising that so little attention was paid to the make-or-buy decision.

The United States has a long history of growing corporate power, dating back to the period immediately following the Civil War, in which emerging national industries were successful in utilizing the 13th and 14th Amendments to establish themselves as legal persons (Reid & Taylor, 2010). This granted corporations greatly expanded powers, and reduced liability, all assisting with the creation of the multinational firms in existence today. The structure of the U.S. government, with such different authorities at the local, state, and federal levels, also served to allow corporations to grow in their power and influence, as corporations are able to work at the level of government that allows them the greatest influence and at which the regulations are less onerous. Savas (1987) describes various pressures for privatization across government programs, including the search for more cost-effective services, ideological bent, the desire to enrich corporations, and the desire for less bureaucracy. These various pressures were all present at the time in which hazard mitigation, and other emergency management programs, were created. All of this affected the eventual push toward privatization of government functions. When it came to discussions regarding planning as a component of emergency management, there were existing interest groups as far back as 1932 looking at public planning as a route to profits (Fischer, 2005).

It is possible, however, to identify clear criteria within the literature related to whether a practice should be privatized and to consider these criteria when evaluating how the various phases of emergency management fall within the typology created by the various authors who address

---

* NPM emerged in the 1980s in response to the high, public expenditures that had characterized the 1980s and grew in momentum through the fiscal crisis of the 1980s and 1990s. Although NPM does not specifically call for privatization, privatization is seen as clearly meeting the efficiency objectives of the NPM (Foster & Plowden, 1996).

the make-or-buy decision. These criteria are illustrated in Table 0.1. One example of these criteria is John Chamberlin's and John Jackson's 1987 article on privatization, which provides an analysis of the appropriate time for public institutions to pursue the privatization approach. They create a clear dichotomy between a situation in which privatization is appropriate (frequent purchases, abundant information, active competition, and low cost of mistakes) and a situation in which there are collective interests,* distributional goals,† and the presence of natural monopolies—making public provision the best option. Chamberlin and Jackson's work, however, fails to clearly address what should be done with services or goods that have characteristics that do not clearly put them into one of the two groupings. This is the case with the various phases of emergency management. It is unclear to which *provider*—public or private—the function should be assigned.

On the basis of the elements that Chamberlin and Jackson suggest make privatization appropriate, emergency management services are not necessarily a good fit. Communities do not make *frequent purchases* because hazard mitigation planning occurs only every five years at the county level and because projects typically occur after a disaster (Godschalk, 1999). Given the technical nature of data analysis for many hazards and the lack of knowledge at the local level regarding the technical aspects of emergency management, *abundant information* is also lacking. *Competition* can sometimes be in place, but more often than not, a very small range of firms is involved. Finally, *mistakes* can carry high costs because what is at stake is a community's resilience. Thus, the typology suggests that privatization of emergency management services would be considered highly risky.

Several other authors observe the challenges of privatization for services in which there is insufficient information or no clear way for the purchaser to select between options. If the phases of emergency management fit these criteria, then they may be services that ought not to be privatized. One phase of emergency management, hazard mitigation, for example, is a specialized activity, making it nearly impossible for a local government purchaser to judge the product it is receiving or for it to select between providers, especially during the creation of the first plan

---

* Collective interests refer to the need to consider not just individual needs but those of society as a whole.
† Distributional goals refer to the need to ensure fairness in distribution of a good or service.

Table 0.1 Criteria for Privatization Decision

Criteria[a]	Private Provision Recommended	Public Provision Recommended	Application to Hazard Mitigation
Frequent purchases	×		Most communities do not frequently purchase hazard mitigation services. Hazard mitigation plan updates take place every five years at the local level, and major disasters can be infrequent.
Abundant information		×	Hazard mitigation has many technical requirements and is not always fully understood by communities. Those at the local level making the contracting decisions cannot easily evaluate the private sector firms.
Active competition	×	×	The amount of competition varies by the location and size of the community needing hazard mitigation services. Large communities, or states with substantial amounts of money available, may see significant competition. Smaller communities may struggle to receive any bids at all. Additionally, there is a small group of firms that consistently obtains the majority of the larger federal contracts—all of which frequently work together. **There is too much variability in hazard mitigation for these criteria to be fully evaluated.**
Low cost of mistakes		×	Hazard mitigation decisions have a great deal to do with the health and safety of residents, as well as with continuity of government and economic vitality. As a result, the consequences of mistakes can be quite high.
Collective interests		×	Hazard mitigation decisions have to do with the whole community, and must take into account the needs of society as a whole.
Distributional goals		×	Hazard mitigation efforts must strive to ensure that all stakeholders are included and given a voice.

[a] Chamberlin & Jackson, 1987.

done by the community and in the first few subsequent revisions of that plan. Hazard mitigation then may create a market failure,* as is described in Table 0.1.

As Table 0.1 indicates, the criteria provided within the literature would not support the use of the private sector for the provision of hazard mitigation. Yet many authors argue that the private sector is inherently better suited to the provision of some services (perhaps mitigation) despite these concerns and that the private sector is more efficient and is better able to mobilize resources (Foster & Plowden, 1996; Trebilcock & Iacobucci, 2003) regardless of the concerns mentioned by Chamberlin and Jackson. In fact, it is argued that as government budgets continue to be reduced, the private sector may have a much greater capacity than the public sector to provide good quality services (Frederickson & Frederickson, 2007). In the case of hazard mitigation, it is not clear that the public sector could provide these services without private assistance due to the costs, to the infrequent need for the expertise, and to the technical nature of the service.

The notion of market failure is worth revisiting. As Bozeman (2007) points out, market failure theory states that the market is the best tool for the provision of services unless there is a monopoly or a lack of information to customers. Warner (2010) has predicted that lack of competition in local government service markets will actually lead to a reversal of the privatization process. When the characteristics are present for market failure to take place (such as a monopoly or inability to accurately judge between service providers), the inherent regulatory functions of the market, which are typically considered to be the best and most efficient providers of quality goods, do not operate. If this is the case, then the use of the private sector to ensure that a service is provided by the most efficient means possible is not feasible.

It is worth examining whether the phases of emergency management fit these criteria. Given the relatively small number of major firms involved and given the challenges of judging the quality of services provided or of evaluating consultants, it would appear that emergency management is an industry in which market failure is taking place and that the market is not able to ensure that the best quality services are provided. If this is indeed the case, then one of the major arguments in favor of privatization, that of increased efficiency and quality through the market, does not hold true for emergency management.

---

* Market failure takes place when the free market cannot efficiently allocate goods and services.

Another cause of market failure listed by Bozeman is the concept of externalities. Some examples are benefits provided to persons who do not pay for the goods or costs taken on by society as a whole for the decisions or benefit of a minority (e.g., construction in unsafe areas). In a sense, public services such as hazard mitigation do just that. The current mechanisms for disaster recovery, including the hazard mitigation component, provide assistance to those who have experienced damages, even if those damages were preventable and were the result of poor decisions. The costs of bad decisions by one community are born by taxpayers in general. Additionally, the benefits of mitigation planning and projects accrue to the community as a whole regardless of who pays for the services or participates in the process. If it is the case that market failure is indeed occurring and that hazard mitigation does not meet the criteria in the literature for privatizing a service, then the question must be raised as to whether hazard mitigation ought to be provided by the public sector. Again, this conclusion might have to be tempered by the potential inability of the public sector to provide these services, regardless of who ought to be providing them. The conundrum of mitigation appears to be that even if it is a service that should not be privatized, the public sector may not be able to otherwise provide it.

Returning to the question of whether hazard mitigation is a service that meets the criteria for privatization, it is important to note that the Disaster Mitigation Act of 2000 (DMA 2000),* which amended the Stafford Act, came about at a time in which privatization was seen as desirable and unquestionably accepted. In Europe, many government functions had been sold to the private sector as early as the late 1970s. In the United States, privatization began to gain momentum following the NPM movement, as described previously. However, the U.S. model was more focused on contracting and not on wholesale transfer of government functions (Henig, 1989–1990). Both models still favor private sector provision of public services. The literature described above does not always distinguish between the privatization model being used, a fact that may limit the direct applicability of the recommendations discussed earlier. However, the literature describing the evolution of privatization clearly shows that the federal hazard mitigation programs came about at a time when private sector provision was becoming the norm, both nationally and internationally. Although there may have been some concerns expressed in the theory, contracting was rapidly growing and was heavily promoted as

---

* DMA (2000) established the requirement for hazard mitigation planning.

a means to reduce government spending. The mitigation programs that focus on disaster recovery also saw heavy private sector involvement, as did those providing mitigation services.

The social sciences literature on natural hazards describes these privatization trends following disasters (Klein, 2007). In particular, the discussion regarding the pros and cons of privatization and the one regarding the evaluation criteria for the make-or-buy decision take into consideration potential outcomes. In their discussion of the decision to make or to buy a good or service, Chamberlin and Jackson (1987) divide goods and services into three categories: government-owned assets, goods and services consumed by government agencies, and goods and services delivered directly to private citizens and firms. They suggest that the third category provides more challenges for the use of private sector contracts, a suggestion that is similar to that made by the various theorists described previously; they suggest that there may be challenges related to equity and distribution in services provided directly to the public. Many of the hazard mitigation activities that are typically managed by private sector firms following a disaster fall into the third category, that of goods and services delivered directly to the community, although a great deal of planning might fall into the second. This appears to indicate that there may be particular challenges in ensuring accountability and equity in the private sector provision of these services. In particular, one interesting observation by Chamberlin and Jackson (1987) regarding the use of the private sector for the third category is that the practice of paying a flat rate per person served discourages corporations from serving those clients with the greatest needs and who will require the most investment of time. This earlier finding has implications for the research reported herein. This exact allegation was made against the Road Home program (a private sector firm had been contracted to manage distribution of recovery dollars) in Louisiana following Hurricane Katrina, but there were multiple complaints regarding the appeals process and the ability of the firm to treat all applicants fairly (Scott, 2009). More specifically, there was a concern that the terms of the contract, which were based on a total number of cases, allowed the firm to focus on the easier cases in order to quickly meet the assigned deliverable of cases. Additionally, the Road Home program was not responsive to local concerns and did not take into account the content of local plans. According to FEMA, in a letter dated February 2, 2007, to the Louisiana Governor's Office of Homeland Security and Emergency Preparedness, "Initial Road Home decisions are currently being made without regard for the local communities' development plans and local mitigation plans" (FEMA, 2007).

Many of the challenges with the management of the Road Home program stemmed from the contract between the Louisiana Recovery Authority and ICF International. The contract did not contain clear performance goals and the state was later unable to add them as the program began to be questioned. As one editorial stated, "ICF's abysmal management of the Road Home program hampered people's recovery from the 2005 hurricanes and caused great misery and hardship" (Sisco, 2009). The state of Louisiana also had to enter into disputes with ICF over the billing of legal expenses for ICF to defend itself against lawsuits by employees (Scott, 2009). When ICF was finally replaced, it was replaced by a former subcontractor, HGI, who had initially come onto the ICF team in 2006 with a contract worth over $70 million, despite allegedly having very little experience in the work it was being hired to do (Scott, 2009).

EVALUATING EFFORTS

As the Road Home example illustrates, there are many challenges to evaluating contracts for certain types of hazard mitigation services. Chamberlin and Jackson (1987) propose two types of evaluation criteria for privatization efforts that may prove useful to this discussion: outcome-oriented criteria, which include efficiency, distribution, and innovation, and process criteria, which include decision costs,* due process, and responsiveness. The majority of the literature currently available regarding privatization, including arguments for and against the practice, focuses primarily on outcome criteria, some of which are the focus of the make-or-buy decision and are illustrated in Table 0.1. The criterion cited the most often is efficiency, with several theorists, such as Ronald Moe (1987), describing privatization as originating from the notion that the public sector is less efficient than the private sector and should therefore be replaced by the marketplace whenever possible. However, this research will examine whether responsiveness to the client as well as the other process criteria described by Chamberlin and Jackson (1987) should be the evaluation criteria for an adequate assessment of the role of the private sector in mitigation.

---

* Decision costs (which can be difficult to know beforehand) include the costs or negative impacts that may result from a particular decision or from not selecting a particular option. They also include the unanticipated costs such as the need to invest in management and oversight.

The dichotomy presented by Chamberlin and Jackson (1987) regarding outcomes and process appears to imply that there are fundamental differences between the public and private sectors. However, the article does not clearly articulate what those might be. Other theorists, such as Moe, have attempted to draw a clearer distinction between the two sectors. According to Moe (1987), the federal government has certain rights and immunities as the sovereign* and should retain control of any functions for which these rights and immunities are needed. He argues that between the two sectors, there is a fundamental difference, based on these rights and on the private sector profit motive, which needs to be taken into account any time privatization of a particular service is considered. In the case of hazard mitigation services, one of the most effective hazard mitigation measures (land use) is clearly a function of local government. Also of note is the fact that the livelihoods, safety, and even survival of communities can depend on hazard mitigation decisions.

Another relevant difference that is often cited is the idea that the public sector is better equipped to provide fair and/or equitable distribution of services. In fact, many opponents of privatization are concerned that too many cuts to social services have been made in the name of the market without the private sector or any other entity filling the gaps (Calhoun, 2006). Additionally, several theorists, including those who favor privatization, have observed or admitted that the results are not uniform and that certain groups invariably benefit more than others (Feigenbaum & Henig, 1994). In terms of hazard mitigation, it may be that private sector involvement does not lead to equitable distribution of services. Equality of distribution is a basic tenet of the American political system. Furthermore, inequality is unacceptable, especially when human safety is at stake. This research explores the incentive to service those clients who have lower transaction costs during disaster recovery and preparedness phases and its relationship to issues of equity and fairness.

Also of concern is accountability; there is widespread agreement that accountability is challenging when government services are privatized. In particular, Gormly and Balla (2004) have noted that government officials often lack the information necessary to distinguish between good and bad service providers, and that responsibilities are often vague and therefore difficult to monitor. With little oversight once a contract is awarded, little in-house expertise, and with little competition for certain

---

* This refers to the rights belonging inherently to a government, such as the ability to tax or to declare war.

services, this may well be the case. Hazard mitigation appears to meet this description: The service provided is quite varied (on a case-by-case basis) and relies on a great deal of discretion (which projects to pursue, what groups to involve in the planning process, etc.). Local and state governments have almost no grounds to distinguish between providers because the cost and scope of work are determined by federal grants and because there are very few providers in the market. Lipsky's (1980) description of street-level bureaucracy, which is examined below, notes the ambiguity of performance measures even within the public sector, a challenge that is further amplified by private sector actors who must keep profit in mind in order for their businesses to survive. The wide range of hazard mitigation services and other unique characteristics previously mentioned only serve to make accountability and standardization more difficult (Lipsky, 1980) when the private sector delivers public services.

However, some theorists who also focus on accountability write in favor of privatization. One example is Trebilcock and Iacobucci (2003) who argue that there are two types of accountability: within an organization and of the organization. They contend that there are differences between public and private provision of services but that accountability is not lost through privatization. In response to the various arguments that the public sector is better equipped to pursue social ends, they note that public actors often act out of political self-interest* and propose that the profit motive can actually have a positive effect on social welfare due to the greater discipline that is required to make a profit. In particular, they argue that because of this requirement, the private sector has more experience in using resources wisely. On the basis of this logic, it might be assumed that the private sector would be inherently more efficient because efficiency only serves to increase profit. Additionally, there is an inherent assumption that government is by its nature wasteful of resources and that the market will ensure that only companies that provide a quality product will continue to receive business. This research looks for indicators of market failure but will not establish whether this action is indeed taking place.

---

* This statement is supported by the disaster literature; it notes that the long-term actions required for hazard mitigation are not always in the immediate political interest of those in local government.

Trebilcock and Iacobucci (2003) do admit, however, that in order to have work, the private sector may have incentive to encourage recidivism.* However, they argue that the market provides its own form of accountability and that private corporations do not survive when they perform poorly. In fact, if hazard mitigation creates market failure by its very nature (i.e., the service is being provided for the community rather than the community providing it for itself), then it becomes necessary to question whether their assumption would hold true regarding accountability. Regardless, it is clear that political self-interest does play a role when significant amounts of money are made available to communities following a disaster. These questions too are explored in the context of accountability and equity.

A brief overview of the chapters in this book follows.

- **Chapter 1—Recent Trends in Emergency Management**
  This chapter provides an overview of recent trends in emergency management. These trends include increasing private sector involvement and the development of several national frameworks.
- **Chapter 2—Privatization of Some Emergency Management Functions: Recent Disasters and Case Examples**
  This chapter includes a series of cases showcasing the role of the private sector in all phases of emergency management.
- **Chapter 3—A Primer on Federal and State Disaster Funds and Funding**
  Each year, the federal government funnels billions of dollars in disaster-related grants to state and local governments. These grants are complex and diverse in scope, often requiring the engagement of multiple actors, including those from the private sector. There have been a number of reports issued by the Government Accountability Office (GAO), the Department of Homeland Security (DHS) Inspector General, and the Office of Management and Budget (OMB), which suggest that a lack of capacity at the local and state levels to effectively administer grants significantly hinders their effectiveness. As a result of this lack of capacity, the responsibility to manage these grants at the state and local levels are increasingly being contracted out to the private sector. In addition to grant management, the private sector

---

* This concept stems from private sector involvement in programs for which the goal is to wean clients off a system. Simply stated, if the service provider is being paid per client, then there is no incentive for it to work toward an eventual reduction in the number of clients.

is also heavily involved in providing services financed by these grants. This chapter discusses these issues and presents an overview of the structure of federal grants to state and local government, commonly referred to as the *grant-in-aid* system, and the role of the private sector in disaster funding.

- **Chapter 4—Privatization of Disaster Preparedness: Increasing Resilience through Planning**
Following recent disasters over the last few decades, both natural and man-made, preparedness has gained attention in the United States. Joplin's (Missouri) tornado strike, September 11, the BP oil spill, and Superstorm Sandy are few examples of events not expected but have acted as catalysts in increasing disaster preparedness. State, local, and federal governments no longer bear the burden of disaster preparedness alone. The role of private sector involvement in preparedness has increased, as well as the public sector's appreciation for such assistance. Partnerships with, and the involvement of, the private sector has had a wide array of benefits. Private entities offer an alternative method for a governmental agency to provide a service to its citizens. Innovation and invention, contracting services, collaborative efforts, and offering goods/services that are not available from the government are ways in which the private sector has affected disaster preparedness. This chapter will discuss the changing landscape of preparedness and the role of the private sector.
- **Chapter 5—Private Sector's Role in Emergency Response**
Emergency response by the government has a long and complex history in the United States. It is a critical component of the four phases of emergency management as it often involves life-saving operations following a disaster. Because the hours and days following a disaster can be chaotic and present citizens with uncertain circumstances, the need for concise and efficient emergency response operation plans is paramount. The private sector has always played a role in emergency response. Whether it is a business owner responding to damage to her own business or a large corporation providing resources to its employees following a disaster, the private sector plays an important role in response efforts. Throughout the years, the public, private, and nonprofit sectors have built collaborative and contractual relationships with one another in an effort to respond to disasters and emergencies as quickly and efficiently as possible. This chapter explores both

the role of the private sector in emergency response and the privatization of emergency response operations.

- **Chapter 6—Recovery and Rebuilding with the Private and Public Sectors**

  On a national level, most people first think of FEMA as the key administrator during a disaster response. However, within FEMA's framework is an understanding that the private sector must play a large role in both the planning and preparedness before a disaster and the recovery process after a disaster.

  The scrutiny that comes with that response mandates that the recovery effort be of the highest levels of efficiency, speed, safety, and cost-effectiveness. Other necessary attributes that vendors, both internal and external, must be able to provide is immediacy of availability, versatility of planning and material options, and specificity of expertise of the task at hand. Disaster recovery necessitates collaboration between private and public entities to achieve the most effective results. Choosing to contract services to a private vendor is not an opportunity for governing bodies to relinquish responsibility, but rather it is an opportunity to seek the best strategy to meet recovery expectations. This chapter will identify the role and importance of private entities in disaster management strategies and explore incidents where established relationships between the government entities and the private and public sector have helped produce better and faster results.

- **Chapter 7—Hazard Mitigation**

  This chapter analyzes the role of the private sector in the creation and implementation of federal hazard mitigation programs. It is based on a doctoral dissertation that utilized a mixed-method approach consisting of semistructured interviews, a review of primary sources, and various coding and analysis strategies. Interview respondents were selected through a snowball sample and asked directly about the role of the private sector, including the decision to use private actors and about the results from this decision. Interview respondents are cited anonymously throughout this chapter.

- **Chapter 8—Homeland Security and the Private Sector in Emergency Management Prevention**

  This chapter introduces the principle of prevention/protection and its role in emergency management. In the post-9/11 era of emergency management, prevention has had a considerable amount of attention focused on deterrence of terrorism. The private sector's access to resources useful in achieving the prevention goals has provided a prime option for partnership with government officials on each level. Though the public–private partnership has its clear benefits for achieving the goals of prevention, the risks of unclear transparency, accountability, and the disparity in the demands of stakeholders still present measurable challenges for emergency managers.

- **Chapter 9—Nonprofits, Academic Institutions, and Their Role in the Disaster Management Cycle**
  Nonprofits and academic institutions play an important role in assisting the community throughout the four phases of disaster management. This chapter shows how communities can be helped by the collaboration partnerships of academic institutions and nonprofits as they pool their knowledge and resources to better help the community manage a disaster. Continued collaboration between these entities will result in communities that are more able to successfully get through the disaster management cycle.
- **Chapter 10—Continuity of Operations and Business Continuity**
  This chapter explores the concept of *continuity* in the field of disaster planning and management. The text identifies recurring issues, underscores the importance of public–private partnerships, and discusses the regulatory framework within which all disaster response occurs. As we will see, continuity lies in the interface—the cooperation between public and private sectors and purposeful interjurisdictional communication and planning. This chapter traces the trend toward the privatization of disaster preparation and response over the last two decades and highlights best practices that save lives and property.

REFERENCES

Calhoun, C. (2006). The Privatization of Risk. *Public Culture*, 18(2): 257–263.

Chamberlin, J.R. & Jackson, J.E. (1987). Privatization as institutional choice. *Journal of Policy Analysis and Management*, 6(4): 586–604.

Denhart, R.B. & Grubbs, J.W. (2003). Public Administration and Action Orientation. (4th ed). Thomson: United States.

Feigenbaum, H.B. & Henig, J.R. (1994). The Political Underpinnings of Privatization: A Typology. *World Politics* (46), 185–208.

FEMA. (2007). Letter to Louisiana Governor's Office of Homeland Security and Emergency Preparedness. February 2, 2007.

Franklin, J. (ed.). (1998). *The Politics of Risk Society*. Polity Press: Cambridge, UK.

Giddens, A. (1998). Risk Society: The Context of British Politics. *The Politics of Risk Society*. Polity Press: Cambridge, UK.

Gormley, W.T. & Balla S.J. (2004). *Bureaucracy and Democracy: Accountability and Performance*. Congressional Quarterly Press: Washington, DC.

Healy, A.J. & Malhotra, N. (2008). Preferring a Pound of Cure to an Ounce of Prevention: Voting, Natural Disaster, and Government Response. Retrieved from http://www.sscnet.ucla.edu/polisci/cpworkshop/papers/Healy.pdf (accessed August 5, 2015).

Heclo, H. (1978). Issue Networks and the Executive Establishment. *The new American Political System*, pp. 87–107, 115–124. Edited by Anthony King.

Lipsky, M. (1980). *Street-Level Bureaucracy: Dilemmas of the Individual in Public Services*. Russell Sage Foundation: New York.

Moe, R.C. (1987). Exploring the Limits of Privatization. *Public Administration Review*, 47(6): 453–460.

O'Toole, L.J. (1999). American Intergovernmental Relations: An Overview. CQ Press.

Trebilcock, M.J. & Iacobucci, E.M. (2003). Privatization and Accountability. *Harvard Law Review*, 116(5): 1422–1453.

1

Recent Trends in Emergency Management

John J. Kiefer

Contents

Learning Objectives

- The reader will get an overview and understanding of the most important trends taking place in emergency management.
- The reader will develop an understanding of how these trends affect the relationship between the public and private sectors in the field.

INTRODUCTION

Emergency management in the United States has continued to evolve over the past several hundred years. During its formative years in the nineteenth and twentieth centuries, this evolution was largely characterized by changes in risk: from the burden being borne solely by the individual to that of shared risk by communities, by states, and by the federal government. Over time, disasters and catastrophes spurred governments at all levels to assume increasing amounts of risk through the crafting and implementation of legislation that shifted the immense burden from the individual to the government.

In the late twentieth century, the profession of emergency management became more refined. It moved from a largely unorganized system of individuals or small-unit responders to highly skilled and specialized professionals, led or directed by well-educated managers. It evolved from a largely national defense–focused paradigm to one of natural disasters. It changed from a directive nature to one of collaboration and, to some degree, participation. With the establishment of the Federal Emergency Management Agency (FEMA) in 1979, the federal government began to play an even more significant role in promoting planning, mitigating, responding, and recovering from disasters. As a result of FEMA's professionalization initiatives, a new breed of emergency managers emerged. These men and women drew upon a broad range of academic disciplines to improve their field; public administration, sociology, anthropology, communications, engineering, and computer science were but a few of these disciplines. FEMA's Higher Education Project actively promoted the sharing of cutting-edge scholarship through its website and annual conferences. By the end of the twentieth century, the field of emergency management was increasingly viewed as a separate academic discipline with its own body of theory and research.

The twenty-first century brings new challenges to the profession. According to David J. Kaufmann, the director of FEMA's Office of Policy and Program Analysis,

> The emergency management community faces a future with challenges likely to be far different from those we confront today. Powerful drivers of change such as globalization, technological development, and the changing roles of individuals in society have real potential to reshape the context within which we will operate. Addressing these transformations will be challenging; confronting the complexity that arises from the interaction of multiple drivers—such as demographic shifts,

2

technology, environmental changes, and economic uncertainty—will require entirely new approaches, tools, and capabilities.

Crisis Response and Disaster Resilience 2030
Progress Report Highlighting the 2010–2011
Insights of the Strategic Foresight Initiative, 2012

It is extremely important that emergency managers carefully assess these new trends—trends such as social media, crowdsourcing, cyber-security, mitigation, sustainability, privatization, nongovernmental organizations, climate change, and terrorism—and strategically plan to meet them head on. This chapter will provide an overview of several of the most significant recent trends in emergency management.

SOCIAL MEDIA

Social media has emerged as a powerful communication tool in recent years. It certainly cannot be ignored as a communications channel. Newsrooms around the country, and many emergency operations centers, continuously monitor one or more social media channels. During the past decade, social media has grown not only as another major channel for broadcasting emergency messages to the public, but also as a means of conversing and engaging with the public as a whole community during emergencies. As opposed to the long-established media communication model, where events are driven by *news* that those who control the media think important (top–down driven), social media is driven by the interests of the masses (bottom–up driven; *trending*); that is, the man or woman on the scene becomes the source/input during a crisis. What follows is that interest drives the volume of coverage of the event. No longer are media channels controlled by a relative few, and no longer does a public information officer have a clear method to disseminating information. Anyone with a smartphone, tablet, or computer can and does report events.

The widespread use of social media presents three significant challenges for public officials. Today, users and content generators expect to interact with one another directly, often in real time. Yet the challenge is that information disseminated through official channels must be carefully screened for accuracy. One characteristic of social media is that immediately following an event, social media can be expected to generate a great deal of erroneous information. Yet as time goes on, much of that information will self-correct. If misleading, erroneous, or false information is released, it can be independently checked, verified, and challenged by an army of ordinary passersby and observers, often accompanied by photographs and on-the-scene reports.

The second challenge is presented by the sheer volume of information that social media often generates. Tools like Blogger, WordPress, Twitter, SMS, Flickr, Picasa, YouTube, Vimeo, Facebook, Tumblr, Meerkat, and Periscope can quickly produce a massive amount of information that may be of critical utility to public managers. But before the information can be acted upon, public officials must verify the reliability and accuracy of the daunting amount of reports that can be generated by major events.

A third challenge is what we call the *response expectation*. The nature of social media is that it is interactive. It is not sufficient to simply post information; rather, there is the expectation of constant conversation … feedback, reaction, and clarification. To effectively maximize the utility of social media then, emergency managers and others must carefully monitor and respond to multiple conversations taking place. This is a considerably time-consuming, but necessary, effort needed to maximize the potential of social media in an emergency situation.

CROWDSOURCING

The growing availability and use of social media and other mass collaboration technologies present new opportunities and challenges for disaster management. *Crowdsourcing* is the practice of obtaining needed services, ideas, or content by soliciting contributions from a large group of people. Historically, that sometimes meant a long, arduous process, hindered by the communication challenges one would expect to encounter at a time before the Internet. Crowdsourcing is becoming a primary source of information in planning and preparing for, as well as during disasters such as hurricanes, tornadoes, and earthquakes. Important information from posts and photographs can easily be crowdsourced from areas affected by a disaster. The potential for assisting emergency managers to *get a handle* on the disaster and subsequently respond efficiently and effectively is significant. The critical, basic need in a crisis situation is relevant, timely, and accurate information, filtered to present the most pertinent data to the decision makers. Crowdsourcing provides a useful tool to provide critical raw information.

FEMA has even developed an application (app) for crowdsourcing. It allows users to send disaster-related photos that are hosted on FEMA's website. Descriptions can be added to the photos, and the submissions are subsequently filtered to ensure accuracy and relevance. Yet the challenges to this new technology include exploring ways to integrate crowdsourced data with more traditional sources of data. In addition to the daunting volume of data produced by crowdsourcing (and the previously mentioned need to manage conversations), there is often uncertainty about accuracy, fear of liability, inability to translate research into operational decision making, and policy limitations on gathering and managing data.

The tremendous benefits of crowdsourcing were evident in the aftermath of the Boston Marathon bombing. The first explosion took place at 2:49 pm, and the first tweet about that bombing took place only a minute later at 2:50 pm. By 3:10 pm, the reports of the bombing had been retweeted more than 20,000 times, reaching millions of people. At 3:20 pm, the Boston Police Department, using Twitter, cautioned citizens to stay clear of the area. A little over an hour later, the Boston Police provided additional public guidance and requested photographs and videos of the incident from the community. Boston Police also used crowdsourced data to manage damage assessment and to prioritize response and recovery efforts.

CYBERSECURITY

Cybersecurity is primarily a protection activity as defined in the National Preparedness Goal (FEMA, 2011). It has become a matter of national, economic, and societal importance. Present-day attacks on the nation's computer systems by foreign governments, anarchists, criminal enterprises, terrorists, and thrill seekers do not simply damage an isolated machine or disrupt a single enterprise system. Instead, modern attacks target infrastructure that is integral to the economy, national defense, and daily life. Computer networks have joined food, water, transportation, and energy as critical resources for the functioning of the national economy. When one of these key cyber infrastructure systems is attacked, the same consequences exist as for a natural disaster or other technological attack.

A recent example of this form of attack was in October 2014, when hackers thought to be working for the Russian government breached the unclassified White House computer networks. The result was a temporary disruption to some services. According to the *Washington Post*, "Recent reports by security firms have identified cyberespionage campaigns by Russian hackers thought to be working for the government. Targets have included NATO, the Ukrainian government, and U.S. defense contractors. Russia is regarded by U.S. officials as being in the top tier of states with cybercapabilities" (Nakashima, 2014).

Computer networks are the *central nervous system* of our national infrastructure. It is the expanding use of information technology and computer-based systems that has increased the importance of cyber and logical interdependencies. The use of advanced technologies and the computer-based automation of systems have led to the increased efficiency and reliability of many infrastructures (Rinaldi, Peerenboom, & Kelly, 2001). As Leavitt and Kiefer (2006) argued, "Technology is also primarily responsible for the tightly coupled, interdependent infrastructures we enjoy today." The extensive use of technology has, however, dramatically increased cyber interdependencies across all infrastructures and has contributed to their increased complexity (Rinaldi et al., 2001; Peerenboom, Fisher, Rinaldi, & Kelly, 2002). As Charles Perrow (2014) point out, "The immense complexity of some industrial organizations and their tight internal connections occasionally allowed even some small local failures, inevitable in complex systems, to cascade through the system and bring it down."

We are faced with the difficult task of securing our critical cyber infrastructure from both foreign and domestic attacks. The backbone of emergency management depends on a robust cyber infrastructure. Those responsible for this security are challenged by the uncertainty and amorphous nature of such attacks. The needed level (and commensurate resources required) for security is not clear, making it difficult to plan for the *appropriate* level of protection.

There is also uncertainty about where and which cyber system terrorists and criminals will attack. We can easily apply the displacement theory used by criminologists (that attackers simply move to other, less defended targets if their original target is in some way *hardened*) to cyber systems. In the end, these systems are critical for enabling emergency management agencies to implement and communicate comprehensive approaches to natural disasters, terrorist attacks, and law enforcement events.

There is a general lack of understanding about how to describe and assess the complex and dynamic nature of emergency management tasks in relation to cybersecurity concerns. Ever since the first computer virus traversed the Internet, it has been apparent that attacks can spread quite rapidly. Just as society has benefited from the nearly infinite connections of devices and people, so have malicious parties with the intent of taking advantage of this connectivity to launch destructive attacks.

MITIGATION

Mitigation of disasters is a sustained and ongoing event unlike disaster relief, which is a short-term event (Haddow, 2008). Mitigation is designed to lessen or diminish the negative impacts of a disaster on people, property, and the economy (Clary, 1985; Birkland, 2006). And mitigation is a strategic activity that involves identifying the specific risks posed by disasters and developing policies to alleviate them (Sylves, 2008).

Mitigation brings the private sector into the emergency management system because the economic sustainability of businesses, and the community as a whole, depends on risk reduction. Mitigation, then, promotes private sector support and leadership. Mitigation also provides the entry point to involve the private sector in other phases of emergency management and to understand the private sector's unique needs in response and recovery.

In the late 1990s, business continuity and mitigation planning was the largest growth area for emergency management. This was, and remains, because economic considerations or interest often drive public decisions.

Mitigation works best at the local level and provides a grassroots constituency that can exert political pressure for continued emergency management support. As a result, emergency management has moved from a leadership paradigm that required directive leadership to one of collaboration. Waugh and Streib (2006) point out that, "By the 1990s, professional emergency managers had largely overcome images of the authoritarian air raid wardens and civil defense directors to develop a leadership model emphasizing open communication and broad collaboration."

The Project Impact initiative articulated this concept and made it a reality in more than 225 communities. Although Project Impact was defunded under the Bush administration, the value of community-level efforts was recognized by including the words "building disaster-resistant communities" in the objectives for the new Department of Homeland Security.

SUSTAINABILITY

The ultimate goal of building sustainably has been to construct resilient communities that can survive and recover rapidly from the effects of disasters. Sustainable and resilient communities are defined as societies that are structurally organized to minimize the effects of disasters, and, at the same time, have the ability to recover quickly by restoring the socioeconomic vitality of the community. However, the relationship between community sustainability and hazards is complex, and cannot be adequately addressed without consideration of social, economic, and political factors.

Poor development decisions, social inequalities, and environmental degradation can result in disasters. Weichselgartner (2001) posits that *disasters* are socially constructed—the result of a cumulative set of decisions made by humans over time, before, during, and after a hazard event. Changing the outcomes of possible disasters is a matter of understanding and modifying the processes by which the decisions are made (Weichselgartner, 2001).

Emergency management can achieve those actions through mitigation measures and by building relationships with the private sector to support sustainability. The FEMA defines one of the principles of emergency management as the responsibility to anticipate disasters and take "protective, preventive, and preparatory" actions to build sustainable, disaster-resilient communities (FEMA, 2011).

A sustainable community builds resistance to hazards through effective land-use planning, linking economic development and the environment, while working to eliminate the social vulnerabilities of its citizens (Brett & Oviatt, 2013). Tobin (1999) defines sustainable and resilient communities as having

- Low risk of disasters
- Low vulnerability
- Ongoing planning initiatives
- High levels of government and political support
- Public–private partnerships

Effective emergency management is key to meeting these goals by supporting all phases of the disaster management cycle (preparedness, response, recovery, and mitigation). Yet emergency management has traditionally been more concerned with addressing the preparedness and response components of disasters, perhaps in part because the life-threatening effects of disasters are more obvious during these phases (Brett & Oviatt, 2013). However, since the implementation of the Disaster Management Act of 2000, mitigation has enjoyed increasing emphasis, and communities are now required to submit hazard mitigation plans in order to receive funding in response to a hazard event.

Hazard mitigation actions are taken to reduce long-term risk to communities from hazard events (Godschalk, 2003). Cutter (1996) recommends mapping the biophysical and social risks to create the mitigation plans, cautioning that mitigation efforts can attenuate or amplify risk. By incorporating wise land-use planning through hazard mitigation plans and comprehensive plans, communities can reduce vulnerabilities to hazards, which will ultimately lead to a reduction in loss of life and overall costs of recovery.

PRIVATIZATION

While privatization is a recent trend in emergency management, it is also the main subject of this book. Certainly, there is a global trend toward increasing the involvement of the private sector in functions formerly performed by the government. The involvement of the private sector ranges from direct performance of government functions to collaborative and partnership models; it must also take into account the fact that businesses and infrastructure are controlled by private entities and are key players in emergency management. Yet much of the debate about whether to have government retain control of emergency management in its totality or to privatize some or all emergency management responsibility centers not about whether privatization should occur, but when and how. There have long been public–private sector partnerships to deal with flood and other weather warnings. But recently, emergency management has become increasingly private as the concept of emergency planning expands to include economic health, business continuity planning, and community safety.

NONGOVERNMENTAL ORGANIZATIONS

There is evidence that the voluntary community is becoming more involved in domestic disasters in the aftermath of Hurricane Katrina. The National Voluntary Organizations Active in Disasters (NVOAD) reports that participation in conference calls over the three months after Katrina struck rose from the usual 40 participants to nearly 120 participants representing a very broad range of nongovernmental organizations (NGOs) that had not historically been involved in domestic disasters (Government Accountability Office, 2008). NGOs such as Save the Children, Oxfam,

CARE, and others sent response teams to the Gulf Coast and are actively pursuing becoming involved in future domestic disasters.

Yet NGOs face many of the same challenges of scale that traditional governmental organizations do. A recent study by RAND indicated that coordination and response, as well as partnerships, remain problematic. The study provided several important areas that required the attention of federal, state, and local policy makers and leaders. Selected items included the following:

- Clearly delineate roles and responsibilities for NGOs during each phase of disaster
- Examine how NGOs leverage routine practice for disaster planning, and identify where opportunities exist for dual benefit in emergency preparedness and daily operations
- Improve information exchange among NGOs and between NGOs, governmental agencies, and community residents
- Increase community capacity to deliver seamless, evidence-based services before, during, and after a disaster through NGO partnerships
- Create guidance about how to allocate resources for NGOs (both financial and nonfinancial)
- Pursue a research agenda that focuses on the implementation of these policy changes and the evaluation of the costs and benefits of NGO engagement (Acosta, Chandra, Sleeper, & Springgate, 2011)

CLIMATE CHANGE

Many scientists and emergency managers have recognized that storms are becoming more intense, and that adapting and planning for more and possibly new weather-related threats need to be incorporated into preparedness procedures. In 2012, FEMA issued a policy statement establishing an agency-wide directive to integrate climate change adaptation planning and actions into agency programs, policies, and operations (FEMA, 2012).

States have been developing climate action plans and some, like California, are taking it a step further by including climate change in their emergency planning and hazard mitigation plans. Our neighbor to the north, Canada, has long recognized climate change—its current, ongoing, and future impacts—and have included it in their national agenda as a national security threat.

The effects of climate change can include intensified wildfires, higher sea levels, extreme rainfall, windstorms, drought, diseases spreading to new areas, heat waves, more frequent and intense hurricanes, social unrest, and more. Although climate change may not specifically be identified in emergency preparedness plans, its ramification will affect emergency managers in many ways. The all-hazards emergency management community plans for just that—all types of emergencies, whether manmade or natural. Although scientists and planners have advice for how the changing climate can be included in emergency preparedness, the field is continuing to evolve as more information becomes available and agencies begin to develop best practices.

Planning for climate change can mean looking at a state or jurisdiction's current natural hazards and anticipating which of them will become more extreme in the future. A good example of this is the increase in sea level. At one time, this was viewed as problematic only in the long term, yet new data has suggested that the increase is occurring more rapidly than anticipated (see Chart 1.1).

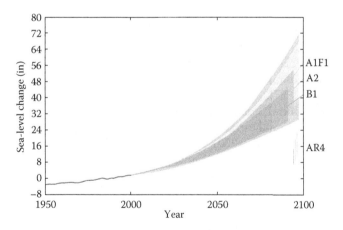

Chart 1.1 Projection of sea-level rise from 1990 to 2100, based on three different emissions scenarios. Also shown: observations of annual global sea-level rise over the past half century, relative to 1990. (From Vermeer, M. & Rahmstorf, S. *Proc. Natl Acad. Sci. USA* 106, 21527, 2009.)

For other hazards, the barrier to the new planning considerations is the relatively long-term timescale of the change. The future being planned for is not likely to be next year, but many years from now. But traditionally, the emergency management paradigm has been mostly focused on response; this paradigm can be a detriment to how agencies include climate change in their planning.

TERRORISM

The genesis of modern terrorism in the United States was the bombing of New York's World Trade Center in 1993. This bombing incident was the largest international terrorist attack ever conducted in the continental United States until the World Trade Center attack on September 11, 2001. In 1994, the Federal Bureau of Investigation (FBI) successfully thwarted an attempt by terrorists to detonate a bomb in the Lincoln Tunnel. The 1995 Oklahoma City bombing was one of the largest explosions ever investigated by the FBI before the 9/11 attacks. It demonstrated, for the first time, the real and deadly threat of terrorism to urban America.

The Nunn–Lugar–Domenici amendment to the FY97 National Defense Authorization Act, in response to concerns about domestic terrorism, provided authority for the Defense Department to address domestic vulnerabilities (Department of Defense, 1997). Yet the more than $40 million allocated was used, according to H. Allen Holmes, assistant secretary of defense for special operations and low-intensity conflict, only for training, access to federal assistance (after an incident), and exercises (National Defense Panel, 1997).

Since the initial bombings of the World Trade Center in 1993, the threat of international terrorism became the primary threat to the nation. In the aftermath of the 2001 attacks on the World Trade Center and Pentagon, the Department of Homeland Security was created in 2003 to prevent attacks to the homeland. A major focus of the new agency was on intelligence gathering, sharing, dissemination, and collaboration among a broad range of agencies at all levels of government.

After 2010, a new threat emerged, that of the *lone wolf* terrorist. Unlike more organized terrorism, the lone wolf makes it much more difficult for law enforcement to identify long-term patterns of aberrant and/or criminal behaviors that may provide useful intelligence for intercepting the terrorist before an attack. According to Jeffrey D. Simon, "Lone wolves think 'outside the box' because that is where they always are; namely, outside the box. They are loners who have to operate by themselves. That means there is no group decision-making process or group pressure that might stifle creativity" (Simon, 2013).

On the other side of the political spectrum, right-wing extremist groups—which generally adhere to an antigovernment or racist ideology—continue to gain supporters. Many of these recruits feel displaced by rapid changes in the U.S. culture and economy, or are seeking some form of personal affirmation (DeHennis, 1997). As the American society continues to change, the potential for hate crimes by extremist right-wing groups is an increasing concern to emergency planners and others.

Terrorism is a criminal act, and, as with other criminal acts, strategies can be undertaken to mitigate the impact of this form of crime. Governments are simultaneously confronted with a rapidly growing number of potential terrorist targets that must be secured and constrained by democratic principles from utilizing many technological devices to secure those targets. Creating an effective security system that protects against a wide range of terrorist attacks while it continues to afford a maximum exercise of democratic freedoms and privileges is a formidable task indeed.

The major characteristic of contemporary terrorism is its unexpectedness. The time and manner of attacks are unpredictable and catch targeted communities—normally innocent civilians—by surprise. In the past, the targets were often political and symbolic figures, not the general public, and the perpetrators proudly notified of who they were and why they had acted. The purposes and targets of contemporary terrorism, on the other hand, are often very unclear. Terrorists attack innocent civilians indiscriminately without prior notification, making attacks more difficult to prevent. For these reasons, it is necessary that emergency planners build strong relationships across levels of government and through public, private, and nongovernmental agencies. According to the Council on Foreign Relations,

> An improved information sharing environment also will be constructed upon a foundation of trusted partnerships among all levels of government, the private sector, and our foreign allies—partnerships based on a shared commitment to detect, prevent, disrupt, preempt, and mitigate the effects of terrorism.

The White House
National Strategy for Information Sharing: Successes and Challenges in Improving Terrorism-Related Terrorism Information Sharing, 2007

CONCLUSION

The recent trends in emergency management outlined in this chapter are important issues that shape the future of emergency management in the United States. Some, like mitigation and sustainability, provide challenges for emergency managers and planners simply because of the long-term time frame required to effectively implement successful plans. Others, like climate change, are made more difficult to address because of caustic political polarization. And some of these trends change, or morph, into other related issues quite rapidly. Take, for example, the shift from the state-sponsored terrorism of the 1970s and 1980s to the domestic terrorism of the Symbionese Liberation Army and Timothy McVey, to the *stateless* terrorism of Al Qaeda. Most recently, we have seen terrorism change yet again, with lone-wolf terrorists providing no clear warnings and indicators to law enforcement officials.

Social media, while continuing to evolve as a useful tool for emergency managers, is also being used quite effectively as a fruitful recruiting tool for international terrorist organizations, particularly by ISIS (Islamic State in Iraq and Syria), the even more violent successor to Al Qaeda. To best prevent or mitigate terrorism, new challenges are presented for law enforcement and intelligence officials when gathering intelligence from social media, crowdsourcing, or other sources such as telephone and wireless communications. These challenges include how best to collect and act upon warnings and indicators without violating constitutional protections.

As emergency managers seek to mitigate, prepare for, respond to, and recover from disasters, these new trends will heavily influence their decisions about privatization. They will have to carefully address questions such as

- Should I privatize?
- What should I privatize?
- Do I have the expertise to address important emergency management responsibilities within my organization?
- Should I seek to develop this expertise internally?
- Can I afford to *contract out*? Can I afford not to?
- How much oversight do I have? Should I have? Will I have?
- And many others

The remainder of this book will seek to provide some useful tools for answering these questions.

CHAPTER QUESTIONS

True or False

1. Over time in the United States, individuals assumed a larger and larger share of risk from disasters.
2. Collaborative skills are very important for modern emergency managers.
3. Social media has caused news events to become more *top–down* driven.
4. The accuracy of information produced by social media is always reliable.
5. FEMA has rejected crowdsourcing because it is often unreliable.
6. Crowdsourcing proved to be ineffective after the Boston Marathon bombing.
7. Cybersecurity is a matter of national, economic, and societal importance.
8. Cyber attacks target infrastructure that is integral to the economy, national defense, and daily life.
9. Fortunately, cyber attacks do not spread rapidly.
10. Mitigation is usually done in the aftermath of a natural disaster.

REFERENCES

Acosta, J., Chandra, A., Sleeper, S. & Springgate, B. (2011). *The Nongovernmental Sector in Disaster Resilience Conference Recommendations for a Policy Agenda.* Arlington, VA: RAND Corporation.

Birkland, T.A. (2006). *Lessons of Disaster: Policy Change After Catastrophic Events.* Washington, DC: Georgetown University Press.

Brett, J. & Oviatt, K. (2013). The intrinsic link of vulnerability to sustainable development. In *Social Vulnerability to Disasters (2nd ed.)*, Eds. D.S.K. Thomas, B.D. Phillips, W.E. Lovekamp & A. Fothergill. Boca Raton, FL: CRC Press.

Clary, B.B. (1985). The evolution and structure of natural hazard policies. *Public Administration Review, 45,* 20–28.

Crisis Response and Disaster Resilience 2030: Forging Strategic Action in an Age of Uncertainty. (2012). Progress Report Highlighting the 2010–2011 Insights of the Strategic Foresight Initiative.

Cutter, S.L. (1996). Vulnerability to environmental hazards. *Progress in Human Geography, 20,* 529539.

DeHennis, P.M. (1997). *Terrorism: National Security and Strategy and a Local Threat Response.* Carlisle Barracks, PA: U.S. Army War College; Pittsburgh: General Matthew B. Ridgway Center for International Security Studies.

Department of Defense (1997). Report of the National Defense Panel, Transforming Defense-National Security in the 21st Century. Retrieved from http://www.ists.dartmouth.edu/docs/trf_def1.pdf. Accessed June 2, 2015.

FEMA EMI 230b. (2011). Fundamentals of emergency management. *Federal Emergency Management Agency.* Retrieved from https://training.fema.gov/is/courseoverview.aspx?code=is-230.d. Accessed June 2, 2015.

FEMA (2011). National Preparedness Goal. U.S. Department of Homeland Security. Retrieved from http://www.fema.gov/media-library-data/20130726-1828-25045-9470/national_preparedness_goal_2011.pdf. Accessed November 19, 2014.

FEMA (2012). Administrator Policy 2011-OPPA-01.

Godschalk, D.R. (2003). Urban hazard mitigation: Creating resilient cities. *Natural Hazards Review, 4,* 136.

Government Accountability Office GAO-08-369 (2008). National Disaster Response: FEMA Should Take Action to Improve Capacity and Coordination between Government and Voluntary Sector. Retrieved from http://www.gao.gov/assets/280/272664.html. Accessed November 19, 2014.

Haddow, G. (2008). *Introduction to Emergency Management.* Amsterdam: Elsevier/Butterworth-Heinemann.

Leavitt, W. & Kiefer, J.J. (2006). Infrastructure interdependency and the creation of a normal disaster: The case of hurricane katrina and the city of New Orleans. *Public Works Management and Policy, 10*(4), 306–314.

Nakashima, E. (2014). Hackers breach some White House computers. *Washington Post:* http://www.washingtonpost.com/world/national-security/hackers-breach-some-white-house-computers/2014/10/28/2ddf2fa0-5ef7-11e4-91f7-5d89b5e8c251_story.html. Accessed November 19, 2014.

Peerenboom, J., Fisher, R.E., Rinaldi, S.M. & Kelly, T.K. (2002). Studying the chain reaction. *Electric Perspectives, 27*(1), 22–35.

Perrow, C. (2014). Getting to catastrophe: Concentrations, complexity and coupling. *The Montréal Review:* http://www.themontrealreview.com/2009/Normal-Accidents-Living-with-High-Risk-Technologies.php. Accessed November 19, 2014.

Rinaldi, S., Peerenboom, J. & Kelly T. (2001). Complexities in identifying, understanding, and analyzing critical infrastructure interdependencies. *IEEE Control Systems Magazine,* 11–25.

Simon, J.D. (2013). *Lone Wolf Terrorism: Understanding the Growing Threat.* Amherst, NY: Prometheus Books.

Sylves, R. (2008). *Disaster Policy and Politics: Emergency Management and Homeland Security.* Washington, DC: Sage Publications.

Tobin, G.A. (1999). Sustainability and community resilience: The holy grail of hazards planning? *Environmental Hazards, 1,* 1325.

Vermeer, M. & Rahmstorf, S. (2009). Global sea level linked to global temperature. *Proceedings of the National Academy of Sciences of the United States of America, 106,* 21527–21532.

Waugh, W.L.J. & Streib, G. (2006). Collaboration and leadership for effective emergency management. *Public Administration Review, Special Issue, 66,* 131–140.

Weichselgartner, J. (2001). Disaster mitigation: The concept of vulnerability revisited, *Disaster Prevention and Management, 10,* 8594.

The White House. (2007). *National Strategy for Information Sharing: Successes and Challenges in Improving Terrorism-Related Terrorism Information Sharing,* Washington, DC.

2

Privatization of Some Emergency Management Functions
Recent Disasters and Case Examples

John J. Kiefer, Kimberly VanWagner, Jeremiah Jones, and Melissa Wilkins

Learning Objectives

- The reader will get an overview and understanding of the important role played by private contractors in debris removal.
- The reader will understand how to balance key trade-offs in public–private partnerships.
- The reader will examine the decision-making process when contracting for the use of private organizations to provide public services.

In this chapter, we present several case studies that illustrate the often complex relationship between public and private organizations during and after disasters.

In the first case, Kimberly VanWagner looks at the important role played by private contractors in debris removal after Hurricane Sandy devastated the East Coast. This case clearly shows the benefits of a rapid response to debris removal resident in the private sector, aided by federal public assistance grants. Yet the case also suggests that the cost (to the federal government) is often significantly higher, and fraud may be more common, than if debris removal was undertaken by the municipality alone.

The second case provides some important considerations in an apparently successful public–private relationship centered on emergency notification through commercial billboards. Jeremiah Jones analyzes the key issues, and provides some cautions for the future of the relationship.

Finally, Melissa Wilkins presents a case for the benefits of the privatization of emergency medical services. Melissa is a long-time public administrator, working for parish government in Louisiana. Her experience includes the time frame of Hurricane Katrina. This case study gives an in-depth look into the decision process for government agencies, and presents the important factors to be considered regarding either utilizing public personnel to provide emergency services or choosing to contract services out to private agencies and firms.

CASE STUDY   Innovative of Fraudulent?: The Role of Private Contractors in Post-Disaster Cleanup

Kimberly VanWagner

ABSTRACT

Post-disaster debris removal is big business for private contractors. Local governments can use their own resources to clear debris after a natural hazard but are often overwhelmed with the breadth of the task after a large-scale disaster such as a hurricane, tornado, or flood. Through a Federal Emergency Management Administration (FEMA) reimbursement program, local and state governments can contract with private debris removal firms. Those contractors provide the administrative and logistical expertise, manpower, and equipment needed to haul away tons of storm detritus. They often bring vast and nuanced experience navigating FEMA's difficult and seemingly arbitrary debris removal guidelines. However, the power these contractors holds has led to some controversies and cases of fraud, frustrating the efficiency of this model and costing taxpayers millions of dollars.

INTRODUCTION

From 2000 to 2010, the Federal Emergency Management Administration (FEMA) reimbursed more than $8 billion for debris removal from natural hazards (Jadacki, 2011). In fact, disaster debris accounts for almost one-third of all post-disaster recovery costs (Fetter & Rakes, 2013). The largest amount of debris caused by a disaster in the United States to date was along the Gulf Coast following Hurricane Katrina; more than 100 million cubic yards was collected and processed (Lipton & Semple, 2012). As of April 30, 2013, 75% of the $178 million in FEMA aid for Hurricane Sandy had been paid for debris removal (Herbert & Crichton, 2013). By November 13 of the same year, a federal audit by the Office of the Inspector General (OIG) for the Department of Homeland Security found that FEMA had awarded more than $463 million in debris removal reimbursements—90% of the debris removal costs (Mullen, 2014).

Debris cleanup following a disaster often presents significant challenges for local governments, ranging from a lack of equipment and manpower to the challenges of dealing with a complex reimbursement system. Disaster debris is a waste stream resulting from a natural disaster and can include building and construction materials; sediments, soils, and sand; vegetative matter; personal property; and other materials, and can be comingled with various hazardous wastes (Environmental Protection Agency, 1995; Jadacki, 2011). The debris can overwhelm existing landfills and recycling facilities. Effective debris response can be a determining factor in how quickly and safely residents can return to live and rebuild following a disaster (Jadacki, 2011).

On October 29, 2012, Hurricane Sandy made landfall in southern New Jersey, battering the coastal areas with 80 mph winds and record-level storm surge. More than 8.5 million customers lost power. FEMA eventually approved more than $2.1 billion in emergency work, debris removal, and replacement of infrastructure funds to help the dozens of states affected rebuild (FEMA NR-239, 2013). During the first 100 days of cleanup in New Jersey, more than 8 million cubic yards of debris was removed (Davis, 2013).

DEBRIS REMOVAL THROUGH FEMA'S PUBLIC ASSISTANCE GRANT FUND

The Stafford Act authorizes FEMA to respond to disasters to save lives and protect public health, safety, and property. FEMA operates under specific regulations found in Section 206.224 of Title 44 of the Code of Federal Regulations (CFR). Within the CFR and the Stafford Act, *debris removal* denotes the entire process of removing, handling, recycling, and disposing of debris. Debris removal needs to be *in the public interest* to protect life, health, and safety and to ensure the economic recovery of the community (Jadacki, 2011).

FEMA expects state and local governments to anticipate debris removal as part of an emergency response plan for a natural hazard (FEMA 327, 2010). Whether through a debris management plan or after a disaster, communities need to decide how best to use their existing facilities for waste management, including recycling, composting, and combusting. Where and how to deal with the substantial increase in debris generated by a disaster event, especially since a municipality's current facilities may not be sufficient, are key components to post-disaster response and recovery. A community must identify additional sites (landfill, compost, recycling) for debris.

When a community's capacity to recover from a natural hazard occurrence is overwhelmed by the magnitude of the hazard, the community must make a declaration of a natural disaster to the state emergency management agency. The state's governor must then request through FEMA that the president declare the affected area a disaster. Once the president declares the area a disaster, the local government becomes eligible for reimbursement of some portion of its debris management costs (and other recovery costs) (Jadacki, 2011) through public assistance grant funding (FEMA 327, 2010).

Once a federal declaration of a disaster is made, FEMA negotiates disaster relief efforts with the state emergency management agency. Local communities are represented by the state during these discussions. FEMA staff advise local officials regarding the activities eligible for reimbursement. To be eligible for funding assistance for debris removal, the activities must be the direct result of a federally declared disaster, occur within the disaster area, be the legal responsibility of the community applying for assistance, and be in the public interest (Jadacki, 2011).

FEMA categorizes debris removal operations in two phases: (1) initial debris clearance necessary to eliminate threats to safety and (2) debris removal activities related to recovery. Successful debris removal operations are usually the result of a local government having a debris management plan in place before a disaster. Once a disaster strikes, decision makers are often overwhelmed by the many immediate problems affecting the safety and health of the citizens.

In the first few days after a disaster, roadways to lifeline services such as hospitals and other vital routes must be cleared. Critical services must be restored. The majority of the contractor work is for the second phase; however, the greatest cost–value for reimbursement from FEMA is usually within the first ninety days of a disaster. FEMA's rules governing debris removal are extensive, affecting the collection, hauling and staging, and sorting and processing of debris.

The FEMA Debris Management Guide has been criticized by the OIG of the Department of Homeland Security as being complex and unwieldy (Jadacki, 2011). The guide is more than 230 pages long with appendices, and the rules within are confusing or even ambiguous. Nevertheless, local governments must follow these rules precisely to be eligible for debris removal reimbursement through the Public Assistance grant fund. *Gray areas* in the regulations include the eligibility of tree and stump removal, assisting the elderly in moving their debris to the curb, whether gated communities or trailer parks are eligible to be included despite their lack of public roads, and whether new landfills are acceptable (Jadacki, 2011). Private sector consultants with prior experience in debris removal can be an asset in navigating these regulations.

The Stafford Act authorizes FEMA to pay for debris removal, transportation, volume reduction at staging areas, and disposal when the debris poses an immediate threat to the public. To ensure compliance, FEMA requires exacting record keeping regarding a community's expenditures on debris management before granting reimbursement. The rules regarding what is reimbursable in part depend on the community's policies in place before the disaster or the community's ability to demonstrate cost-effectiveness for debris management methods. For example, if the local government has previously emphasized recycling in the community or if it can show the cost-effectiveness of recycling disaster debris, costs incurred recycling the debris can be reimbursed (Jadacki, 2011).

The overwhelming amount of debris and the complexity of FEMA's reimbursement process cause many communities to turn to private contractors for debris management (Jadacki, 2011). One recommendation from FEMA is for local or state government to prequalify debris contractors to ensure the immediate response of coordinated debris removal support following a disaster. However, FEMA does not provide a list of preapproved contractors (FEMA Debris Removal Contractor Registry, 2013, https://asd.fema

.gov/inter/drcr/home.htm); municipalities are encouraged to vet contractors in advance of a disaster to save time and ensure quality. Contracts are often structured to go into effect only when a disaster event is declared (prevent contracts or mutual aid agreements). Unfortunately, communities sometimes contract with firms that do not deliver the expected results—and they lack the knowledge to adequately select between firms.

BENEFITS OF CONTRACTING OUT DEBRIS MANAGEMENT

The Office of Inspector General of the Department of Homeland Security found that in some instances, FEMA debris management specialists were not on the ground until three or more weeks after a disaster event. In addition, FEMA officials designated to respond immediately to disasters to help the state with coordination, such as Incident Management Assistance Teams, do not have adequate knowledge of debris removal regulations. When debris specialists are not *boots on the ground* for more than twenty-one days after a disaster, and local officials are confused or overwhelmed by FEMA's reimbursement regulations for debris, the local governments could end up footing the bill for any mistakes they make. Many opt to hire private contractors as a safer choice.

Because FEMA will reimburse direct administrative costs through the public assistance grant fund program, local governments can contract out all aspects of the debris operations, including management and oversight, and be reimbursed at the cost–share rate established for the particular disaster declaration. Understanding this arrangement, contractors secure work managing all aspects of the debris removal, appealing to local governments that do not have the staff or upfront funding to handle the operations on their own (Jadacki, 2011).

Private debris management contractors can bring experience in establishing staging areas, separating debris, and coordinating FEMA's reimbursement process. Contractors can bring efficiency and speed to disaster cleanup, providing equipment, staff, and the relationships necessary for a successful operation. The large contractors who operate nationwide have the capacity to handle complicated subcontracting with local work crews. They can secure the large amounts and varying types of debris cleanup equipment required. These factors—expertise, efficiency, effectiveness, capacity, and speed—often combine to save the government money.

Local governments could choose to do the work themselves, and many do. But given FEMA's difficult regulations regarding debris and the lack of debris management specialists from FEMA on the ground immediately following a disaster, more and more municipalities are choosing to work with private contractors. When the duties of local officials in the wake of a disaster include soliciting bids, executing emergency operations, and rebuilding other parts of the community, the decision to contract with professionals for debris removal seems obvious. However, it is critical that local jurisdictions adequately screen contractors and be very explicit in their contracts.

CONTROVERSIES WITH PRIVATE DEBRIS REMOVAL MANAGEMENT FIRMS

There are times when private contractors, despite being lauded for saving money, actually cost the federal government more. Most commonly, the contractors will bill for administrative costs at a higher rate for their staff than a local government would charge for its. On a large scale, FEMA officials report that the reimbursement rates for administrative costs are disproportionately higher when municipalities use private contractors (Jadacki, 2011).

In addition, the drive for profits has led to a variety of fraudulent acts by private contractors, frustrating the potential benefits of using contractors and costing taxpayers millions of dollars. For example, auditors found $5.4 million in unsupported debris removal costs in Gulfport after Katrina cleanup (Jadacki, 2011; Herbert & Crichton, 2013). Examples of fraud by private contractors firms includes

- Posing as FEMA-certified debris removal contractors, despite the fact that FEMA does not endorse or certify any particular contractors
- Collecting ineligible debris to compensate for purposefully *lowballed* bids
- Collecting debris created by the contractor, for example, by clear-cutting public lands
- Coordinating bids between companies

When paid for the mileage accumulated during operations, some contractors have purposefully added unnecessary miles to their reimbursement requests. Contractors have falsified load tickets or stacked debris in trucks in such a way as to appear full.

One way FEMA combats fraud is through the use of independent monitors. The independent monitors are also hired by the local or state government. Debris monitors are responsible for recording quantities of debris, completing incident reports, daily logs, GPS reports, and other monitoring duties required to track debris removal operations. The independent monitors look for possible safety risks or violations, and they verify overall compliance with public assistance grant eligibility criteria. The monitors also validate the truck and trailer capacity used for debris removal (FEMA 327, 2010). Unfortunately, some contractors hired for debris removal promote their own companies to act as the independent monitor without disclosing the relationship.

In addition to collusion between the monitoring company and the debris removal company, monitors may overstate the volume of debris for a number of reasons. Some contractors cheat the system by installing false bottoms in their trucks or falsify the volume certification for a truck (Jadacki, 2011). Monitors may lack the training required to accurately assess the volume of an individual truck or the percentage load of trucks entering the landfill or other staging area. A report by the OIG of the Department of Homeland Security found that monitors can overstate the volume of debris by 20% or more, and estimates that FEMA may have overpaid $20 million in debris removal for Hurricanes Gustav and Ike due to the lack of qualified monitors (Jadacki, 2011).

Incidents of fraud, collusion, and conflicts of interest injure the public trust and call into question the criteria needed for success when government contracts out emergency management functions: accountability, equity, affordability, efficiency, and effectiveness. These criteria can be evaluated through the following case study, which briefly explores New Jersey's contract with AshBritt Environmental for debris management and removal after Hurricane Sandy in 2012.

NEW JERSEY'S CONTRACT WITH ASHBRITT

Immediately after Hurricane Sandy made landfall, New Jersey contracted with AshBritt Environmental, an established disaster debris management company, to handle the debris removal operations in the first ninety days of the recovery (New Jersey Office of Recovery and Rebuilding, 2013). There are several concerns with New Jersey Governor Chris Christie's decision to contract with AshBritt: a *no bid* contract was issued; the firm has a history of potential fraudulent charges from Hurricane Katrina cleanup; the firm was investigated for overcharging municipalities hauling rates during Hurricane Sandy cleanup; and the firm's work for New Jersey was monitored by a partner corporation, Arcadis. Not one of these concerns has resulted in any serious finding of wrongdoing on the part of the company. However, the concerns regarding one contractor provide a useful look at the myriad ways contractors and government can improve the disaster debris removal system to uphold the public's trust.

- AshBritt was criticized for securing a *no bid* contract with New Jersey, leading to questions of equity, affordability, and accountability.

On October 31, 2012, the state of New Jersey entered into an emergency debris removal contract with AshBritt (Boxer, 2013). The contract was not competitively bid in New Jersey; rather, it was *piggybacked*, or taken from a competitively bid contract, between the state of Connecticut and AshBritt. That contract was signed in 2008 and scheduled to become effective in the event of a disaster. New Jersey changed the contract to defer to New Jersey law in the case of any conflicts with state regulations (Kaltwasser, 2012), but otherwise kept the contract as it was.

Towns and counties in New Jersey could choose to hire AshBritt and use the contract as a ready-made framework (Kaltwasser, 2012). Fifty-three local governments chose to do so. Those that did not had to take time to solicit bids and hire contracting firms. FEMA did reimburse the state of New Jersey for work done through this contract, despite its discouragement of *piggybacking* and *no bid* contracts (FEMA 327, 2010).

However, firms that would have been eligible to bid on the immediate debris removal work were left out of the hiring process, despite their lower costs (Renshaw & Baxter, 2013). To some contractors, the *piggybacking* led to an unfair advantage for AshBritt. Ninety days after the storm, the state solicited bids for the remaining debris removal. AshBritt, the highest bidder, was one of the four firms chosen (Renshaw & Baxter, 2013). AshBritt's advantage may have come in part through other political connections. Its lobbying group, BGR, held a fundraiser for New Jersey Governor Chris Christie on February 28, 2013 (Reitmeyer & Hayes, 2013). Following an investigation, the OIG of the U.S. Department of Homeland Security found that New Jersey's contract award process with AshBritt complied with state law (Kelly, 2014; Mullen, 2014).

- AshBritt was also criticized during cleanup of Hurricane Katrina for increasing costs and decreasing the affordability of contracting out debris removal.

AshBritt had secured a $500 million contract for emergency debris removal in Mississippi following Hurricanes Katrina and Rita (Kopecki, 2006). AshBritt was among several debris contractor firms, including CERES Environmental Services Inc., Environmental Chemical Corp., and Phillips & Jordan Inc. (Myers, 2006), criticized during the cleanup of debris after Hurricane Katrina for hiring many layers of subcontractors (Committee on Government Reform, 2006). By hiring multiple layers of subcontractors, AshBritt was able to inflate the cost of its services to the federal government (Myers, 2006).

Immediately after Congress investigated, AshBritt eliminated the multiple layers of subcontractors (Lipton & Semple, 2012).

- AshBritt was accused of overcharging for cleanup of Hurricane Sandy debris.

New Jersey's contract with AshBritt was *piggybacked* onto an existing contract AshBritt had with Connecticut, and both contracts lacked clear language about which specific route the debris removal trucks needed to take (Boxer, 2013). AshBritt was able to charge for the mileage incurred within the landfill, an extra 2.5 miles for each load. Debris hauled up to 15 miles is charged at a lower rate than debris hauled 16–30 miles. The extra mileage bumped each trip to the next bracket of rates, 30% higher, resulting in AshBritt overbilling some towns by more than $300,000 (Boburg, 2013b).

The New Jersey comptroller investigation concluded that AshBritt's overbilling had not been intentional. AshBritt agreed to repay the $300,000 in extra charges (Boburg, 2013c).

- AshBritt's work in New Jersey was monitored by its own former subcontractor, Arcadis, leading to questions of accountability and conflict of interest.

On November 1, 2012, the state of New Jersey sent a request for a quotation to potential debris monitors. Three proposals were received, and Arcadis U.S. and Science Application International Corporation were subsequently awarded eight-month contracts (Kelly, 2014) to monitor the debris removal contractors, including AshBritt. Back in 2010, Arcardis had worked for AshBritt's Haiti Recovery Group in Haiti (Renshaw, 2013). Arcadis provided monitoring services and its proprietary software to track debris removal.

According to *The Star-Ledger*, a FEMA spokesman said, "It is the applicant's responsibility to ensure that any debris monitoring contractors are not employed by or affiliated with their debris removal contractor and that they are following all federal, state, and local procurement policies and all federal, state, and local regulatory requirements" (Renshaw, 2013).

Although subject to audit by the U.S. Department of Homeland Security's OIG, no action has been taken to address this relationship by the OIG; however, the Department of the Treasury found no conflict of interest (Renshaw, 2013).

INNOVATIONS OF PRIVATE DEBRIS REMOVAL MANAGEMENT FIRMS

The private sector approach is used to achieve the highest profit, but that is not necessarily a negative attribute when considering government contracting. Private debris removal contractors have a vested interest in reducing costs—so that they may secure the contract through lower bids without reducing their profit margins. This need to reduce costs drives the private sector toward innovation—creating new products to increase the efficiency, effectiveness, and affordability of their services.

Debris removal contractors provide cost-cutting innovations in at least two ways: positioning themselves as debris removal experts and creating proprietary software to track debris more accurately. As stated above, contractors provide guidance and clarification for FEMA's debris removal regulations, but they also have the expertise to file appeals for communities when FEMA underestimates reimbursement rates. Obviously, this skill benefits both the community and the contractor, leaving only the federal government responsible for extra costs.

Arcadis, an international consulting and engineering firm, has created HaulPass, its proprietary software program that uses Geographic Information Systems (GIS) and other digital technologies to track debris removal in real time. The system was used during the cleanup from Hurricane Sandy to monitor the truckloads of debris in an effort to reduce costs and increase efficiency (Havins, 2012). HaulPass eliminates the paper ticketing system that so easily lends itself to fraud; instead, data is entered into tablets and uploaded immediately (Rosania, 2012). Similar programs, such as Recovery Management Inc.'s software, DIRT (Disaster Incident Removal and Tracking), and DebrisTech Electronic Debris Management System, have been helpful in eliminating fraud and waste—even securing GIS coordinates and digital imagery of potentially fraudulent acts (see Jadacki [2011] for examples). This also improves reporting to FEMA and can therefore speed up reimbursement submissions.

UPHOLDING THE PUBLIC TRUST

When a community declares disaster, its resources are overwhelmed, and it needs assistance in responding to the devastation. Because there are significant technical aspects to debris removal after disasters, many communities choose to contract with debris removal management firms. These firms are hired for their expertise in following EPA guidelines for disposing of various materials, navigating FEMA's nuanced regulations, and coordinating equipment, personnel, and disposal sites. Outsourcing government functions is often touted for its flexibility, cost cutting, and access to industry expertise. However, these benefits must align with the public integrity values of accountability, fairness, efficiency, affordability, and effectiveness.

ACCOUNTABILITY

A competitively bid contract has the weight of a vetting process, transparency, and benefit–cost analysis. Unfortunately, New Jersey contracted with AshBritt without utilizing a competitive bidding process, a decision that raised the ire of taxpayers and undermined the public trust. Also, the public's interest in accountability is undermined when an independent monitor has a business relationship with the entity it is supposed to be tracking. New Jersey hired Arcadis to monitor AshBritt, a company with a record of inflating costs through subcontractor layering.

At the same time, Arcadis' proprietary software, HaulPass, was used to increase accountability and cut costs. The software was able to verify the mileage AshBritt truckload drivers submitted, and helped build the case for communities that were overbilled.

AFFORDABILITY

Evaluating competitive proposals in advance of hiring a contractor prevents the public from overpaying and is one way to help ensure that the government gets the most bang for its buck. By accepting the Connecticut contract without more careful scrutiny, New Jersey inherited a poorly written contract with a lack of specific standards for payment calculation, resulting in overbilling for mileage. As noted above, however, GIS tracking software programs like HaulPass were used to verify the overbilling, resulting in a $300,000 savings for communities.

EQUITY

The question of fairness and accessibility in this case can be applied to other qualified contractors who did not have the opportunity to secure the most lucrative contract since AshBritt was chosen within hours of Sandy's landfall (see Renshaw & Baxter, 2013). Also, the Committee on Government Reform (U.S. House of Representatives, 2006) found that large contractors who rely on layers of subcontractor inflate their bill to the federal government by up to almost 50%—from $15 per cubic yard of debris removed to $31 during cleanup of Hurricane Katrina (see also Myers, 2006). While the citizens of New Jersey were denied accountability through the contracting process, they may also have been denied equity when AshBritt hired subcontractors; at least one of the subcontractor companies (County Waste) hired was owned by AshBritt's chief executive, Randal Perkins (Boburg, 2013a; Jordan, 2013).

At the same time, contractors can improve the fairness of FEMA's debris estimates by providing subject matter experts and technology to counter the federal estimates. This can result in additional reimbursements for communities.

EFFICIENCY

Private debris removal contractors can save the local government affected by disaster time and money because of their expertise and ability to handle the entire operation, including administrative tasks and FEMA reimbursement paperwork. But ultimately, the contractors may cost the federal government more, in part due to the inflated rates the contractors charge to hire layers of subcontractors and in part due to the administrative costs that would otherwise be paid for by the local government. The complexity of FEMA's reimbursement policies create a situation whereby local governments are more likely to receive reimbursements when they hire private contractors, but those reimbursements will cost more. In addition, the loose regulations surrounding the independent monitor contracting and qualifying process means many discrepancies that could be found out in advance are missed. Overall, the current system is probably, therefore, not the most efficient (maximum productivity with minimum waste) model for disaster debris removal. Some contractors are improving the efficiency of the model through innovative software tracking systems, providing real-time data and digital imagery to verify completed work.

EFFECTIVENESS

Using private contractors for debris removal is effective. According to FEMA NR-156 (2013), 95% of Hurricane Sandy debris in New York was removed and processed within ninety-five days. However, the significant amount of inquiry necessary to determine if a company such as AshBritt is colluding with the independent monitor, securing a contract underhandedly, or overbilling municipalities undermines the effectiveness achieved when using private contractors and adds time and expense to the overall disaster response and recovery.

CONCLUSION

Private contractors can help or harm a community's efforts to recover after a disaster. More specifically, debris removal management firms are often available immediately after a disaster declaration, and they offer expertise, equipment, and innovation to tackle the overwhelming task of hauling, sorting, and disposing of storm debris. However, they have a track record as a group of seeking to *game* the system by overstating the volume of debris, falsifying mileage records, or increasing their fees through layers of subcontractors.

FEMA has addressed these concerns through the use of independent monitors, but even that adjustment, emphasized after the problems with Hurricane Katrina cleanup efforts, needs improvement. Communities are on their own to verify the quality of both monitors and debris removal managers, and are encouraged to engage in a vetting process that includes competitive bidding. In addition, communities are on their own to write strong contracts using clear language to prevent being overcharged for mileage or otherwise.

One solution is for a community to create a strong pre-disaster debris management plan with contract templates. By developing a debris management plan, communities can expedite the recovery process and save time after a disaster. In addition, having a debris management plan in place should enhance the community's ability to document its costs, reducing the administrative time required to apply for Public Assistance grant funding (Jadacki, 2011).

In what are considered the most significant improvements to FEMA's powers since the Stafford Act (FEMA, 2013), President Barack Obama signed the Sandy Recovery Improvement Act in January 2013. The additional legislation addresses several of the recommendations and concerns cited in the OIG's 2011 report on debris removal contracting (see Jadacki, 2011). Specifically, FEMA is now piloting alternative procedures, including providing incentives to local government, to have FEMA preapproved debris management plans and prequalified contractors in place before a disaster declaration.

CASE STUDY   Digital Highway Notification: A Look at the Privatization of Emergency Notification through Commercial Billboards

Jeremiah Jones

ABSTRACT

In times of emergency (hurricanes, extreme winter conditions, AMBER alerts, wanted fugitive postings, and other such crises), the local government needs/wants to disseminate pertinent information to its citizens. As the need for alerting the affected population can be infrequent, unforeseen, and sometimes not deemed a priority until it is needed, the local agencies may not possess the capabilities or resources to best notify the public. One such case where the government has turned to a private entity for such disaster preparedness is in Florida. The state of Florida has used privately owned digital billboards in an attempt to improve its residents' preparedness before an emergency, as well as to provide information afterward during the response to/relief of an event. This case study will look into the success and shortfalls of privatization in the realm of emergency notification and disaster preparedness.

BACKGROUND

The geography of Florida makes it susceptible to a variety of natural disaster events. Since 1851, the 1200 miles of the coastline of Florida has been affected by 40% of all hurricanes that have made U.S. landfall, to include eight tropical storms in the last six years. Besides the more rare occurrences, the state can also fall victim to more everyday hazardous weather events such as tornadoes and flash flooding following a severe rainfall. In a state with a combined resident and visitor population totaling more than 18 million annually, the need to notify the populous of upcoming dangerous situations is critical.

The state of Florida has created a Public–Private Partnership (P3) in an attempt to better alert its population of coming hazards, and to continually notify the citizenry of up-to-date information regarding actions to be taken following such hazards. This P3 system has been achieved through an agreement between the Florida Division of Emergency Management (FDEM, 2015) and the Florida Outdoor Advertising Association (FOAA, n.d.). The FOAA has donated the use of its digital billboards, normally used for commercial advertising, to the FDEM to display emergency messages. As of June 4, 2008, the FOAA had fifty-two market billboards, with a total of sixty-one facings. These signs allow the FDEM to alert Floridians and tourists about warnings and suggested courses of action for a hazardous event. The first *real-world* application of the digital billboard warning system was for Tropical Storm Fay, in August 2008.

ISSUES

The FDEM and FOAA partnership has apparently been one of assistance to the population, resident and visiting, of Florida. With the presence of highway digital billboards, people on the roadways are better informed and aware of potentially hazardous situations. A careful study of this partnership revealed several important issues, among the most important of which are as follows:

- *The hollow state.* The current arrangement of the FDEM–FOAA P3 offers an example of the hollow state in governance. Here, the public sector becomes a revolving door for entry-level professionals to gain the required experience to move to more lucrative positions in the private sector. As a result, the public sector is left lacking the needed expertise to properly serve its constituents.
- *Market failure.* The FDEM has no direct control over the FOAA and their billboards. The FOAA has donated the usage of their billboards in times of crises. Such charity cannot always be seen as free and limitless. Should any factor change for the FOAA and their financial status, they could either cease to provide such a service or begin to charge the state of Florida for their usage. In either such case, the FDEM would have to readdress their program of public notification. The implication here is that the citizens of Florida that have been accustomed to such a system for nearly six years would suddenly be

without the familiar billboard warnings. Subsequently, if the FDEM were to attempt to either carry out such a program by themselves, or pay the FOAA for usage, the cost would have to be borne by the state. This may result in cuts in another program or generated by the taxpayers. Neither of these situations is favorable; however, should something alter the current arrangement, these critical decisions would need to be made by the FDEM.

- *Contract management.* The donation of FOAA digital billboards in times of emergency are not tied to any contract with the FDEM. This lack of control in the activity leaves the FDEM, and local emergency managers, powerless in the long-term arrangement with the FOAA. This P3 is not guaranteed by any means to continue, and as a result could leave the public without the service at a moment's notice. This lack of surety is a liability to the residents of Florida. Without any security of continuation, the FDEM may be without the current *crutch* of having such a widespread and free system of notifying the public in times of crisis.

- *Accountability.* The local level's role in the warning system is either to up channel the information to the FDEM to then disseminate to the FOAA, or the local emergency management officials contact local FOAA partners directly to tell of notification needs. On the local level, the partnership has been one of mutual cooperation and ease. The partnership is one that has been of reciprocated trust and communication. These attributes have allowed the local officials to maintain their accountability to the public by having the proper oversight and input required of the warning system collaboration.

- *Equity.* The accessibility of the digital billboard warning system contains little to no barriers, except for that it only reaches individuals on the selected highways. This barrier affects the members of the population that either do not drive, do not drive on the highways, or are not literate enough to understand the warning. The language barrier is also a consideration. For Florida, there is a large Spanish-speaking contingency, as well as others not primarily speaking English. If the individual counties do not specifically approach the language barrier, there could be a large portion of the population becoming vulnerable when otherwise they would not. Language and literacy aside, for the highway-riding masses, the signs offer a high degree of equity in the public service of providing warnings and notifications. As the highway signs are just that—signs on the highway—the issue of reaching those not on the roads is a moot point. However, the potential issue of a language and literacy barrier is one that has not yet been standardized since each locality is responsible for its desired message.

- *Affordability/best value.* The FOAA-donated digital billboards are of the best level of affordability—free. This is the ultimate value for the FDEM and local emergency managers. With the potential for millions of Florida residents and visitors to be warned of any possible disastrous situation at no extra cost, this partnership is a definitive best buy for the local and state governments. The lack of cost also increases the equity of the program, as it is not discriminatory toward jurisdictions that cannot afford to support the finances of such a system. This value is passed from the government and on to the citizens of Florida.
- *Quality/effectiveness.* The FOAA digital billboards cover situations including, but not limited to, directions to emergency shelters, evacuation routes, emergency-related road closures, AMBER alerts, wanted fugitive postings, and boil advisories. Such a widespread range of public notifications increases the overarching effectiveness of the digital billboard warning system. According to local emergency managers, there are no criticisms about how the P3 could improve to better serve the public. With the first-hand account from the boots on the ground, it is a very telling sign that the FDEM and FOAA partnership provides a high quality of service to at-risk Floridians.
- *Efficiency.* One aim for the public sector is to offer the most services at as little cost as possible. This allows for even more services to be provided, in theory better serving the community and making it *better.* This constant bargain hunting is best epitomized by the FDEM and FOAA arrangement. Neither the taxpayers nor the government are dedicating extra funds and, in return, are receiving a highly effective system promoting public safety. The situation is the very definition of efficiency,

getting more than what is expended. With zero expended on the FOAA billboards, the FDEM and other agencies are able to fully capitalize on offering public warnings to ensure the highest levels of safety.

CONCLUSION

The public–private partnership of the FDEM and FOAA has improved the safety of Florida's residents and visitors through offering emergency warnings on digital highway billboards. This arrangement has allowed for an increased awareness to those who are (or possibly) in affected areas of Florida. As this system is designed to alert travelers on the state's highways, it is not a ubiquitous warning system. Also, the FOAA has donated the usage of the billboards with no contractual agreement or long-term understanding. However, it has thus far seemed to be a partnership of mutual trust, understanding, respect, cooperation, and communication. This highly effective and efficient manner of warning the public has been regarded by local emergency managers as a great idea. With the individuals that are closest to ground zero singing the praises of such a system and no words from detractors, this public–private partnership is a prime example of how such arrangements can benefit emergency management.

CASE STUDY Benefits of Privatization of Emergency Medical Services

Melissa Wilkins

ABSTRACT

The history of established emergency medical services (EMS) and the role governments take on in the deciding process of providing services publicly or through private contracts are based on several factors. This study will show how privatizing emergency services can be beneficial to a constituency because of affordability, efficiency, quality effectiveness, area, public needs, and the challenges municipalities face in implementing new technologies or innovative services.

In addition to providing emergency services, municipalities must also plan for area needs in the event of natural disasters, such as hurricanes or tornadoes. Community needs have also grown to include emergency assistance with hazardous materials, disaster medicine, toxicology, infectious disease care, and more. The increased needs in these specialty areas result in existing medical staff having to be trained in these areas. As a direct result, additional funding is needed (Chiang, David, & Housman, 2006). Supporting information will show that the choice between public and private services is determined by looking at the net result obtained when measuring city/community demographics such as population, crime percentage, age, and urban density. The likelihood of major emergency events and infrastructure costs are also important factors. Polled results of areas currently using both private and public services will provide essential insight into the areas of affordability, efficiency, and quality effectiveness.

BACKGROUND

Municipalities and government agencies became accountable and responsible for providing the public with emergency services in November 1973, with the passing of the Medical Services Systems Act. The new guideline, according to the act, stated that government agencies must provide assistance and encouragement for the development of comprehensive area-wide emergency medical systems (Chiang et al., 2006). The new provision did not require government agencies to provide services; it only ensured that services were provided to the public. This could include ambulance services, fire rescue services, or both (Balaker & Summers, 2003). Contracts were required to be in place to provide services through public entities or private providers—an easier task to accomplish with federal funding.

Before passing the EMS Act, personnel only provided transportation services. Prehospital care or services were not administered owing to the lack of training. In addition to responding to emergency-based fire calls, local fire departments were also included within the emergency services realm. New guidelines and infrastructure developments led to including first response or emergency care and transportation services.

For private companies or firms, reimbursements from both Medicare and Medicaid encouraged agencies to compete with public entities that relied solely on federal funding. Private agencies began to gain momentum in providing transportation services and first response care, as well as bidding for contracts to exclusively provide services. These factors would ultimately decide whether government agencies would contract services from outside private agencies or use in-house services. Available resources, revenue, cost analysis, and infrastructure needs are just a few of the aspects officials would need to examine. This opened the door for more private firms to develop (Chiang et al., 2006).

INTRODUCTION

City- or area-based conditions, infrastructure, and funding are just a few of the components government agencies and officials have to consider before choosing to contract services out to private firms or provide services in-house. Outsourcing emergency medical services (EMS) is a growing trend in the United States for government agencies because they can offer more flexibility, assist larger areas, implement advanced technology faster, and respond to emergencies more rapidly. Contracting out for private services is often an approach used by smaller, rural areas like Abilene, Texas (Chiang et al., 2006). Customer satisfaction is imperative to private entities in building a good reputation and subsequently leading to more contract opportunities like taking over entire areas, partial services, or working alongside already existing public services. It is likely that municipalities will need both public and private agencies to help with the increased rates of widespread chronic medical conditions, natural disasters, and even domestic terrorism (Balaker & Summers, 2003).

EMERGENCY RESPONSE TIME AND TRANSPORTATION

The nature of an emergency call cannot be predicted. A fast response time is necessary to ensure a high survival rate of those exposed to an emergency. Because it depends on how quickly care is administered to patients, the National Institutes of Health suggests emergency service personnel should aim to arrive at the scene within five minutes. For best results, patients must receive care within nine minutes. Exceeding the nine-minute mark approaches a critical time, causing further damage that can lead to cardiac arrest (International Association of Fire Fighters®, 1997).

Fire department personnel administer 80% of prehospital care to patients or the community (International Association of Fire Fighters, 1997). Although prehospital care can be provided by fire department personnel, transportation services to trauma centers or hospitals is not an option. Private firms offer fully equipped vehicles for transportation; public-operated departments or personnel such as fire departments do not always have the resources available on the scene of an extreme emergency. Approximately 57% of emergency calls result in transporting patients for urgent care. Emergency transportation would require special vehicles that are American with Disabilities Act (ADA) compliant and EMS specific (fully equipped with necessary supplies) (Chiang et al., 2006).

In data compiled from the 200 largest cities in the United States, 96% of residents preferred public-based services for the first response only. The same information revealed that private-based transportation services were preferred by 45.5%, 4% higher than residents who preferred public transportation. The remaining 13% preferred a mix of both public- and private-based services. Polled results show that private services are chosen over public services in the area of transportation, while fire department services are maintained publicly. This results in a public–private relationship (Williams, 2004). Overall, approximately 37% of government municipalities and counties contract ambulance services privately (Balaker & Summers, 2003). Areas with fewer trauma centers or long transport times prefer private companies for these services (Chiang et al., 2006).

AFFORDABILITY

It is vital that government agencies examine all aspects of the equation when providing emergency service or asking for bids from private firms. Although federal funding is available, local taxpayer dollars also contribute to the overall associated costs (Chiang et al., 2006). The costs to provide emergency services and transportation publicly are considerably higher than when those services are contracted out. Equipment, personnel, training, and maintenance fees are just a few of the associated expenditures. With new technology and advanced machinery comes a necessary level of more highly qualified staff members. This causes maintenance costs to climb on a yearly basis. Operating with old equipment and less skilled crewmembers can diminish the chances of those in need of emergency services.

Poor performance from public services only affects those served in that particularly designated area. An incident in Detroit, Michigan, showcased the governing municipalities' challenges to perform at EMS standards. Owing to the lack of available resources, a gunshot victim was unable to receive medical attention for twenty-eight minutes after a 911 call was made. This resulted in the death of the victim who suffered from multiple gunshot wounds. The delayed response was due to the fact that 60% of the ambulances were out of service. The remaining vehicles, a total of 24, were reported to have several mechanical issues, such as broken dispatch equipment or brake problems (Balaker & Summers, 2003). Although public entities can purchase new vehicles to comply with upgrades, the cost associated with keeping vehicles in proper working condition is considerable too. Owing to more available resources, private agencies are able to offer better care at a reasonable rate with advanced, cutting-edge technology.

Although federal funding is available to assist municipalities, the process of implementing advanced technologies or system upgrades occurs more slowly when compared with private firms. Public agencies are at the mercy of government assistance that may not have a fast processing time for the requested items. Public agencies are often simply waiting for financial assistance. Private providers have more incentives available than public providers to develop and offer superior medical services (Chiang et al., 2006).

EFFICIENCY AND EFFECTIVE MEASURES

To provide around-the-clock emergency care, personnel must be ready to assist immediately. To promote the most efficient approaches for accomplishing this, private firms are frequently looking to implement new system designs. Among the most popular are Event-Driven Deployment, Flexible Production Strategy, and Peak-Load Staffing (Balaker & Summers, 2003).

By studying traffic congestion patterns, highly populated areas, and other important factors, private providers have had great success in performing effectively with the Event-Driven Deployment technique. The compiled data is able to assist providers by determining where services will be needed. Instead of choosing to stay at stationary locations such as a fire department, providers opt to have emergency vehicles located near freeways in larger areas or alternative routes during rush-hour traffic. This technique may change on a daily basis to comply with current events, infrastructure improvements, and city-level characteristics.

One tactic the federal government has used to increase efficiency is to have different teams or personnel specially trained to meet nonemergency calls, or teams more suited to handling severe life-threatening calls. An emergency operator would decide between dispatching the Basic Life Support team for nonemergency calls or the Advanced Life Support team for more severe calls. There is no guarantee that the operator answering the emergency call would have enough information to release the correct team. It would be a huge risk and responsibility in that the operator could make a life-saving decision in a moment's notice. Maintaining this method of operation required more staff, funding, and training just to keep up with medical demands. The tactic was proven to be less effective in performance measures (Balaker & Summers, 2003). Private providers, on the other hand, have found a way to offer flexibility and better care to those in need (Chiang et al., 2006). Unlike the federal government, some private firms use the Flexible Production Strategy, which treats every call as life threatening. Every employee is exposed to a highly skilled training associated with Advanced Life Support. Ensuring that personnel can adapt to handling both nonemergency and life-threatening calls has proved to be an efficient method for private firms (Balaker & Summers, 2003).

The average shift or schedule for public-based services is twenty-four hours on and forty-eight hours off (Williams, 2004). The average represents approximately 84% of the total emergency personnel—a figure that can cause operating costs to increase. A more efficient system design that contributed to higher performance standards became the deciding factor in Pinellas County, Florida, where officials received a bid from a public agency and another from a private entity. Like the average shift schedule, the public agency scheduled personnel in twenty-four-hour shifts with the following forty-eight hours off. This proved to be a costly approach. The private firm used an approach called Peak-Load Staffing, which allowed the company to essentially do more with less. The company added additional staff at peak times and operated with smaller crews on slower days and times. They were able to respond to more calls with one-third less employees at only two-third of the cost. Faster response times and better software helped the Pinellas County's EMS receive several awards including Florida's Provider of the Year Award (Balaker & Summers, 2003).

Most insurance companies will cover costs associated with emergency transportation to hospitals. The average collection rates reported for emergency transport providers are approximately 55% of billed charges. In an emergency, health care cannot be denied to those in need. Even with the knowledge that hospitals will not receive payments for a large percentage of emergency room visits or administered care, hospital administrators still understand that they will turn an overall profit by those who can pay or those who are covered by Medicare or Medicaid (Williams, 2004).

ECONOMY

Those municipalities with a constituency on the lower end of the socioeconomic scale are faced with economic challenges that may affect the decision process of choosing to privatize services. Private companies are able to divide costs of services across all areas to decrease payments (Chiang et al., 2006). Low urban density, smaller populated areas, severe weather conditions, and poor access to health care often contribute to choosing private firms. Data shows that people with greater wealth have a longer life expectancy than those with less financial means. It can be construed from that statistic that the quality of health is directed related to a household's financial situation. Data shows that healthier cities are more prone to using private providers and less healthy cities tend to use public providers (Chiang et al., 2006).

PLANNING AND RECOVERY

Supporting documentation shows that areas less likely to be exposed to extreme weather such as tornadoes, natural disasters, or terrorist attacks prefer private services (Chiang et al., 2006). However, some agencies currently operating under public funding during natural disasters have to deal with unpredicted hurdles that make recovery efforts more difficult to accomplish. During Hurricane Katrina, the city of New Orleans operated the EMS services with local taxes and federal funding. Although the area was able to function without any issues, the collapse of the city's infrastructure, due to extensive flooding from Katrina and Hurricane Rita, delayed its recovery efforts (National Association of Community Health Centers, 2006).

Owing to law enforcement and infrastructure limitations, a privately run emergency management operation would not have provided a quicker or more efficient response. Ultimately, the administrative duties will have to lie with public entities because there are hurdles that private organizations cannot overcome because they do not have legal jurisdiction. Yet, government agencies do recognize the growing need of assistance from privatized firms to assist with recovery efforts. Through third-party logistics, FEMA officials believe transporting supplies and the process to receive items can be shorter and quicker. Reaching out to large retailers after Hurricane Katrina may have improved recovery efforts in terms of providing bottle water, ice, and other necessary items (Phillips, 2007).

City governments must also consider planning for unexpected events an essential duty as the community relies heavily on officials to ensure the safety and survival of its constituents. There were a number of components that contributed to the government's failure in the aftermath of Hurricane Katrina in 2005. Flooding alone caused several health-care facilities and medical centers to close. Although the degree of severity that the impact of breached and overtopped levees had was somewhat unpredictable, New Orleans' city government still did not have an effective emergency recovery plan in place to help the area rebuild and recover.

For the economically challenged, getting medical attention after the hurricanes in New Orleans was close to impossible as Charity Hospital, the primary hospital that catered to the uninsured and income-challenged residents, was forced to close. Approximately two-third of patients at the Medical Center of Louisiana (MCLNO) were forced to seek medical attention at other places. Finding the same services offered at Charity Hospital was just an additional problem they would have to solve. The percentage of those uninsured increased from 6% to almost 40% (National Association of Community Health Centers, 2006). Most of these residents lived on the eastern side of New Orleans, making it difficult to travel to appointments for care. Before the storms, about sixteen ambulance units assisted residents. That number decreased to seven after the hurricanes. Several medical facilities and centers were severely affected by Hurricane Katrina and Rita, resulting in their closure (National Association of Community Health Centers, 2006).

Many New Orleanians were without medical attention or care for weeks and even months following the storm. Before Hurricanes Katrina and Rita, New Orleans functioned with approximately twenty-three hospitals. During the immediate aftermath, only one emergency trauma center and a few volunteer-based medical centers were operational and available to residents (Health and Medical Services, 2006). Immediately after the storm, six centers were completed destroyed and about eighty centers damaged.

Eight years later, there are only three trauma centers available, two medical facilities, and fourteen clinics open and in full operation. Many nursing homes or assisted living facilities had also closed, leaving only six from more than fifty facilities that had been previously available to serve the elderly patients of Orleans, Jefferson, Plaquemines, and St. Bernard Parishes (Health and Medical Services,

44

2006). After Hurricane Katrina, Louisiana fell to the forty-ninth spot on the national rankings for health-care infrastructure.

The City of New Orleans created a nonprofit agency after Hurricane Katrina to help recover, rebuild, and plan for future natural disasters. Bring New Orleans Back, created by Mayor Ray Nagin's administration, focused on assisting with the many infrastructure and medical care needs of the city (National Association of Community Health Centers, 2006).

During such catastrophes as Hurricanes Katrina and Sandy, the U.S. government has called upon seventeen different health-care facilities to enact much more elaborate and long-term emergency preparedness plans. In addition, the government would require facilities to maintain generated power, emergency lighting, and more to ensure patients could be served and treated in a comfortable and safe setting. This includes hospitals, outpatient facilities, hospice operations, and nursing homes. The new guidelines could affect as many as approximately 70,000 medical facilities or offices (Fink, 2014: 1–5).

CONCLUSION

Providing emergency care to its constituency is one of the most essential duties any municipality has. Privatized services provide the right balance of cost-effectiveness, efficiency, quality service, and streamlined operations. Their ability to adjust practices and methodology at a more rapid pace allows them to adapt to a situation more readily based on a situation's needs. Public emergency services are often bogged down with systems and protocols in place that may be outdated and no longer the most efficient. The flexibility and adaptability that privatized companies provide are why they are the preferred choice for emergency services.

CHAPTER QUESTIONS

True or False

1. Post-disaster debris cleanup is usually facilitated by a straightforward reimbursement system.
2. Communities need to decide how best to use their existing facilities for waste management.

3. When a community's capacity to recover from a natural hazard occurrence is overwhelmed by the magnitude of the hazard, the FEMA must make a declaration of natural disaster to the state emergency management agency.
4. The state's governor must request through FEMA that the president declare the affected area a disaster.
5. The state of Florida has used state-owned digital billboards to improve its residents' preparedness before an emergency.
6. With the presence of highway digital billboards, people on the roadways are better informed and aware of potentially hazardous situations.
7. FOAA digital billboards in times of emergency are tied to a contract with the FDEM.
8. The public–private partnership of the FDEM and FOAA has improved the safety of Florida's residents and visitors.
9. Municipalities and government agencies became accountable and responsible for providing the public with emergency services in November 1973, with the passing of the Hatch Act.
10. Before passing the EMS Act, personnel only provided transportation services.

REFERENCES

Balaker, T. & Summers, A. (2013). Emergency medical services privatization: Frequently asked questions. Reason.org. Reason Foundation. Retrieved from April 5, 2014, http://reason.org/files/ca8a6bf4603054c96fdde11c70329187.pdf.

Blake, E.S., Gibney, E.J. & Landsea, C.W. (2011). The deadliest, costliest, and most intense United States tropical cyclones from 1851 to 2010 (and other frequently requested hurricane facts). NOAA Technical Memorandum NWS NHC-6.

Boburg, S. (2013a). A second payday for Sandy cleanup contractor. *The Record.* Retrieved from http://www.northjersey.com/news/nj-state-news/a-second-payday-for-sandy-cleanup-contractor-1.615419. Accessed July 9, 2015.

Boburg, S. (2013b). Debris haulers' windfall: Odd math jacks up Sandy tab. *The Record.* Retrieved from http://www.northjersey.com/news/nj-state-news/debris-haulers-windfall-odd-math-jacks-up-sandy-tab-1.166824. Accessed July 9, 2015.

Boburg, S. (2013c). AshBritt to repay $300,000 after comptroller finds Sandy contractor mileage errors not intentional. *The Record.* Retrieved from http://www.northjersey.com/news/ashbritt-to-repay-300-000-after-comptroller-finds-sandy-contractor-mileage-errors-not-intentional-1.604251#sthash.vYHXE15v.dpuf. Accessed July 9, 2015.

Boxer, M. (2013). Mileage charges associated with the hauling of Superstorm Sandy debris. State of New Jersey Office of the State Comptroller. Investigative Report. Retrieved from http://www.nj.gov/comptroller/news/docs/report _sandy_debris_removal_charges.pdf. Accessed July 9, 2015.

Chiang, A., David, G. & Housman, M. (2006). The determinants of urban emergency medical services privatization. Critical Planning. Retrieved from April 5, 2014, http://www.researchgate.net/publication/228172145_The_Determinants_of _Urban_Emergency_Medical_Services_Privatization. Accessed July 9, 2015.

Committee on Government Reform (2006). Sifting through Katrina's legal debris: Contracting in the eye of the storm. U.S. House of Representatives One Hundred Ninth Congress. Serial No. 109-160. Retrieved from http://www .gpo.gov/fdsys/pkg/CHRG-109hhrg28897/html/CHRG-109hhrg28897.htm. Accessed July 9, 2015.

Davis, T. (2013). Sandy, One year later: Post-storm debreis removal completed. Toms River Patch. Retrieved from http://patch.com/new-jersey/tomsriver /sandy-one-year-later-poststorm-debris-removal-completed. Accessed July 8, 2015.

Environmental Protection Agency (1995). Planning for disaster debris. EPA 530-K-95-010. Retrieved from http://www.epa.gov/wastes/conserve/imr/cdm/pubs /disaster.htm. Accessed July 9, 2015.

FEMA 327 (2010). Public assistance debris monitoring guide. Department of Homeland Security Federal Emergency Management Agency. Retrieved from http://www.fema.gov/pdf/government/grant/pa/fema_327_debris _monitoring.pdf. Accessed July 9, 2015.

FEMA article. Public Private Partnership Case Study: Digital Billboards Deliver Emergency Messages. Retrieved from http://www.fema.gov/pdf/privatesec tor/fdem_foaa_case_study.pdf. Accessed July 9, 2015.

FEMA Debris Removal Contractor Registry (2013). Department of Homeland Security Federal Emergency Management Agency. Retrieved from https:// asd.fema.gov/inter/drcr/home.htm. Accessed July 9, 2015.

FEMA NR-156. (2013). Sandy debris removal passes 95 percent in 95 days. Retrieved from http://www.fema.gov/news-release/2013/02/01/sandy-debris-removal -passes-95-percent-95-days. Accessed July 9, 2015.

FEMA NR-239. (2013). A year after Hurricane Sandy, more than $2.1 billion in FEMA Public Assistance Grants in New York helps clear debris, reopen public facilities. Retrieved from https://www.fema.gov/news -release/2013/10/24/year-after-hurricane-sandy-more-21-billion-fema -public-assistance-grants-new.

FEMA. (2013). Sandy Recovery Improvement Act of 2013 progress update. Retrieved from https://www.fema.gov/sandy-recovery-improvement-act-2013.

Fetter, G. & Rakes, T.R. (2013). An equity approach to contractor assignment in post-disaster debris disposal operations. *International Journal of Emergency Management*, 9(2), 170–186.

Fink, S. (2014). Citing urgent need, U.S. calls on hospitals to hone disaster plans. *New York Times*, sec. A-19, 5.

Florida Division of Emergency Management (FDEM). (2015). Florida Disaster. Retrieved from http://www.floridadisaster.org/index.asp. Accessed July 9, 2015.

Florida Outdoor Advertising Association (FOAA). (n.d.). Welcome to FOAA. Retrieved from http://www.foaa.org/. Accessed July 9, 2015.

Havins, D. (2012). ARCADIS assists storm affected municipalities in debris removal. *Business Wire*. Retrieved from http://www.businesswire.com /news/home/20121129005231/en/ARCADIS-Assists-Storm-Affected -Municipalities-Debris-Removal#.U13V5K1dWXS. Accessed July 9, 2015.

Health and Medical Services. (2006). Louisiana Speaks Long-term Recovery Planning. City of New Orleans. Retrieved from April 3, 2014, http://www .louisianaspeaks-parishplans.org/IndParishHomepage_BaselineNeeds Assessment.cfm?EntID=11.

Herbert, K. & Crichton, S. (2013). Suffolk DA probes Sandy work in Brookhaven, Islip, Babylon. Retrieved July 19, 2015 from http://www.newsday.com/long-island /suffolk-da-probes-sandy-work-in-brookhaven-islip-babylon-1.5033528.

International Association of Fire Fighters® (1997). Emergency medical services privatization and prehospital emergency medical services. Retrieved from April 1, 2014, http://www.iaff.org/tech/pdf/monograph1.pdf.

Jadacki, M. (2011). FEMA's oversight and management of debris removal operations: OIG 11-40. Assistant Inspector General, Office of Emergency Management Oversight. U.S. Department of Homeland Security. Retrieved from http:// www.oig.dhs.gov/assets/Mgmt/OIG_11-40_Feb11.pdf. Accessed July 9, 2015.

Jordan, B. (2013). Watchdog: Two paydays for AshBritt in some Sandy-damaged towns. *Asbury Park Press*. Retrieved from http://www.app.com/arti cle/20130402/NJNEWS1002/304020025/Watchdog-Two-paydays-AshBritt -some-Sandy-damaged-towns. Accessed July 9, 2015.

Kaltwasser, J. (2012). No bids, no problem in Sandy cleanup. *NJBiz*. Retrieved from http://www.njbiz.com/article/20121126/NJBIZ01/121129942/No-bids-no -problem-in-Sandy-cleanup. Accessed July 9, 2015.

Kelly, J.V. (2014). New Jersey complied with applicable federal and state procure-ment standards when awarding emergency contracts for Hurricane Sandy debris removal activities. OIG-14-45-D. Office of the Inspector General, U.S. Department of Homeland Security. Retrieved from http://www.oig.dhs.gov /assets/GrantReports/2014/OIG_14-45-D_Feb14.pdf. Accessed July 9, 2015.

Kopecki, D. (2006). Cashing in on the Katrina cleanup. *Bloomberg Business Week*. Retrieved from http://www.businessweek.com/stories/2006-04-09/cash ing-in-on-the-katrina-cleanup. Accessed July 9, 2015.

Lipton, E. & Semple, K. (2012). At landfill, storm cleanup is military-style effort. *New York Times*. Retrieved from http://www.nytimes.com/2012/11/17 /nyregion/cleanup-from-hurricane-sandy-is-military-style-operation .html?pagewanted=all&_r=0. Accessed July 9, 2015.

Mullen, S. (2014). Feds: No wrongdoing in Sandy debris-removal contract. *Asbury Park Press.* Retrieved from http://www.app.com/article/20140306/NJ NEWS33/303060151/Feds-No-wrongdoing-Sandy-debris-removal-contract. Accessed July 9, 2015.

Myers, L. (2006). Is Katrina cleanup a fleecing of America? *NBC News Investigates.* Retrieved from http://www.nbcnews.com/id/13153520/ns/nbc _nightly_news_with_brian_williams-nbc_news_investigates/t/katrina -cleanup-fleecing-america/#.U17YAa1dWXQ. Accessed July 9, 2015.

National Association of Community Health Centers. (2006). One year later. National Association of Community Health Centers. Retrieved from April 8, 2014, http://www.nachc.com/client//CHCKatrinaReport.pdf. Accessed July 9, 2015.

New Jersey Office of Recovery and Rebuilding. (2013). Taking emergency and long-term action to assist debris removal. Retrieved from http://www.state .nj.us/governor/news/news/552013/approved/20130205f.html.

Phillips, Z. (2007). FEMA looks to private sector for disaster provisions. *Government Executive.* Retrieved from May 3, 2014, http://www.govexec .com/defense/2007/08/fema-looks-to-private-sector-for-disaster-provisions /25168/.

Politicker, N.J. (2013). Democrats find an opening with AshBritt. *PolitickerNJ.* Retrieved from http://www.politickernj.com/62955/democrats-find-opening -ashbritt. Accessed July 9, 2015.

Reitmeyer, J. & Hayes, M. (2013). Lobbyist for Florida Sandy cleanup firm hosting Christie fundraiser. *The Record.* Retrieved from http://www.northjersey .com/news/nj-state-news/lobbyist-for-florida-sandy-cleanup-firm-hosting -christie-fundraiser-1.540680. Accessed July 9, 2015.

Renshaw, J. & Baxter, C. (2013). Firm offered cheaper rates to clean up after Sandy, but Christie stuck with AshBritt. *The Star-Ledger.* Retrieved from http://www .nj.com/politics/index.ssf/2013/02/hurricane_sandy_debris_removal.html.

Renshaw, J. (2013). Once employed by AshBritt, monitoring firm is now fiscal watchdog over its operations in NJ. *The Star-Ledger.* Retrieved from http:// www.onenewjersey.org/2013/02/18/once-employed-by-ashbritt-monitoring -firm-is-now-fiscal-watchdog-over-its-operations-in-nj/. Accessed July 9, 2015.

Rosania, S.M. (2012). State of New Jersey request for qualifications for Disaster debris management monitoring operations by ARCADIS. State of New Jersey Department of the Treasury. Retrieved from http://www.state.nj.us/trea sury/purchase/notices/pdf/arcadisproposal.pdf. Accessed July 9, 2015.

Williams, D. (2004). JEMS emergency medical services. *JEMS 200-City Survey.* Retrieved from April 5, 2014, http://www.jems.com/sites/default/files/2004 -200CitySurvey04_tcm16-12234.pdf. Accessed July 9, 2015.

3

A Primer on Federal and State Disaster Funds and Funding

Race A. Hodges

Contents

Learning Objectives

- The reader will be able to describe the structure of federal and state disaster funds and funding.
- The reader will develop a working knowledge of the federal grant-in-aid system and of some specific emergency management–related grant opportunities.
- The reader will understand the role of the private sector in disaster funds and funding.
- The reader will be able to explain the typical role of state government in the field of emergency management and identify the opportunities and challenges associated with the relationship between local and state government.

INTRODUCTION

Each year, the federal government funnels billions of dollars in disaster-related grants to state and local governments. These grants are complex and diverse in scope, often requiring the engagement of multiple actors across the public and private sectors. Despite this complexity, the Government Accountability Office (GAO) offers a clear definition of a grant as "a financial assistance award comprised of payments in cash or in kind for a targeted purpose" (GAO, 2005). In fiscal year 2011, the amount of grants awarded to state and local government approximated

$606 billion, a figure that has dramatically increased in constant dollars over the past three decades (GAO, 2012).* While the proportion of federal outlays for disaster-related grants constitutes less than 5% of this amount, these grants are nevertheless instrumental in achieving goals and objectives across all areas of emergency management.

There have been a number of reports issued by the GAO, the Department of Homeland Security (DHS) inspector general, and the Office of Management and Budget (OMB) that suggest that a lack of capacity at the local and state level to effectively administer grants significantly hinders their effectiveness. As a result of this lack of capacity, the responsibility to manage these grants at the state and local level are increasingly being contracted out to the private sector. In addition to grant management, the private sector is also heavily involved in providing services financed by these grants. This chapter discusses these issues and presents an overview of the structure of federal grants to state and local government, commonly referred to as the *grant-in-aid* system, and the role of the private sector in disaster funding.

INTRODUCTION TO THE FEDERAL GRANT-IN-AID SYSTEM

Federal grant-in-aid programs constituted a notable 26.3% of the 2011 federal government budget, indicating the significance of grants as a mechanism for distributing federal funds. According to the Catalog of Federal and Domestic Assistance (CFDA), which is a compendium of all federal grants available to state and local governments, more than 2000 federal grant-in-aid programs currently exist. Nearly a quarter of these programs were managed by the Department of Health and Human Services (492), with the Departments of the Interior (274), Agriculture (272), Justice (136), and Education (120) rounding out the top five federal departments with the most grant-in-aid programs. Within the realm of emergency management, the CFDA lists eighty-two grant-in-aid programs under the purview of the DHS, of which the Federal Emergency Management Agency (FEMA) plays a critical role in administering. While this chapter will focus primarily on grants administered by FEMA, other departments

---

* Between 1980 and 2012, this amount has an average annual growth rate of 4.58%, in 2011 constant dollars.

and agencies, such as the Department of Housing and Urban Development (HUD), are also involved in awarding disaster-related grants.

As the federal grant-in-aid system constitutes such a high percentage of government expenditures, the federal government has implemented stringent regulations and processes guiding the management of these funds to ensure that they are used for their intended purposes. While much of the terminology behind grant management is intricately complex and beyond the scope of this chapter, there are some general characteristics common to federal grants, which are briefly outlined below.

Federal grants can generally be understood to fall into one of two categories:

1. Categorical grants

    Categorical grants are narrow in scope and restricted to fund a very specific set of activities. FEMA's Flood Mitigation Assistance (FMA) program uses categorical grants to fund a specific set of flood mitigation activities.
2. Block grants

    Block grants are broad in scope and fund a wide range of activities. HUD's Community Development Block Grant (CDBG) program is often used to finance a broad range of disaster recovery projects.

Likewise, grants generally use one of two methods to determine the allocation of funds to applicants:

1. Project grants

    Project grants are competitive. They fund specified, time-bound projects via a benefit–cost-based selection process. FEMA's FMA program uses this approach.
2. Formula grants

    Formula grants are noncompetitive. The grant award amount is determined using a preestablished formula based on a set of criteria. HUD's CDBG program uses a formula-based approach for awarding funds.

While federal grants may initially be grouped into the aforementioned categories, it is important to note that their status may change once they are circulated through various levels of government. For example, while HUD's CDBG is first characterized as a formula grant, once the funds are awarded to a particular state, the state may subsequently choose to redistribute these funds as project grants.

For a more detailed description of the type of federal grant opportunities offered by the federal government, please see the CFDA's database at http://www.cfda.gov.

FEDERAL GRANT-IN-AID LIFE CYCLE

While the type and characteristics of different grants play a critical role in defining how they are administered, the federal grant-in-aid life cycle typically follows a predictable series of steps. First, all grant-in-aid programs are initiated by some federal enabling legislation. For example, FEMA's Hazard Mitigation Grant Program (HMGP) was first authorized by the Robert T. Stafford Disaster Relief and Emergency Assistance Act in 1988. The programmatic details and rules are then incorporated into the Code of Federal Regulations (CFR), which, once installed, can be difficult to change. Following enabling legislation, federal departments or agencies must develop the administrative mechanisms necessary to administer the relevant grant-in-aid program. For FEMA in particular, the Grants Program Directorate (GPD) is in charge of overseeing the administration of their grant programs. In addition, Congress must routinely authorize fiscal appropriations for multiple grant programs in order for these programs to have funds to disperse.

Once these requirements are in place, grant-in-aid programs generally follow a predicable series of four stages, with the private sector involved at each of these stages in varying capacities. In the *pre-award stage*, eligible applicants submit their application, which is followed by a review process. For some local government that may lack administrative capacity to submit full applications for these grants, these applications are written by private firms on their behalf, either for a fee or with the expectation that the firm will be contracted to perform additional work funded by the grant award. Next, successful applicants enter the *award stage* involving the notification of the award. Next, the *implementation stage* involves fund dispersal and receipt by the applicant, grantor oversight, project administration, and report development. The implementation stage is where the private sector is most heavily involved. For example, for a community that receives a grant to elevate homes in a floodplain, the elevation services may be contracted to a private firm. Finally, the federal grant life cycle concludes with the *closeout stage*, which involves auditing and fiscal reconciliation. Many FEMA nondisaster grants follow this life cycle as well. Figure 3.1 is a modified version of the grant management life cycle published by FEMA's Grant Program Directorate.

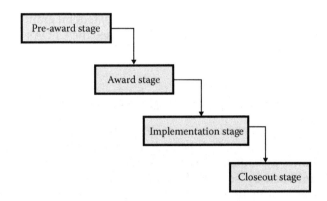

Figure 3.1 Federal grant-in-aid life cycle. Requirements for grant: Enabling legislation, fiscal appropriation, and grant administration capabilities developed.

Federal Grant-in-Aid Life Cycle of Post-Disaster Funding

The life cycle of the majority of federal grants, including those related to emergency management, can be characterized by the aforementioned illustration and discussion. However, within the realm of emergency management, the life cycle of post-disaster grants in particular varies considerably. One important reason for this variation is their dependence on disaster declarations to be in place. For example, FEMA's Public Assistance (PA) program, HMGP, and others only become available when these declarations are issued. While the private sector can be involved at any stage and for any disaster-related grant, these post-disaster grants often involve the private sector to the greatest degree because of the surge in funding available. Furthermore, local capacity can be overwhelmed following a disaster, and the desire for an expedient response and recovery often requires assistance from nongovernmental actors. The general life cycle of post-disaster grants is outlined below (GOHSEP, n.d.).

1. Local emergency disaster declaration
2. Governor's emergency declaration
3. Initial damage assessment
4. Preliminary disaster assessment
5. Request for presidential disaster declaration
6. Granting of presidential disaster declaration
7. Delivery of FEMA programs: IA, PA, HM

8. Applicant's briefings
9. Kickoff meetings (scope of work defined)
10. Project approval; funds obligated
11. Project execution (procurement, record keeping)
12. Applicant applies for reimbursement

Grant Management Requirements

Various requirements for federal grant-in-aid management are put in place at different levels of government.

Federal Level

The OMB is a critical figure involved in developing rules and regulations for the federal grant-in-aid system. For all policies related to ensuring proper oversight and accountability related to grant management, the OMB is the central governmental leader. Following President George W. Bush's E-government initiative, OMB launched Grants.gov (http://www.grants.gov) to allow for a central forum for which grantors and grantees can access more information regarding the federal grant-in-aid process. The OMB also regularly issues grant management circulars to federal agencies regarding updates to grant management policy.

While the OMB sets broad-level policies, federal agencies and departments also develop rules and regulations for grant management. The GPD, which is housed within the FEMA, administers the majority of DHS grants to state and local governments and is often referred to as the *one-stop-shop* for grant management (FEMA, 2011). The GPD plays an essential role in FEMA operations. In 2013, FEMA grant programs accounted for 15.38% of the agency's entire operating budget (FEMA, 2013; DHS, 2014b). In accordance with the Post-Katrina Emergency Reform Act of 2007, Congress created the GPD by synthesizing the FEMA Grants Management Branch, the DHS Office of Grants and Training-Office of Grant Training, and the DHS Office of Grants and Training-Preparedness Programs Division. The mission of the GPD is to "ensure that, through the strategic use of federal funding, our nation is well prepared to respond to and mitigate all-hazard events" (The Future of FEMA's Grant Programs Directorate, 2011).

While the vast majority of emergencies and disasters that have occurred since 9/11 have been nonterrorist related, the majority of DHS grants to state and local government have been focused on terrorism preparedness (Congressional Research Service [CRS], 2009). In 2010, 60% of grant outlays to state and local governments were for terrorism-focused programs, such as the Urban Areas Security Initiative (UASI), which appropriated close to $1 billion in grants during FY 2013. The federal government first made terrorism preparedness grants available to state and local governments following the 1993 bombing of the World Trade Center; however, since 9/11, the proportion of emergency management grants available for all hazard programs has steadily decreased (CRS, 2009).

State Level
Few emergency management grants are offered directly from the federal government to local recipients. Rather, many state emergency management agencies or State Administration Agencies (SAAs) serve as intermediaries between these federal grants and recipients at the local level. For example, a significant number of emergency preparedness grants limit applicant eligibility to SAAs, which may increase the opportunity for FEMA to monitor grant administration, rather than dealing directly with multiple localities. This intermediary step also allows the state to place additional requirements that subrecipients are required to comply with. For example, in 2011, the state of Louisiana passed Revised Statutes 38 and 39, which contain important information on public finance and public contracts that grant recipients are required to follow. California and Florida, along with many other states, also have additional requirements that localities must comply with during the HMGP application procedure. The capacity of states, like localities, may also be overly taxed in the post-disaster environment, leading many to hire administrative firms to assist in the grant administration process.

An additional authority at the state level is their ability to actually set grant award priorities. For example, while local governments may submit an HMGP application for any project, the state selects applications based on predetermined priorities as outlined in their mitigation strategy, before forwarding these applications to FEMA for final approval.

Local Level
Since most emergency management grants are made available to government entities, local governments have little discretion in terms of complying with grant requirements imposed by state and federal agencies. Many state and federal agencies collaborate with localities in the development of grant applications, as well as in the monitoring and implementation of the grant award. Therefore, the majority of grant management

requirements at the local level involve adhering to procurement law and complying with those requirements put forth at higher levels of government. In Texas, for example, local governments are required to comply with the Uniform Grant Management Standards, which place strict oversight rules regarding the tracing of funds and require the maintenance of financial records, source documentation, and other requirements that grantees must comply with. Additionally, during the closeout process of the grant, local governments may be required to submit financial status reports, final performance reports, cash/cost adjustments, and other activities.

CURRENT TRENDS AND CHALLENGES

Both the GAO and other agency-level inspector generals have identified a number of recurring challenges involving grant management by state and local governments. Of particular interest are findings that claim that intergovernmental collaboration, internal control weaknesses, and a lack of agency or recipient capacity are recurring problems associated with the federal grant-in-aid system (Farris & Jerolleman, 2012). As such, these challenges may prompt government to outsource grant management and procurement to private agencies, whose role in this process has increased significantly over the past few decades (Farris & Jerolleman, 2012).

In light of these problems, there have been a number of attempts by the GPD to improve the administration of FEMA grants to state and local governments. In 2008, the GPD created the short-lived Cost-to-Capability (C2C) evaluation to measure a potential grant recipient's ability to handle and respond to disasters. The purpose of this evaluation was to better understand areas where grant recipients needed assistance, and to more effectively allocate funding as a result (DHS, 2008). However, the C2C was fraught with problems from its initiation. In light of a GAO report outlining the questionable mechanisms for assessing local disaster response capability, the C2C program was discontinued, with no current successive mechanism in place (Morton, 2012).

This ongoing problem takes on an additional level of concern when coupled with findings presented in a 2009 CRS report regarding the DHS's assistance to states and localities. The report notes that between 2002 and 2009, the number of DHS assistance programs increased from nine to fifteen, coupled with an increase of $34 billion in appropriations during this same period. Thus, while the administrative mechanisms were already recognized as being insufficient in grant management, the number of grants and amount of funding continued to increase. Other reports conducted by the CRS and GAO have garner similar findings, such as that a lack of coordination across grant programs has led to a duplication of activities, which suggests that there may be a wasteful and inefficient allocation of funds appropriated to state and local governments (CRS, 2009). Finally, in a report completed by the Brookings Institution reviewing federal post-disaster recovery programs, more than fifty stakeholders and federal agency representatives identified key barriers to administering effective post-disaster recovery efforts at the state and local levels. Of their findings, the report argued that the high number of federal categorical grants can be challenging for local leaders to both comprehend and manage. These reports, like many others before them, strongly suggest that Congress, DHS, and FEMA must work more closely together to reconsider critical issues regarding federal homeland security assistance and their federal grant-in-aid system.

Despite identifying these problems, the increased involvement of the private sector may not necessarily be the best answer. Numerous reports suggest that contracting consultants in the work of disaster management may lead to a decreased level of community input and sustained local interest. In a survey of State Hazard Mitigation Officers nationwide, Smith et al. (2013) found that many attributed the lack of local commitment to hazard mitigation as a result of an overreliance on consulting work. Furthermore, the quality of consultant work in writing hazard mitigation plans for a community may be of mediocre quality, as consultants "seek to do the minimum required to meet FEMA standards while still 'breaking even' or garnering a profit from what often amount to low-cost planning grants" (Smith et al., 2013). Therefore, developing grant management requirements to ensure that the private sector performs high-quality project work is a recurring challenge in disaster grant management.

UTILIZING THE PRIVATE SECTOR
TO ADDRESS THESE CHALLENGES

Despite attempts to improve administrative efficiency, recurring problems with grant administration in the public sector continue to go unresolved. The increased role of the private sector in terms of grant administration also comes at a time when FEMA is actively promoting that the private sector play a larger role in emergency management. For example, FEMA has suggested that teaming with the private sector can improve disaster management decision making and resource availability, and increase the overall effectiveness of emergency management efforts (DHS, 2012). Additionally, a 2012 publication issued by the DHS acknowledges that, "when the public and private sectors bring their knowledge and resources to the table as part of the same team, we are better able to serve our neighbors, fellow citizens, and disaster survivors in particular" (DHS, 2012). This report also brings attention to the 2012 DHS Appropriation bills, which states that, "disaster preparedness, mitigation, response, and recovery are efforts that particularly lend themselves to public and private partnerships" (DHS, 2011).

This rhetoric, which is something of a new phenomenon, is now commonplace in many contemporary emergency management publications. While the private sector had been importantly involved in the recovery efforts of the Great Chicago Fire of 1871, the first indication of the private sector managing and disaster funding came after the 1906 San Francisco Earthquake and the 1927 Great Mississippi Flood. Busch and Givens (2012) report that post-disaster reconstruction funding regularly changed hands between the federal and private sectors following these two historic events. The role of the private sector in federal disaster funding also underwent a change following the creation of FEMA during the Carter administration, which saw an increase in outsourcing government office job functions to private contractors. Busch and Givens argue that one reason that the private sector is involved in disaster management involves its ability to "more effectively fill personnel needs" than the government acting independently. As the bureaucratic hiring process can often take much longer in government agencies, the ability of the private sector to streamline this process in time-pressing situations is a critical ability needed during certain types of disasters.

The private sector played perhaps its most critical role in emergency management during the George W. Bush administration. Despite the proliferation of DHS programs following 9/11, the Bush administration was able to convey that the size of government was shrinking in part because of the proliferation of DHS contracts to the private sector (Priest & Arkin, 2011). Today, the private sector's administrative role in the grant-in-aid system can also be seen by examining the proliferation of Request for Proposals (RFPs) issued by local governments. RFPs are mechanisms for which local governments solicit the services of an independent party. Many local governments that effectively manage to win an emergency management grant issue RFPs for private organizations to play a multitude of roles during the administration of the grant.

For example, following Hurricane Sandy, the Township of Little Falls, New Jersey, issued an RFP for a *FEMA and CDBG Disaster Recovery Project Manager* to assist the municipality with the coordination of services from a variety of professionals to acquire, demolish, or elevate identified properties in the municipality. The Township of Little Falls received this grant from Passaic County, which was a subgrantee of the state of New Jersey for funding provided by HUD. Similar to many RFPs, this RFP contained a variety of sections, such as the official legal notice to bidders, instructions to proposers, statutory requirements, information regarding how proposals would be scored, scope of work requirements, and many other terms and conditions.

DHS/FEMA Emergency Management Grants

The following section provides a concise overview of a variety of FY 2014 FEMA or HUD grants related to emergency management. These different programs are categorized as Preparedness, Recovery, or Mitigation focused. Given the immediate nature of emergency response, grant programs that seek to improve local response capabilities are discussed under the Preparedness section. Similarly, grant programs that provide reimbursement funding for certain response-related activities, such as the FEMA PA program, are discussed in the Recovery section.

Introduction to Preparedness Grants

FEMA offers a wide variety of preparedness grant programs to state and local governments. In 2011, the DHS released its National Preparedness Goal in an attempt to unify preparedness grant programs. These grants seek to achieve the National Preparedness Goal, which is to achieve "A secure and resilient Nation with the capabilities required across the whole community to prevent, protect against, mitigate, respond to, and recover from the threats and hazards that pose the greatest risk." (DHS, 2011). This document further offers five core capabilities across the areas of Prevention, Protection, Mitigation, Response, and Recovery, each of which have targets and performance measurements that influence the allocation of resources to different preparedness grants. For FY 2014, FEMA offered eight preparedness (nondisaster) grants, which are briefly outlined below.

Emergency Management Performance Grants Program
The Emergency Management Performance Grants Program (EMPG) was authorized by the Robert T. Stafford Disaster Relief and Emergency Assistance Act. The EMPG provides funding to state, local, tribal, and territorial governments to support the National Preparedness Goal. In FY 2013, the total amount of federal outlays for the EMPG totaled approximately $332 million, a figure that has grown considerably in constant dollars since 2005 (see Figure 3.2). Examples of activities that have been funded by the EMPG program include a wide range of emergency management preparedness programs, such as (CFDA, 2014a)

- Developing and maintaining community emergency plans and mitigation plans
- Preparing and approving ordinances to comply with the National Preparedness Goal
- Conducting or participating in all-hazards based exercises
- Continuity of Operations (COOP) and Continuity of Government (COG) activities
- Completing of the Threat and Hazard Identification and Risk Assessment (THIRA) process (pre-disaster recovery planning)
- Recovery planning

Each of these bulleted points often relies heavily on the involvement of the private sector.

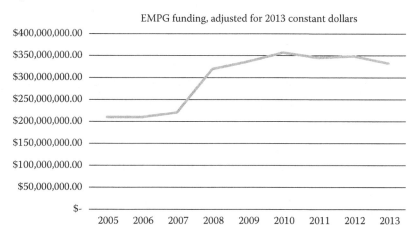

Figure 3.2 EMPG funding FY 2013.

The EMPG program requires a cost-matching agreement of 50% and quarterly reporting requirements. More information on the EMPG program can be found at http://www.cfda.gov and http://www.fema.gov /grants. More information on the National Preparedness Goal can be found at http://www.fema.gov/national-preparedness.

Homeland Security Grant Program

The Homeland Security Grant Program (HSGP) was established by The Homeland Security Act of 2002 to support the National Preparedness System and National Preparedness Goal. The HSGP provides formula grants across the following three interrelated subgrant programs: (1) the UASI, (2) the State Homeland Security Program (SHSP), and (3) Operation Stonegarden (OPSG). In 2014, the combined federal outlays for these programs totaled $968,389,689. Grants are awarded to State Administrative Agencies (SAAs), which then must pass 80% of funding to local governments. Each of the HSGP programs fund different types of activities, and are outlined below:

1. *The UASI.* The UASI accounts for more than half of all HSGP funding. The UASI issues funds to SAAs, which may subsequently allocate these funds to assist high-density urban areas in terrorism preparedness programs. In 2013, the DHS identified twenty-five high-threat/high-density urban areas that were eligible to participate in the program. Examples of activities that UASI funds include, but are not limited to, training exercises, planning, and equipment purchasing.
2. *The SHSP.* The SHSP account for approximately one-third of all HSGP funding. The SHSP issues funds to SAAs, which then obligates these funds to local government units. SHSP funds can be used for activities that help build local capacity related to terrorism preparedness. Such activities may include trainings, exercises, planning, and others.
3. *OPSG.* OPSG began in 2010, replacing the Metropolitan Medical Response Team and Citizen Corps Program. OPSG accounted for approximately 6% of all HSGP funding. OPSG issues funds to SAAs located in areas that share international borders. OPSG funds activities to increase intergovernmental coordination in order to better secure the U.S. borders. Example of activities with

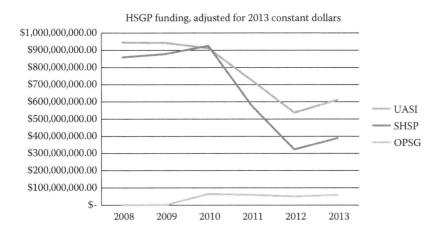

Figure 3.3   HSPG funding FY 2013.

the OPSG may fund activities that enhance cooperation between law enforcement agencies and increase their operational capabilities to secure the country's border.

Unlike most disaster grants, the HSGP program does not require cost-sharing or matching funds from state or local governments. Figure 3.3 illustrates how funding for these programs has changed since 2008.

More Information on HSGP is available at http://www.fema.gov/fy-2014-homeland-security-grant-program-hsgp.

Intercity Passenger Rail Program

The Intercity Passenger Rail Program (IPR) was established by the 9/11 Commission Act of 2007, Section 1406, Public Law 110-53 to support the National Preparedness Goal. The IPR provides project grants to the National Passenger Railroad Corporation (Amtrak) with a specific focus on terrorism preparedness activities for the U.S. passenger rail infrastructure for terrorism. If Amtrak is awarded an IPR grant, funds are transferred and administered by the Department of Transportation Federal Railroad Administration (DHS, 2014). In FY 2014, the combined federal outlays for these programs totaled $10,000,000. Examples of projects that the IPR program funds include, but are not limited to

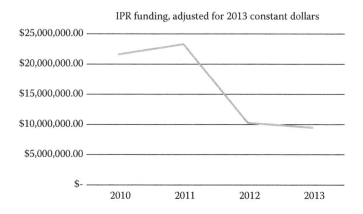

Figure 3.4 IPR funding FY 2013.

- Developing emergency management capabilities through emergency-preparedness drills and exercises
- Protecting high-risk/high-consequence underwater and underground rail assets
- Planning
- Public awareness and preparedness campaigns
- Protecting high-risk, high-consequence areas or systems

Like the HSGP, the IPR program does not require cost-sharing or matching funds from state or local governments. Figure 3.4 illustrates how funding for this program changed between 2010 and 2013.

More information on the IPR is available at http://www.fema.gov/fy -2014-intercity-passenger-rail-ipr-amtrak.

Nonprofit Security Grant Program

The Nonprofit Security Grant Program (NSGP) was established by Section 2003 of the Homeland Security Act of 2002 (Public Law 107-296) to support the National Preparedness Goal. The NSGP provides project grants to nonprofits at high risk of terrorist attack located in areas that have been identified as eligible for an Urban Area Security Initiative grant program (CFDA, 2014b). An SAA may apply to this program on behalf of nonprofits with Section 501(c) (3) status. In FY 2014, the combined federal outlays for these programs totaled $13,000,000. Examples

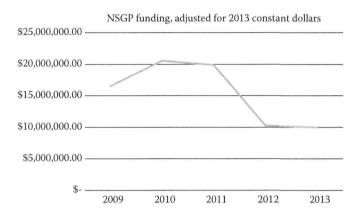

Figure 3.5 NSGP funding FY 2013.

of projects that the NSGP program funds include, but are not limited to (CFDA, 2014b)

- Target hardening
- Physical security enhancements
- Integrating nonprofit preparedness activities with state and local preparedness activities
- Supporting collaboration between private and public representatives

Unlike most disaster grants, the NSGP does not require cost-sharing or matching funds from state or local governments. Figure 3.5 illustrates how funding for this program changed between 2009 and 2013.

More Information on NSPG is available at http://www.fema.gov.

Port Security Grant Program

The Port Security Grant Program (PSGP) was established by Section 102 of the Maritime Transportation Security Act of 2002 (Pub. L. No. 107-295) (46 U.S.C. § 70107) to support the National Preparedness Goal. The PSGP provides project grants to port authorities, facility operators, ferry systems, and government agencies that provide port security services in the nation's highest-risk ports. In 2014, the DHS identified 146 ports eligible to receive PSGP funding. In FY 2014, the combined

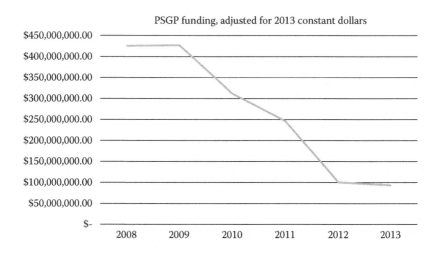

Figure 3.6 PSGP funding FY 2013.

federal outlays for these programs totaled $100,000,000. Examples of projects that the PSGP program funds include, but are not limited to

- Maritime prevention, protection, response, recovery, and mitigation capability development
- Enhancing cybersecurity capabilities
- Training and exercises
- Supporting governance integration

In FY 2014, the PSGP required that public organizations provide matching funds of at least 25% and that private organizations provide matching funds of at least 50%. Figure 3.6 illustrates how funding for this program changed between 2008 and 2013.

More Information on PSPG is available at http://www.fema.gov/fy -2014-port-security-grant-program-psgp.

Tribal Homeland Security Grant Program

The Tribal Homeland Security Grant Program (THSGP) was established by the Homeland Security Act of 2002 to support the National Preparedness System and National Preparedness Goal. The THSGP provides formula grants to tribal nations in the United States. In 2014, the

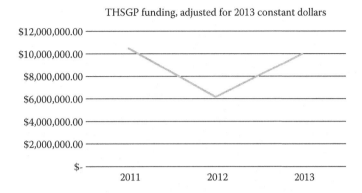

THSGP funding, adjusted for 2013 constant dollars

Figure 3.7 THSGP funding FY 2013.

combined federal outlays for these programs totaled $10,000,000. The THSGP funds different types of activities, and are outlined below:

- Planning, training, exercise, and equipment activities
- Law enforcement terrorism prevention

Unlike most disaster grants, the THSGP does not require cost-sharing or matching funds from state or local governments. Figure 3.7 illustrates how funding for this program changed between 2011 and 2013.

More Information on THSGP is available at http://www.fema.gov /fy-2014-tribal-homeland-security-grant-program-thsgp.

INTRODUCTION TO RECOVERY GRANTS

As mentioned earlier, federal grants that assist in disaster recovery generally require a Presidential Disaster Declaration. The president is granted this authority by the Robert T. Stafford Emergency Relief and Disaster Assistance Act. Unlike preparedness grants, which have a set amount of annual federal outlays, the amount of funding available for recovery grants can fluctuate immensely depending on the scale of the disaster experienced. For example, following the 2005 Hurricane Season, FEMA's PA program, which is outlined below, dispersed well over $11 billion to Gulf Coast affected communities (GAO, 2008). The funding for many recovery-related grants is extracted from the disaster relief fund, which is funded annually but allows unused funds to carry over to subsequent years. Historically, the involvement of the private sector in the administration of recovery grants has been more notable than in preparedness grants. This section concisely outlines three significant recovery-related grants.

CDBG Disaster Recovery Assistance Program

The CDBG Disaster Recovery Assistance Program was established by Title I of the Housing and Community Development Act of 1974. The CDBG Disaster Recovery Assistance is a noncompetitive, formula-based block grant that allows Congress to appropriate money to assist in the recovery process following a disaster. This funding amount has historically varied significantly; following Hurricane Katrina and Hurricane Sandy, funding for this program exceeded $16 billion. Since 1993, the least amount of money appropriated totaled $39 million in 1993, to assist in the recovery of the Oklahoma City Bombing.

The Office of Community Planning and Development, a subsidiary of HUD, administers the program and notifies governments of their eligibility to apply for funding. For communities with populations of more than 200,000, funds are typically administered directly to the local government. For communities under this population level, funds are directed toward state governments, which then oversee the process of allocating the funds to these smaller communities.

The CDBG Disaster Recovery Assistance Program requires that the majority of funds be spent on activities that assist low- to medium-income-level communities. Examples of activities that this program has funded in the past include debris removal, acquisition of property in floodplains, home and infrastructure rehabilitation, business assistance, etc. Planning and administration of this program is limited of 20% of allocated funding (Table 3.1).

More information on this program can be found at http://portal.hud .gov/.

Public Assistance Program

The largest grant program that FEMA administers is the PA program. The PA program was established by the Robert T. Stafford Disaster Relief and Emergency Assistance Act (Stafford Act) to provide direct assistance to state, tribal, and local governments, as well as nonprofit organizations,

Table 3.1   CDBG Disaster Recovery
Assistance Program Appropriations
by Year, 1993–2013

Year	Amount Appropriated
1993	$85,000,000.00
1994	$830,000,000.00
1995	$39,000,000.00
1996	$50,000,000.00
1997	$500,000,000.00
1998	$130,000,000.00
1999	$20,000,000.00
2000	–
2001	$7,000,000.00
2002	$2,783,000,000.00
2003	–
2004	–
2005	$150,000,000.00
2006	$16,700,000,000.00
2007	–
2008	$9,400,000,000.00
2009	–
2010	$100,000,000.00
2011	–
2012	$400,000,000.00
2013	$16,000,000,000.00

following a presidentially declared disaster. Between 2000 and 2010, the amount of funding appropriated to the PA program has exceeded $30 billion (DHS, 2009).

Following a presidentially declared disaster, FEMA may issue PA grants to states, which then administer the funds to local government and nonprofit organizations as subgrantees. To receive funding, FEMA requires that PA Project Assistance worksheets be completed, which provide a damage assessment, cost estimate, and scope of work for proposed projects. Examples of projects that the PA program has funded include emergency work, such as debris removal and emergency protective measures, and permanent work, such as the repair of critical infrastructure.

The process for administering the PA program is lengthy and complex; however, an abbreviated process is outlined below (GAO, 2008):

1. The Presidential Disaster Declaration is issued.
2. Applicant submits PA request to the state, which in turn reviews and submits it to FEMA.
3. FEMA, the state, and the applicant work to discuss projects, provide needed documentation, and develop the project worksheet.
4. FEMA obligates funds to the state.
5. The state obligates funds to the applicant and monitors use.
6. The applicant uses funds to complete approved projects.
7. Final audit by the state and FEMA and fiscal reconciliation.
8. Projects are closed out.

The PA program has been criticized by both internal and external investigations. In 2008, the GAO reported the PA program experiences a number of challenges in Gulf Coast rebuilding following the 2005 Gulf Coast hurricanes. Problems identified included a lack of stable FEMA personnel, information sharing, and proper reporting practices (GAO, 2008). In 2009, these concerns were echoed when the DHS inspector general found deficiencies in the program's management, the program's measurement of objectives, as well as in the high turnover rate of personnel (DHS, 2009).

FEMA uses the PA Technical Assistance contract (PA–TAC) to obtain professional services from architects, engineers, consultants, and others in developing grant applications for state and local governments for PA funding. This funding is limited for the repair of the government's infrastructure that was damaged by natural or man-made disasters. In 2011, the DHS OIG conducted a report on FEMA's PA–TAC and raised concerns on how the government was awarding these contracts, and speculated that they may not be properly evaluating the performance of contractors. The DHS OIG made a series of recommendations relating to how performance expectations were implemented to evaluate the work of these contractors.

Individual Assistance
Following a Presidential Disaster Declaration, FEMA's Individual and Household Assistance Program (IHP), formerly known as the Individual Assistance (IA) program, can provide direct assistance to individuals and households with property damage losses not covered by insurance. This assistance generally takes the form of housing assistance, which can include providing temporary housing, funding housing repair, or housing

replacement. Other non-housing-related activities that the IA program funds include disaster-related medical costs, funeral and burial costs, legal services, unemployment assistance, crisis counseling, clothing, housing fuel, vehicle damage, and others (LEPA, n.d.). In FY 2014, the total amount of IA funds eligible to any single household was $32,400 (KYEM, 2014). For all non-housing-related activities, FEMA requires states to pay 25% of awarded assistance.

The private sector has been heavily involved in managing temporary housing programs funded by IA–TACs in the past. Following Hurricane Katrina, FEMA awarded noncompetitive contracts to manage these temporary housing programs to large private firms such as the Shaw Group, CH2M Hill Constructors Inc., Bechtel National Inc., and others. FEMA also awarded contracts to the Partnership for Temporary Housing LLC following the 2009 Alaska floods and the 2009 American Samoa tsunami and earthquake (DHS, 2011). FEMA requires that private sector recipients of IA–TACs be able to deliver a wide array of services, such as "comprehensive emergency management, project management, and program management services, as well as construction, architectural, and engineering capabilities" (DHS, 2011).

Despite billions of dollars being awarded the private sector through IA–TACs, the private sector needs to improve to manage these funds effectively. In 2011, the DHS OIG conducted a report on FEMA's IA–TAC and raised concerns over the contract recipient's emergency readiness capabilities and the level of accountability and oversight involved.

INTRODUCTION TO MITIGATION GRANTS

The FEMA offers a number of other grants that fund mitigation-related activities; however, four constitute the most significant sources of funding. The four mitigation-oriented grant programs are the FMA, Repetitive Flood Claims (RFC), Severe Repetitive Loss (SRL), and HMGP. The first three of these grants are classified as nondisaster grants, meaning that funding for these programs are available continuously so long as the broader programs are funded. The Hazard Mitigation Grants Program (HMGP) is the only mitigation program that is classified as a post-disaster grant.

To be eligible to apply for funding, FEMA requires that states take proactive steps in addressing hazard mitigation in their communities, as evidenced by developing a FEMA-approved hazard mitigation plan. Communities that do not develop a hazard mitigation plan will be ineligible to apply for mitigation-related grants whether before or following a disaster. Due to the technical nature of many hazard mitigation plans, plan development is often contracted out to the private sector. In addition to managing the planning process and writing the actual hazard mitigation plans for communities, the private sector is also frequently contracted to carry out mitigation actions that are proposed in these hazard mitigation plans.

Hazard Mitigation Grants Program

The HMGP provides funding for a wide array of mitigation projects and is only available to communities that have received a presidential disaster declaration. As such, the amount of money available for the program has fluctuated annually based on the number and severity of disasters. Originally authorized by Section 404 of the Stafford Act, the program is mandated to be cost-effective and to focus on the long-term reduction to the loss of life and property in the aftermath of a disaster (GAO, 1999). Successful applicants typically receive 75% of project funding from the federal government, with the remaining 25% of funding from the local level.

Unlike many other grant programs, the State Hazard Mitigation Officer reviews all applications and has the ability to prioritize which mitigation actions should be funded. FEMA requires that before receiving an HMGP grant, the state must have an administrative plan in place that outlines the way in which projects will be selected and prioritized.

In FY 2013, the CFDA reports that there were $482 million in FEMA HMGP–obligated funds, which resulted in $964 million in disaster losses avoided. The CFDA projects a 17% decrease in HMGP obligated funding for FY 2014 (Figure 3.8).

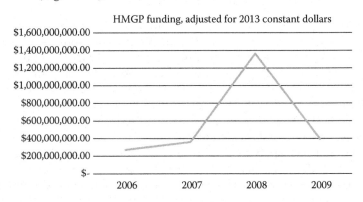

Figure 3.8   HMGP funding FY 2013.

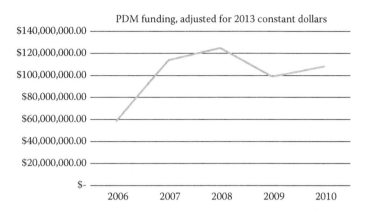

Figure 3.9   PDM funding FY 2013.

Pre-Disaster Mitigation Grants Program

The pre-disaster mitigation (PDM) grants program provides funding for a wide array of mitigation activities; however, unlike HMGP, these funds are continuously available and not contingent on a disaster declaration. The PDM grants program was authorized by Section 203 of the Stafford Act. Eligible applicants include the state emergency management agency or federally recognized tribal nations. Subapplicants, such as state agencies, local governments, academic institutions, and others, can apply through their city or county.

In FY 2013, the CFDA reports that there were $31,272,087 million in FEMA PDM-obligated funds, which resulted in $62,544,174 million in losses avoided. The CFDA projected a 100% increase in PDM obligated funding for FY 2014 (Figure 3.9).

FMA Program

The FMA program is authorized by Sections 1366 and 1367 of the National Flood Insurance Act of 1968, 42 U.S.C. 4104c and 4104d. The CFR states that the purpose of the program is to "assist state and local governments in funding cost-effective actions that reduce or eliminate the long-term risk of flood damage to buildings, manufactured homes, and other insured structures." Examples of common activities that the FMA provides funding for are surveying at-risk structures, property acquisition and elevation, demolition, and minor structural flood mitigation

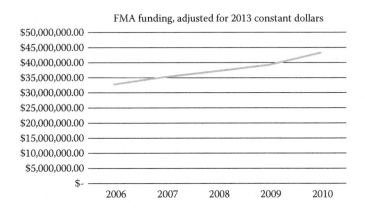

Figure 3.10 FMA funding FY 2013.

activities. Applications for this program are restricted to the 50 states, the District of Columbia, American Samoa, Guam, the U.S. Virgin Islands, Puerto Rico, the Northern Mariana Islands, and federally recognized Indian tribal governments; however, smaller communities may serve as subgrantees. Figure 3.10 indicates how funding for the FMA program steadily increased from 2006 through 2010.

Severe Repetitive Loss Program

The Severe Repetitive Loss Program was authorized by the Bunning–Bereuter–Blumenauer Flood Insurance Reform Act of 2004, as an amendment to the National Flood Insurance Act of 1968. The program provides funding to states and communities to undertake mitigation actions for SRL properties that meet the following criteria.

A residential property that is covered under a National Flood Insurance Program (NFIP) policy and (FEMA, 2014b)

a. That has at least four NFIP claim payments (including building and contents) more than $5000 each, and the cumulative amount of such claims payments exceeds $20,000.
b. For which at least two separate claims payments (building payments only) have been made with the cumulative amount of the building portion of such claims exceeding the market value of the building.

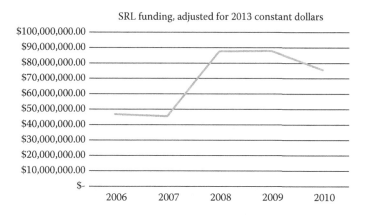

Figure 3.11 SRL funding FY 2013.

c. For both (a) and (b), at least two of the referenced claims must have occurred within any ten-year period, and must be greater than ten days apart.

Examples of activities that the SRL program funds include, but are not limited to, elevation of SRL-designated properties, relocation of SRL properties, acquisition of SRL properties, and others.

Figure 3.11 indicates how funding for this program has varied since 2006.

Leveraging the Private Sector in Mitigation

The private sector can be involved in hazard mitigation in a number of ways. Pursuant to the DMA 2000, governments that wish to be eligible for a number of hazard mitigation grant-related programs are required to develop hazard mitigation plans every five years. For governments that may lack the capacity to do this internally, RFPs may be issued in order from private firms to develop these plans on the local government's behalf. Also, government that have the capacity to do this internally but wish to focus on other issues may also hire private firms to write hazard mitigation plans. At the state level, a handful of large engineering related firms are often contracted to provide these services. At the regional, county, and municipal level, smaller firms are often involved in developing these plans.

These firms are often also involved in providing consultation regarding different mitigation projects that may be useful for communities, and mechanisms through which they may be funded. Firms that are interdisciplinary may also seek to apply from mitigation project funding on behalf of the local government after a plan is completed, in anticipation that their firm will be able to help the local government initiate a mitigation action. See Chapter 7 of this book for an in-depth discussion regarding how the private sector can be leveraged in hazard mitigation.

SUMMARY

Each year, the federal government funnels billions of dollars in disaster-related grants to state and local governments. These grants are complex and diverse in scope, often requiring the engagement of multiple actors across the public and private sector. This chapter has outlined basic components of the federal grant-in-aid system, with particular attention given to how this system is involved in disaster management within the United States. To effectively and more efficiently manage disasters, governments have sought the assistance of the private sector. While the private sector is heavily involved in disaster management, this chapter has discussed the advantages and disadvantages of this involvement. This chapter concluded with outlining a number of DHS/FEMA grant opportunities that were in operation during FY 2014, with an additional discussion regarding how the private sector is involved across each stage of emergency management. This chapter has provided a brief overview of each of these areas. Moving forward, this text develops this discussion in a more in-depth manner.

CHAPTER QUESTIONS

1. How does the grant life cycle differ for pre-disaster and post-disaster grants?
2. What grants are only available in the post-disaster environment? What conditions must be met in order for these grants to be awarded?
3. What have been some of the problems associated with grant management by the federal government?
4. What is the role of State Administrative Agencies in grant management?

REFERENCES

Busch, N.E. & Givens, A.D. (2012). Public-Private Partnerships in Homeland Security Opportunities and Challenges.

Catalog of Federal Domestic Assistance (CFDA). (2014a). Emergency Management Performance Grants (EMPG). Retrieved July 9, 2015, from http://www.cfda.gov.

Catalog of Federal Domestic Assistance (CFDA). (2014b). Non-profit Security Program (NSGP). Retrieved July 9, 2015, from http://www.cfda.gov.

Catalog of Federal Domestic Assistance (CFDA). (2014c). Port Security Grant Program (PSGP). Retrieved July 9, 2015, from http://www.cfda.gov.

Catalog of Federal Domestic Assistance (CFDA). (2014d). Rail and Service Security Grant Program (TSGP/IPR). Retrieved July 9, 2015, from http://www.cfda.gov.

Congressional Research Service (CRS). (2009). Department of Homeland Security assistance to states and localities: A summary and issues for the 111th Congress. (R40246; Shawn Reese).

Farris, M. & Jerolleman, A. (2012). The growing role of the private sector in mitigation. In *Natural Hazard Mitigation*, Eds. A. Jerolleman & J. Kiefer (p. 83). Boca Raton, FL: CRC Press.

Federal Emergency Management Agency (FEMA). (2011). Grants Program Directorate Fact Sheet. Washington, DC: U.S. Government Printing Office.

Federal Emergency Management Agency (FEMA). (2013). FEMA FY 2013 Budget. Washington, DC: U.S. Government Printing Office.

Federal Emergency Management Agency (FEMA). (2014a). FY 2014 Port Security Grant Program (PSGP). Accessed September 3, 2014, from http://www.fema.gov/fy-2014-port-security-grant-program-psgp.

Federal Emergency Management Agency (FEMA). (2014b). Severe Repetitive Flood Loss Program (SRL). Accessed September 3, 2014, from http://www.fema.gov/fy-2014-port-security-grant-program-psgp.

FEMA (2011). The Future of FEMA's Grant Programs Directorate. (2011). Hearing before the Subcommittee on Emergency Communication, Preparedness, and Response. 111th Congress.

Government Accountability Office (GAO). (1999). Disaster Assistance. Information on the cost effectiveness of hazard mitigation projects. (GAO Publication No. T-RECD-99-106). Washington, DC: U.S. Government Printing Office.

Government Accountability Office (GAO). (2005). A glossary of terms used in the Federal budget process. (GAO Publication No. 05-734SP). Washington, DC: U.S. Government Printing Office.

Government Accountability Office (GAO). (2008). Disaster recovery. FEMA's Public Assistance Grant Program experienced challenges with Gulf Coast rebuilding. (GAO Publication No. 09-129). Washington, DC: U.S. Government Printing Office.

Government Accountability Office (GAO). (2012). Grants to state and local governments: An overview of the Federal funding levels and selected challenges. (GAO Publication No. 12-1016). Washington, DC: U.S. Government Printing Office.

Governor's Office of Homeland Security and Emergency Preparedness (GOHSEP). (n.d.). Procurement desk reference: Avoiding DHS-OIG audit findings: Procurement. Accessed September 1, 2014, from http://www.gohsep.la.gov /workshops/procurement/Desk_Reference.pdf.

Kentucky Emergency Management (KYEM). (2014). Individual and Household Assistance Program (IHP). Accessed September 16, 2014, from http://kyem .ky.gov/recovery/Pages/IndividualAssistance.aspx.

Louisiana Emergency Preparedness Association (LEPA). (n.d.). FEMA Public & Individual Assistance Programs. Accessed September 15, 2014, from http:// www.lepa.org/Data/Sites/6/Certification/public-individual-assistance.pdf.

Morton, J. (2012). *Next-Generation Homeland Security: Network Federalism and the Course to National Preparedness*. Annapolis, MD: Naval Institute Press.

Priest, D.P. & Arkin, W.M. (2011). *TopSecret America: The Rise of the New American Security State*. New York: Little, Brown and Company.

Smith, G., Lyles, W. & Berke, P.R. (2013). The role of hazard mitigation planning in building local capacity and commitment: A tale of six states. International Journal of Mass Emergencies and Disasters 32(2):178–203.

U.S. Department of Homeland Security (DHS). (2011a). DHS Appropriates Bill, 2012. 112th Congress, 112–174. Washington, DC: U.S. Government Printing Office.

U.S. Department of Homeland Security (DHS). (2011b). *National Preparedness Goal*, First Edition. Washington, DC: U.S. Government Printing Office.

U.S. Department of Homeland Security (DHS). (2012). Homeland Security Grant Program. Supplemental resource: Support for public–private collaboration. FY 2012. Washington, DC: U.S. Government Printing Office.

U.S. Department of Homeland Security (DHS). (2014a). FY 2014 Intercity Passenger Rail (IPR) Amtrak. Accessed September 13, 2014, from https://s3-us-gov -west-1.amazonaws.com/dam-production/uploads/1406301756822-adc 433e01a473ce8723134155017cde8/IPR_Fact_Sheet_Final.pdf.

U.S. Department of Homeland Security (DHS). (2014b). Budget-in-brief: Fiscal year 2014. Washington, DC: U.S. Government Printing Office.

U.S. Department of Homeland Security, Federal Emergency Management Agency. (2014). Funding opportunity announcement: FY 2014 Port Security Grant Program.

U.S. Department of Homeland Security, Federal Emergency Management Agency. Office of Inspector General (2009). Assessment of FEMA's public assistance program policies and procedures (OIG Publication 10-26). Washington, DC.

U.S. Department of Homeland Security, Federal Emergency Management Agency. Office of Inspector General (2011). Improving FEMA's individual assistance, technical assistance contracts (OIG Publication 11-114). Washington, DC.

U.S. Department of Homeland Security, Office of Congressional Affairs. (2008). The Cost-to-Capability Initiative (C2C): Connecting local investment strategies to the Nation's Homeland Security priorities, Fact Sheet (p. 1). Washington, DC.

4

Privatization of Disaster Preparedness
Increasing Resilience through Planning

Jeremiah Jones

Contents

Learning Objectives

- What is disaster preparedness and how is it accomplished?
- Why has the private sector come into play with disaster preparedness?
- How has the private sector become involved with disaster preparedness?
- What impact on disaster preparedness has the private sector had, both positive and negative?

"[T]he most important failure was one of imagination," 9/11 Commission findings reflected upon by the House Select Committee when considering the poor response to Hurricane Katrina.

W.L.J. Waugh and G. Streib
Collaboration and Leadership
for Effective Emergency Management, 2006, p. 135

INTRODUCTION

What Is Disaster Preparedness?

In an effort to minimize damage and save lives, disaster preparedness is the process of emergency management that "contributes to sound emergency *response* and *recovery* from a disaster" (Sylves, 2008, p. 23). According to the Department of Homeland Security (DHS), national preparedness is defined as "the actions taken to plan, organize, equip, train, and exercise to build and sustain the capabilities necessary to prevent, protect against, mitigate the effects of, respond to, and recover from those threats that pose the greatest risk to the security of the Nation" (DHS, 2011, p. A-2). These actions should be taken by all levels of government, as well as other stakeholders with the capability to best prepare an area for a disaster. Overall, disaster preparedness is having taken all precautionary steps to ensure that a disaster is less likely to occur, and if it does, that an area is better equipped to handle the circumstances. By taking into account the traditional aspect of preparedness, as actions taken in the face of a disastrous event in an attempt to lessen the impact, in combination with the more recent concept that preparedness is all-encompassing of disaster planning, disaster preparedness can be defined as follows. The processes taken by a community, government, business, or other entity intended on decreasing the potential for loss of life and damage to property associated with a disaster. Preparedness must also involve actions that result in increasing the ability to handle a disastrous event, to include proper response during an event and in relief efforts, which result in a higher disaster resilience.

Preparedness has gained a great deal of attention in the United States in recent years, following recent disasters over the last few decades, both natural and man-made. These events have made the country aware that no place is 100% inherently safe from a disastrous event. Joplin, Missouri's tornado strike, September 11, the BP oil spill, and Superstorm Sandy are a few examples of events not expected by the general population (although plans were in place that acknowledged the risks and the potential impacts of the natural hazards) that have acted as catalysts in increasing disaster preparedness. Tornadoes are the most violent of nature's storms and pose a risk to every state in the United States (Ready.gov, 2014). However, the massive destruction of these twisters has made apparent that "lightning (or a series of intense tornadoes) can strike twice, or more, in the same spot." The attacks on 9/11 could never have been truly anticipated but could have happened in any city in America. Such a devastating attack was considered all but impossible before September 11, 2001. The terrorist attacks brought to light the possibility of such a tragedy on American soil. The BP oil spill caused damages across the entire coast of the Gulf of Mexico when the Deepwater Horizon drilling platform sank and allowed for the release of nearly 5 million barrels of oil into the Gulf (National Oceanic and Atmospheric Administration [NOAA], 2014). This accidental, man-made disaster was another such unprecedented and unexpected event. Without even considering such a possibility of a massive offshore, deep-water oil spill, any such plans to remedy the situation were nonexistent. These disastrous events have caught cities, states, regions, and even the entire nation by surprise. The misconception of "it can't happen to me" has been replaced by "I hope it *doesn't* happen to me." With what would have previously been thought of as an impossibility now becoming reality, the notion that extreme disaster can strike in just about any place or come in any form is gaining acceptance. This realization, and added focus on recent disasters by the media, has increased the public's appreciation and desire for preparedness. With an increasing priority in public interest, government officials have increased the disaster preparation policy agenda.

Outsourcing Preparedness

State, local, and federal governments no longer bear the burden of disaster preparedness alone. The role of private sector involvement in preparedness has increased, as well as the public sector's appreciation for such assistance. The private sector, considered everything outside of government, can offer expertise, physical manpower, technology, equipment, transportation, food and water, and other resources in times of disaster. Partnerships with, and the involvement of, the private sector have had a wide array of benefits. Public–private partnerships (PPP) in disaster preparedness may take a variety of forms. The private sector may be contracted out completely, perhaps in the writing of a hazard mitigation plan for a municipality. Also, private businesses may simply make themselves more available to the public in times of emergency to better serve the community in terms of goods or services. Another form of PPP is a more collaborative effort, such as hired consultants or experts to deal with more specific matters in an interactive way. Private entities offer an alternative method for a governmental agency to provide service to its citizens. Innovation and invention, contracting services, collaborative efforts, and offering goods/services that are not available from the government are ways in which the private sector can positively influence disaster preparedness. The potential benefits of the private sector's role in preparedness are not without concern, however. Such outsourcing can come with the costs of decreased accountability, lack of transparency, or simply subpar services when the contract goes to the lowest bidder.

The private's level of involvement varies by location, role, and entity. Other factors to be considered, in regard to the private sector in disaster preparedness, are the questions of accountability, level of government oversight, public–private collaboration, and where funding will come from and go to. These issues are dealt with in a variety of manners depending on the actors involved, perceived level of threat to an area, fallout from negative consequences, and the overall dynamic of the area and situation.

There are many different reasons for why the private sector can be a key partner in disaster preparedness. The resources available to the private realm differ from that of the public sector, and at times the private sector is more readily able to engage in preparedness activities. However, this is influenced by scale, as small businesses may require government assistance. The interoperability and interdependence of private and public sectors are critical in emergency management and preparedness. With 85% of critical infrastructure falling under the ownership of the private sector (PwC, 2013), the importance of the two worlds' intertwining is made abundantly clear. Critical infrastructure is defined as "systems and assets, whether physical or virtual, so vital to the United States that the incapacity or destruction of such systems and assets would have a debilitating impact on security, national economic security, national public health or safety, or any combination of those matters" (Koenig & Wolff,

2010, pp. 2–3). Such policies as the National Infrastructure Protection Plan (NIPP), Homeland Security Presidential Directive 7 (HSPD-7), Critical Infrastructure Partnership Advisory Council (CIPAC), and the National Response Framework (NRF) highlight the importance of PPPs for the protection of the nation's infrastructure (Koenig & Wolff, 2010). Using infrastructure as an example, the interdependence and need for interoperability between private and public can be made highly visible. With such a majority of critical infrastructure privately owned, it is in the interest of the public to ensure that it is properly cared for. These assets are vital to the continuity of the government's ability to ensure public safety and the provision of basic human needs (Kallam, 2010), and therefore must be protected and cared for. The private sector, with its critical infrastructure, must reciprocate this aid. By allowing government use of the infrastructure, as well as ensuring that it is properly maintained, the private entities are helping out twofold: (1) the public sector's ability of providing the services of which it is expected and obligated to is greatly enhanced, and (2) the private sector benefits the entire community in an affected area. With the infrastructure being readily available to citizens and government of an area, an area's overall resilience can be increased significantly. This increase in resilience is the end goal of disaster preparedness.

Disaster preparedness procedures, to include private sector involvement, have been outlined in the DHS's National Preparedness Framework (NPF). The details of the NPF are given in the National Preparedness Report (U.S. Department of Homeland Security, 2014) and the National Preparedness Goal; however, the exact steps taken to fill in this framework are not prescribed. As no area shares identical demographics, geographic features, or social aspects, it cannot be expected that a universal plan to prepare for disaster response and recovery would be effective nationwide. Likewise, the role of the private sector in disaster preparedness is also not to be approached with a one-size-fits-all attitude.

U.S. DISASTERS AND SUBSEQUENT POLICY ACTION

The development and evolution of disaster policies has been predominately reactive, rather than proactive. The cause for this is, oftentimes, it is either not known what disastrous event could affect an area, or that the possibility is downplayed or disregarded. For policy to become enacted, there must first be an open policy window. This occurs when three factors—problem, policy, and politics—all intersect at a given moment

(Sylves, 2008, p. 10). When a problem has arisen, a policy (solution) is available, and the political atmosphere is just right, a policy window has been opened. This window also allows for the private sector to enter and offer their assistance. If or when there is governmental uncertainty about what or how to proceed with an action, the private sector may be included. The policies of disaster preparedness follow the policy window cycle, as described in the succeeding sections. The U.S. disaster preparedness policy has, in varying degrees, utilized the private sector in order to carry out suitable solutions to the problems facing the nation. The following examples illustrate such disaster policy evolution, as often it has come on the heels of a disastrous event.

Flood Control Acts of 1928 and 1936

Following the massive flooding of the central United States in 1927, the Flood Control Acts of 1928 and 1936 were enacted. These Acts were aimed at the federal government taking a larger role in flood prevention and inland water control. Following the Lower Mississippi River Flood Control Act of 1928, whereas the federal government now has ultimate responsibility for flood control measures, the issue of revetments on the river had become an economics problem (Harrison, 1951, p. 305). The concrete mats were expensive, as was the process of laying the mats on the banks of the river. To accomplish such a feat, local levee boards and the federal government had to hire out labor and use currently owned equipment. The process of flood control, following the policy action, brought to light the fact that the public sector may have ideas of what they want accomplished but are not fully able to make such decisions come to fruition.

National Flood Insurance Program

The National Flood Insurance Act of 1968 came on the heels of the devastation following Hurricane Betsy. This Act brought about the National Flood Insurance Program (NFIP) as a way for those who lived in flood-prone areas to attain federally subsidized flood insurance coverage, due to the large inability and willingness of the private sector to do so (Platt, 1976, p. 304). For a community to be eligible for NFIP coverage, steps to mitigate flood damages must be adhered to. Because of massive loss in times of flooding, private insurance holders are not financially able or willing to subject themselves to the potential heavy cost of paying out claims. The private sector has not been totally aloof on this subject of flood preparedness. The Write Your Own (WYO) program has enabled private sector insurers to handle flood insurance, with the same subsidization as individuals (Lowe, 2003, p. 24). By allowing a WYO middleman, privatization of flood preparedness has freed up government resources from the daily workings of flood insurance.

Disaster Relief Acts of 1969 and 1974

Four years after the devastation of Hurricane Betsy, Hurricane Camille came through and spurred yet more federal action to improve resilience. The Disaster Relief Act of 1969, and also of 1974, improved upon the earlier 1950 version by expanding the level and amount of federal disaster relief available to an area. The Acts of 1969 and 1974 set in motion the processes of the federal government's responsibility for large-scale disaster relief (Clary, 1985). These Acts have had heavy impact on the private sector by creating assistance programs that are aimed at helping maintain business and daily-life continuity. Through the collaborative efforts of the federal government relief and private-entity support, community resilience can be improved and maintained.

Flood Disaster Protection Act

Following the inception of the NFIP in 1968, those who lived within a flood-prone area were able to purchase federally subsidized insurance, some of which came from private insurers as members of the WYO program. Communities located within a Special Flood Hazard Area (SFHA) that were participating in the NFIP were not obligated to purchase the federal flood insurance. This lack of enforcement threatened to put unnecessary strain on the federal purse strings should a disaster strike. If an individual, or entire community, in an SFHA is not mandated to purchase flood insurance, the federal government will pay more for the relief efforts. This is in part due to not collecting a premium throughout the year, and also because participation in the NFIP requires certain mitigation efforts by the community. To remedy this possible problem, the Flood Disaster Protection Act (FDPA) of 1973 was enacted (Federal Deposit Insurance Corporation [FDIC], 2014). The FDPA leans on both federal regulatory agencies and private lenders to help enforce the participation in the NFIP for those within an SFHA. The FDPA aims to (FDIC, 2014, p. V-6.1) (1) provide property owners within the SFHA, within an NFIP participating community, with the ability to purchase flood insurance;

(2) require flood mitigation measures to be taken by a community before federally subsidized flood insurance is made available; (3) ensure that federal financial regulatory agencies enforce that no loan shall be renewed or extended on a property in an SFHA, of an NFIP-participating community, without the property being covered by flood insurance; and (4) require that any federal agency that insures, guarantees, or subsidizes a property loan does not do so if the property is within an SFHA and the community is not NFIP participating. Private lenders that dealt with federally backed loans (SBA, FHA, and VA) were placed into the regulatory cycle of enforcing federal flood protection. Without the involvement of private lenders to mandate flood insurance coverage where applicable, the NFIP would be a dog without any teeth. The FDPA formed a partnership between the WYO private insurers, federal flood insurance regulation, federal lending regulatory agencies, and private lenders.

National Governors' Association Report on Emergency Preparedness

In the wake of nearly two decades with increasing natural disasters, the National Governor's Association (NGA) filed a Report on Emergency Preparedness. As a plea to President Jimmy Carter for a consolidation of more than one hundred federal disaster-related programs, the report eventually led to the formation of the Federal Emergency Management Agency (FEMA) in 1979 (Waugh & Streib, 2006, p. 132). In their report, the NGA insists that "emergency management should be a team effort based on knowledge of resources" (NGA, 1979, p. 9), and this must include existing public and private assistance organizations at the state, local, and federal level. The private sector's unique materials, workforce expertise, and technical know-how are a critical aspect of the disaster preparedness partnership between them and the public. This report emphasizes the importance of such partnerships where the private sector and local governments can best prepare an area for a disaster. The private entities are often embedded within an area and have valuable resources that can make a positive difference when local governments are planning for their constituent's safety in a time of crisis. The NGA Report on Emergency Preparedness has proved to be a critical step in the evolution of disaster preparedness, and is one of the first documents clearly asserting the importance of the private sector in emergency management. See Figure 4.1 for responsibilities/abilities associated with the private sector and state, local, and federal government for emergency management.

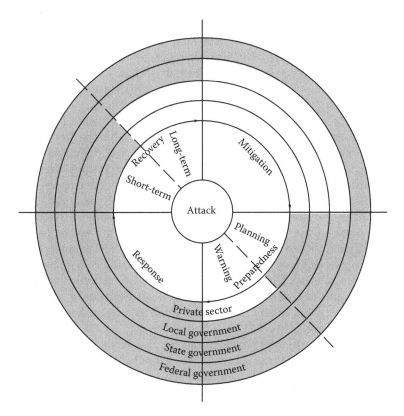

Figure 4.1 Responsibilities of private sector and local, state, and federal government throughout the stages of emergency management. (National Governors' Association. *Comprehensive Emergency Management: A Governor's Guide.* Washington, DC: U.S. Government Printing Office, 1979.)

Stafford Act

The dynamic process of federal disaster preparedness had brought about multiple Disaster Relief Acts, a federally subsidized flood insurance program, and led to the creation of a centralized agency to handle emergency management (FEMA). These policies set the groundwork for a standardized system of emergency management, from the state, local, and federal governmental aspect, as well as the private sector involvement. However, individual discretion and interpretation of policies was present. In 1988, President Ronald Reagan signed into law the Robert T. Stafford Disaster and Emergency Assistance Act. The Stafford Act essentially was a continuation of the Disaster Relief Acts, as it amended and improved upon the current manner of federal disaster relief (Sylves, 2008). The primary aspect of the Stafford Act is presidential declarations. These declarations of *emergencies* by the president aimed at taking the ambiguity out of disastrous events and, in turn, defining moments that were qualified and needing federal assistance. For a locale to be eligible for federal relief dollars, the president would have to deem that area to be under the circumstances of when "federal assistance is needed to supplement state and local efforts and capabilities to save lives and protect property and public health and safety, or to lessen or avert the threat of catastrophe" (Sylves, 2008, p. 60). Presidential declarations are often politicized and energized. The nuances that are involved in presidential declarations involve partisanship, personal and governmental interest, and even include the private sector and its ability to market its home turf. As an effort to ensure that the hometown will be given the declaration in times of disaster, private sector entities have acted as lobbyists in Washington, DC. Attempting to prove their worthiness of federal relief spending, private parties have the ability to increase the value of an area in the federal eye, in turn increasing the resilience of an area.

If an area is not so fortunate to receive the declaration, private lawyers have represented these communities (Abbott, 2005, pp. 469–470). The Stafford Act requires certain mitigation actions to take place in order for a community to be eligible for federal relief spending. At times, there have been disputes between the federal government and a community desiring to benefit from the Act. Private lawyers, in the interest of increasing federal relief and eventually community resilience, contest the federal rulings. The legalese used in legislation and court proceedings provide the ambiguity for interpretation. A battle of semantics, between the private interest lawyer and the federal government, holds the resilience of the community in question in the balance. An increase in the resilience of a community is the ultimate goal of disaster preparedness. The Stafford Act, while aimed at improving the resilience of disaster areas, can in fact cause the localities to muddle through with their emergency preparations. If a private entity must represent a locality's interest in order to prove to the federal government that it is *worthy* of disaster funding, trust and transparency has been compromised. The Stafford Act has improved greatly the processes of disaster funding, but is lacking in some collaboration aspects on the local level. Private sector involvement can come to the aid of local governments when such deficiencies exist in the federal system.

Project Impact

The focus on emergency management had shifted away from civil defense and almost entirely toward natural disaster preparedness, with the end of the Cold War in 1991. The mindset was that there was no longer a need to be overly concerned with a Russian threat, or other military-type attack. This swing in preparedness tactics allowed for the federal government to focus the majority of its spending toward natural disaster scenarios. One such program was Project Impact, instituted in 1998. Project Impact was a whole-community "effort to reduce the repeated loss of property and lives every time a disaster struck" (Holdeman, 2005). This federal program incentivized local and state governments to increase community awareness of disaster vulnerability (Sylves, 2008, p. 69). Project Impact, although a short-lived policy, proved to be effective in reducing the vulnerability of communities by community outreach and business leader involvement. This partnership tied local business, citizens, and governments in a concerted effort to improve the community resilience and make their area more prepared for a disastrous event. In particular, the Puget Sound area of Washington State was a participant in Project Impact. The effects of the 2001 Nisqually earthquake were lessened by the education campaigns and structural retrofittings that were a direct result of Project Impact and its private partners (Holdeman, 2005).

Disaster Mitigation Act of 2000

A further continuation of federal disaster policy was enacted with the Disaster Mitigation Act (DMA) of 2000. The DMA was an amending legislation to the existing policy in place by the Stafford Act. The purpose of the law is to increase the resilience and decrease the vulnerability of areas by mandating specific measures to be taken in order to receive federal disaster funding (Sylves, 2008, p. 69). A major stipulation was that state governments, as well as local governments, had to have a federally approved hazard mitigation plan on file. The DMA also provided for pre-disaster mitigation efforts, in hopes of reducing the loss of life and damages to property that can accompany a disaster. The private sector plays a vital role in the mitigation efforts of a community, especially in regard to physical measures. New construction, retrofitting existing structures, and development of previously unused areas are all roles in which the private sector participates. Private industry is only held to follow the regulations and ordinances in place, which are predominately written by local governments. It is the role of the public sector to develop and enforce the rules, and the private sector needs to be in accordance with those rules. The partnership between the private sector and the local government is critical for the best results in mitigation efforts. Through proper mitigation, an area's disaster level of preparedness is raised, in turn increasing its resilience.

The above examples highlight some of the most important or notable policy actions in regard to disaster preparedness. Such policy is driven by external factors, and often, disastrous events must occur to prompt action aimed at alleviating future occasions. Table 4.1 illustrates the history of disasters in the United States and the following legislative actions affecting emergency management policy, starting in 1927 and finishing with Hurricane Sandy.

ROLE OF PRIVATE SECTOR IN PREPAREDNESS

Public–Private Preparedness Framework

Following the terrorist attacks of September 11, the newly found DHS absorbed FEMA. The national shift in attention had gone from natural disasters to concerns regarding terrorists. The DHS's new model of emergency management has revamped the previous: Mitigation, Preparedness, Response, and Recovery. The previous four-element model has been updated to Prevention, Protection, Mitigation, Response, and Recovery. FEMA has done away with considering preparedness as an individual element within the emergency management system, and now views it as an overall goal consisting of the level of readiness and capability of the stated five elements (DHS, 2011, p. 1). The new U.S. National Preparedness System details how a community can achieve a satisfactory level of preparedness. The U.S. National Preparedness Goal, published in 2011, prescribes actions to attain the desired Prevention, Protection, Mitigation, Response, and Recovery for a community. This plan requires participation from the whole community. State, local, and federal government; private sector; and the public are all required to work in conjunction with each other to achieve disaster preparedness. Whether the newer DHS emergency management model of five elements is considered (where preparedness is an overarching goal) or the previous concept (where preparedness is a single objective and one of four elements), it is critical to have intergovernmental and public–private collaboration to best achieve disaster preparedness.

Table 4.1 Timeline of Important Disasters and Following Legislation

Event	Date	Privatization Actions/Side Effects
Great Mississippi River Floods	1927	Flood control was primarily the responsibility of locality and private interest
Lower Mississippi Flood Control Act/Flood Control Act	1928/1936	Usage of private contractors were necessary to properly enact federal flood control measures; private sector was urged (successfully) by federal government to donate for relief of affected areas (FEMA, 2010)
Office of Emergency Management	1940	First inclusion of private organizations in disaster planning; private assets can be of use in emergency management (McReynolds, 1941)
Federal Civil Defense Act	1950	Fallout structures made a responsibility of state and private industry; favored privatization of shelter construction and maintenance over public oversight (Baker, 2001)
Disaster Relief Act	1950	Federal government now responsible for rebuilding of local government facilities, but private business and individual relief still managed by Red Cross (Froot, 2007, p. 315)
National Plan for Emergency Preparedness	1964	Industry, agriculture, labor, and finance leaders deemed integral in planning to ensure expedient restoration of the country's economy (OEP, 1964)
Hurricane Betsy	1965	Private sector focus on development in New Orleans East, lakefront neighborhoods, and the Ninth Ward compromised city's ability for flood control; private *tidewater* protection was insufficient to hold back storm surge (Colten & Giancarlo, 2011)
National Flood Insurance Protection Act	1968	Federally subsidized flood insurance was made available by Write Your Own (WYO) private insurers; this freed up governmental time and resources allowing private sector back into the fold of flood insurance

(*Continued*)

Table 4.1 (Continued) Timeline of Important Disasters and Following Legislation

Event	Date	Privatization Actions/Side Effects
Hurricane Camille	1969	Uncontrolled and unregulated private sector development contributed to subpar construction and poor site planning (Waugh & Streib, 2006, p. 132)
Disaster Relief Acts	1969 and 1974	Further improved upon relations between government and private sector with relief programs (SBA, FHA, USDA, and other special interests) (Barnett, 1999, p. 141)
Hurricane Agnes	1972	Forced the hand of federal government to increase participation in the NFIP, led to FDIP's involvement of private lenders and flood insurance
Flood Disaster Protection Act	1973	Mandated that private lenders, issuing federally backed property loans, ensured that the purchased property be covered with flood insurance, if necessary; made eligibility for NFIP coverage for a community contingent upon a set criteria of mitigation measures, which often involve private sector actions/cooperation
National Governor's Association Report on Emergency Preparedness	1979	Touted importance of private sector involvement with all facets of emergency management; private sector has specialized knowledge, equipment, and rapport with localities that can prove useful in disaster preparedness
Three Mile Island nuclear plant meltdown	1979	Under a fledgling US Nuclear Regulatory Commission, human error, poor planning, and primitive control devices (in an attempt to save money and maximize profits) the Three Mile Island plant melted half of its reactor core (USNRC, 2014)
Creation of Federal Emergency Management Agency	1979	Result of NGA Report on Emergency Preparedness; put into action a consolidated emergency management framework for state, local, and federal government, as well as private sector to work together in times of disaster (NGA, 1979)

(Continued)

Table 4.1 (Continued) Timeline of Important Disasters and Following Legislation

Event	Date	Privatization Actions/Side Effects
Stafford Disaster Relief and Emergency Assistance Act	1988	Required mitigation efforts may not be able to be undertaken by local government, and the private sector might be needed to assist; private sector *lobbyists* can improve the marketability of a disaster declaration for an area in the eyes of the president; private sector legal representation may be required to ensure the area is not passed over for federal aid
Hurricane Hugo	1989	Category 4 hurricane affecting the southeast Atlantic coast; cost more than $7 million, at the time was the costliest storm (Blake & Christopher, 2011, p. 9)
Loma Prieta earthquake	1989	Massive destruction of California's San Francisco Bay area, exposing the vulnerabilities of utilities, water and wastewater, and communications systems (Schiff, 1997)
Hurricane Andrew	1992	Category 5 hurricane, with landfall on Florida and Louisiana, caused $26.5 million in damages (Blake & Christopher, 2011)
Midwest Flooding	1993	Some locations experienced 20 days of consecutive precipitation, resulting in a maximum flood duration of the Mississippi River of 195 days, 1083 of 1571 levees overtopped, 400,000 square miles of inundation, and 50 deaths (Larson, 1996)
Hazard Mitigation and Relocation Act	1993	Amendment to the Stafford Act of 1988; encouraged and funded mitigation measure (mainly relocation out of disaster prone areas and structural actions) through the Hazard Mitigation Grant Program (HMGP) (FEMA, 2010, p. 24)
World Trade Center Bombing	1993	First Middle Eastern–attributed act of terrorism, on American soil, killing six (FBI, 2008)

(Continued)

Table 4.1 (Continued) Timeline of Important Disasters and Following Legislation

Event	Date	Privatization Actions/Side Effects
Murrah Federal Office Building, Oklahoma City, Oklahoma, bombing	1995	"Worst act of homegrown terrorism in the nation's history" (FBI, 2014); FBI's resources and procedures were put to the test in an unprecedented event of domestic terrorism
Defense Against Weapons of Mass Destruction Act	1996	Outlines domestic preparedness to terrorist threat of WMD, response to such events, military assistance to civilian officials, interdiction of such materials, and control and disposition of such materials (United States Congress, 1996)
Project Impact	1997	Promoted public–private partnerships as essential for community mitigation; utilized collaborative efforts between private entities and local governments for mitigation activities (Jerolleman, 2013)
Disaster Mitigation Act	2000	Another Stafford Act amendment; aimed to improve the resilience and reduce the vulnerability of areas by increasing criteria for disaster relief: primarily by mandating that local governments must have a federally approved hazard mitigation plan in order to receive federal assistance (Sylves, 2008)
September 11 airplane hijacking and attack	2001	Brought a large-scale attack to U.S. soil without any warning or preparation for such an event; caused a knee-jerk reaction to all but discard any form of disaster but terrorism
Formation of Department of Homeland Security	2003	Reorganization/merging of any federal agency with ties to emergency management; now include 22 agencies, 40 federal entities, and 180,000 employees (Sylves, 2008, p. 70); shifted federal focus toward terrorism and away from the all-hazards approach
Hurricane Katrina	2005	Costliest storm ever ($108 million in damages and over 1200 casualties) (Blake & Christopher, 2011); exacerbated local, state, and federal capabilities in preparation, response, and relief to the Mississippi Gulf Coast (particularly southeast Louisiana)

(Continued)

Table 4.1 (Continued)   Timeline of Important Disasters and Following Legislation

Event	Date	Privatization Actions/Side Effects
Deepwater Horizon, BP oil spill	2010	Through alleged lack of government oversight, poor safety practices, material failure, and/or human error, 5 million barrels of crude oil was released into the Gulf of Mexico (NOAA, 2014)
National Preparedness Goal, Presidential Policy Directive 8: National Preparedness, DHS	2011	Guidelines for national preparedness with a focus on a shared responsibility of the whole community; every community is different in both needs, vulnerabilities, and abilities, which are all considered to improve local resilience in the hopes of improving the nation's resilience (USDHS, 2011)
Hurricane Sandy	2012	Owing to cold Atlantic waters, Sandy weakened and made landfall as a post-tropical cyclone near Brigantine, New Jersey. The storm's slow movement brought an immense storm surge up the Atlantic coast, inundating primarily the New York and New Jersey areas. Sandy showed what can happen if a known hazard is approaching and either the government cannot handle the situation or residents do not know what to do, or do not take the situation seriously. Sandy cost seventy-two lives, the most deaths by a tropical storm (not in the south) since Hurricane Agnes in 1972 (Berg, Beven, Blake, Cangialosi, & Kimberlain, 2013)

Source: Rubin, C.B. *Emergency Management: The American Experience, 1900–2005.* Fairfax, VA: Public Entity Risk Institute, 2007; Kiefer, J.J. & McCarthy, M.V. A history of hazard mitigation in the United States. In A. Jerolleman & J.J. Kiefer (Eds.), *Natural Hazard Mitigation* (pp. 1–18). Boca Raton, FL: CRC Press, 2013.

Presidential Policy Directive 8: National Preparedness (PPD-8) gives direction for how the United States is to prepare "for the threats and hazards that pose the greatest risk to the security" of the nation (DHS, 2011, p. 1). PPD-8 included the whole community as a critical element for full and proper preparedness. State, local, and federal governments cannot adequately prepare a community for a disastrous event. Such times require the involvement of citizens and the private sector. The National Preparedness Goal (2011) designates specific goals, objectives, and actor roles for preparedness of a community. As stated earlier, the DHS now considers preparedness as an overarching goal that can be accomplished through suitable Prevention, Protection, Mitigation, Response, and Recovery. Throughout the National Preparedness Goal, the cornerstone of implementation of PPD-8 (DHS, 2011, p. 19), ways in which the private sector and its resources are critical to successful emergency management are identified.

Planning: For prevention of terrorist attacks, coordination between state, local, federal, and private sectors are vital to the proper design, implementation, and execution of action.

Intelligence and information sharing: Relevant, timely, and actionable information and analysis to be shared between public and private sectors; public and private partners must possess, or have access to, the ability to relay terrorism/suspicious activity to law enforcement.

Public and private services and resources: Essential public and private resources and services are to be provided to affected and surrounding areas and population, to include critical infrastructure and first responders; public, NGO, and private resources to mobilize within and outside the affected area to save lives, sustain lives, meet basic human needs, stabilize the incident, and transition to recovery; enhance public and private resources and services required for the support of an affected area.

Situational assessment: Public and private resources are needed to relay information that can aid in adequate decision making for life saving and sustaining in and around the affected area; public and private resources can deliver enhanced information to reinforce ongoing life saving and sustaining; ensure affected area's basic human needs are met, incident is stabilized, and a transition to recovery is taking place.

Operational coordination: Public and private sector resources are needed to establish a method and timeline for recovery within a jurisdiction that accomplishes the objectives of leadership.

Private Sector Involvement

There are times when the governmental agencies involved in disaster preparedness are lacking the needed resources, to include technology, manpower, experience, or time required to properly carry out and implement disaster-planning procedures. When this shortfall has happened, or is forecasted, the governmental agency has three options: try and stretch their already insufficient resources, do nothing and let the status quo remain, or attain outside help from the private sector. The first two options, stretching resources and doing nothing, are likely to not have a positive impact on the area affected. Stretching current resources will simply compromise all areas of government, where every sector will suffer and none will best serve the public. Doing nothing, in regard to disaster preparedness, is truly a roll of the dice. This approach would not affect other departments within the government, but the requirements of preparedness would not be addressed. In doing so, the fact of best preparing an area for the potential of a disaster has been outweighed by the lack of resources and/or the low priority placed on preparedness. The private sector offers a solution to the government's lack of resource problem. By tapping into this source of information, technology, and extra manpower, a government can utilize the private sector in a way that yields two beneficial outcomes: (1) the public entity is now freed from the tasking, allowing it to focus its limited resources on other aspects requiring attention, and (2) the private sector oftentimes, but not always, has the potential to be subject matter experts, using the latest technology and the most experience for the associated undertaking. As this is not always the case, the private sector must be treated with both caution and respect in terms of their alleged expertise and capabilities.

Innovation and independence can be associated with features that the private sector may have over that of the government. The ability to spend money on whatever projects the board of directors approve of, over that of pleasing a broad constituency, is more easily gained in the private business world. The successes of such innovation have led to the ability of communities to be better prepared for when disaster strikes. One example of the private's success is the levee monitoring system (developed by Siemens) that utilizes sensors that monitor water pressure and temperature, as well as weather patterns, in order to identify possible breaches (Cho, 2013).

SUMMARY

Disaster preparedness is a term that has now come to mean more than just being ready before an event occurs. The new, dynamic term includes the overall processes of emergency management, in that all aspects must be planned and cared for in order to be properly prepared. Disaster preparedness is now considered the processes taken by a community, government, business, or other entity intended on decreasing the potential for loss of life and damage to property associated with a disaster. Preparedness must also involve actions that result in increasing the ability to handle a disastrous event, to include proper response during an event and in relief efforts, which results in a higher disaster resilience. Such actions cannot always be undertaken by the local, state, or federal government. Either they may be too expensive for the government to afford, out of the experience realm of governmental employees, beyond the technological capabilities of the government, or simply involve more man-hours than the public has available. When public agencies are overwhelmed, private entities can be used to alleviate the situation. In disaster preparation, private entities may offer assistance in various ways, such as their expertise in the hazard mitigation planning process, their technologies in forecasting events and prevention techniques, as well as pure manpower for physical preparations and relief operations. Having the private sector as an option for governments gives the public the ability to prioritize their resources and collaborate with the private. Private sector aid is not without its concerns. They are not all the most knowledgeable or technologically advanced, or even the most scrupulous. Private sector must be looked after, in terms of maintaining accountability and oversight by the public. This could be seen as an added cost to privatization, but must be considered to prevent what could be a worsening of an already disastrous event.

CHAPTER QUESTIONS

True or False

1. Overall, disaster preparedness is having taken all precautionary steps to ensure that a disaster is less likely to occur.

2. Hurricanes are the most violent of nature's storms.
3. With an increasing priority in public interest, government officials have increased the disaster preparation policy agenda.
4. State, local, and federal governments bear the burden of disaster preparedness alone.
5. The role of private sector involvement in preparedness has increased.
6. Private entities offer an alternative method for a governmental agency to provide a service to its citizens.
7. Outsourcing always increases accountability.
8. The resources available to the private sector differ from that of the public sector.
9. Less than 10% of critical infrastructure falls under the ownership of the private sector.
10. The role of the private sector in disaster preparedness is not to be approached with a one-size-fits-all attitude.

REFERENCES

Abbott, E.B. (2005). Catastrophic events: DHS/FEMA responses and recovery issues. *The Urban Lawyer, 37*(3), 467–488.
Baker, S. (2001). Shelters or evacuation?: A critical problem of the Federal Civil Defense Administration. *The Upsilonian*, 13, Cumberland College Department of History and Political Science.
Barnett, B.J. (1999). US government natural disaster assistance: Historical analysis and a proposal for the future. *Disasters, 23*(2), 139–155.
Berg, R.J., Beven, J.L. II, Blake, E.S., Cangialosi, J.P. & Kimberlain, R.B. (2013). Tropical cyclone report: Hurricane Sandy. Miami, FL: National Hurricane Center.
Blake, E. & Christopher, G.E. (2011). The deadliest, costliest, and most intense United States tropical cyclones from 1851 to 2011 (and other frequently requested hurricane facts). NOAA Technical Memorandum NWS NHC-6.
Cho, A. (2013). Disaster resilience: The private sector has a vital role to play. Retrieved July 9, 2015, from http://www.theguardian.com/sustainable-business/disaster-resilience-private-sector-role.
Clary, B.B. (1985). The evolution and structure of natural hazard policies. *Public Administration Review, 45*, 20–28.
Colten, C.E. & Giancarlo, A. (2011). Losing resilience on the Gulf Coast: Hurricanes and social memory. *Environment: Science and Policy for Sustainable Development.* Retrieved July 9, 2015, from http://www.environmentmagazine.org/Archives/Back%20Issues/2011/July-August%202011/losing-resilience-full.html.

Federal Bureau of Investigation (FBI). (2008). First strike: Global terror in America. Retrieved from http://www.fbi.gov/news/stories/2008/february/tradebom _022608.

Federal Bureau of Investigation (FBI). (2014). Terror hits home: The Oklahoma City bombing. Retrieved from http://www.fbi.gov/about-us/history/famous -cases/oklahoma-city-bombing.

Federal Deposit Insurance Corporation (FDIC). (2014). Section V.: Lending—Flood insurance. *FDIC Compliance Manual*, January.

Federal Emergency Management Agency (FEMA). (2010). The federal emergency management agency. *The Federal Emergency Management Agency Publication 1*, November.

Froot, K.A. (2007). *The Financing of Catastrophe Risk*. Chicago: University of Chicago Press.

Government Accountability Office. (2014). Homeowner's insurance: Multiple challenges make expanding private coverage difficult (GAO-14-179).

Harrison, R.W. (1951). The new "Mississippi problem." *Land Economics*, 27(4), 297–305.

Holdeman, E. (2005). Destroying FEMA. *Washington Post*. Retrieved July 9, 2015, from http://www.washingtonpost.com/wp-dyn/content/article/2005/08/29 /AR2005082901445.html.

Jerolleman, A. (2013). The privatization of hazard mitigation: A case study of the creation and implementation of a federal program (Doctoral dissertation). New Orlean: University of New Orleans Theses and Dissertations, Paper 1692.

Kallam, H. (2010). Private sector integration into homeland security. Denver, CO: State of Colorado Department of Local Affairs, Emergency Management.

Kiefer, J.J. & McCarthy, M.V. (2013). A history of hazard mitigation in the United States. In A. Jerolleman & J.J. Kiefer (Eds.), *Natural Hazard Mitigation* (pp. 1–18). Boca Raton, FL: CRC Press.

Koenig, G. & Wolff, E. (2010). The role of the private sector in emergency preparedness, planning, and response. In E.B. Abbott & O.J. Hetzel (Eds.), *Homeland Security and Emergency Management: A Legal Guide for State and Local Governments* (pp. 121–154). Chicago: American Bar Association.

Larson, L.W. (1996). The great USA flood of 1993. IAHS Conference Presentation: Destructive Water: Water-Caused Natural Disasters—Their Abatement and Control.

Lowe, A.S. (2003). May 1, 2004 program changes, Federal Emergency Management Agency memorandum.

McReynolds, W.H. (1941). The Office for Emergency Management. *Public Administration Review*, 1(2), 131–138.

National Governors' Association (NGA). (1979). *Comprehensive Emergency Management: A Governor's Guide*. Washington, DC: U.S. Government Printing Office.

National Oceanic and Atmospheric Administration (NOAA). (2014). Gulf spill restoration. Retrieved July 9, 2015, from http://www.gulfspillrestoration.noaa .gov/.

Office of Emergency Planning (OEP). (1964). *The National Plan for Emergency Preparedness*. Washington, DC: Office of Emergency Planning, Executive Office of the President, December.

Platt, R.H. (1976). The National Flood Insurance Program: Some midstream perspectives. *Journal of the American Institute of Planners, 42*(3), 303–313.

PwC. (2013). *Rebuilding for Resilience: Fortifying Infrastructure to Withstand Disaster.* Retrieved July 9, 2015, from http://www.pwc.com/en_GX/gx/psrc/publi cations/assets/pwc-rebuilding-for-resilience-fortifying-infrastructure-to -withstand-disaster.pdf.

Ready.gov. (2014). Tornadoes. Retrieved July 9, 2015, from http://www.ready.gov /tornadoes.

Rubin, C.B. (2007). *Emergency Management: The American Experience, 1900–2005.* Fairfax, VA: Public Entity Risk Institute.

Schiff, A.J. (1997). The Loma Prieta, California, earthquake of October 17, 1989— Lifelines. *U.S. Geological Survey Professional Paper*, 1552-A.

Waugh, W.L.J. & Streib, G. (2006). Collaboration and leadership for effective emergency management. *Public Administration Review, Special Issue, 66*, 131–140.

Sylves, R. (2008). *Disaster Policy & Politics: Emergency Management and Homeland Security*. Washington, DC: CQ Press.

United States Congress. (1996). 50 USC Ch. 40: Defense against weapons of mass destruction. *Title 50: War and National Defense.*

United States Nuclear Regulatory Commission. (2014). U.S. NRC: History. Retrieved July 9, 2015, from http://www.nrc.gov/about-nrc/history.html.

U.S. Department of Homeland Security. (2011). National Preparedness Goal. Retrieved July 9, 2015, from http://www.fema.gov/media-library/assets /documents/25959?fromSearch=fromsearch&id=5689.

U.S. Department of Homeland Security. (2014). National Preparedness Report. Retrieved July 9, 2015, from https://www.fema.gov/media-library/assets /documents/97590.

5

Private Sector's Role in Emergency Response

Jacqueline Brubaker

Contents

Learning Objectives

- Describe the history of emergency response and the emerging role of the private sector
- Describe the role of each level of government in emergency response
- Describe the role of the private sector and nongovernmental organizations in emergency response
- Identify key legislation guiding emergency response and how it incorporates privatization and the private sector
- Understand the benefits and limitations of privatizing emergency response operations

... I want to just say this about the private sector. In my mind, the government is incapable of responding to its maximum ability without private sector support...

Tom Ridge (Busch & Givens, 2012)
Former Secretary, U.S. Department of Homeland Security

INTRODUCTION

Emergency response by the government has a long and complex history in the United States. It is a critical component of the four phases of emergency management as it often involves life-saving operations following a disaster. Because the hours and days following a disaster can be chaotic and present citizens with uncertain circumstances, the need for concise and efficient emergency response operation plans is paramount. The private sector has always played a role in emergency response. Whether it is a business owner responding to damage to her own business or a large corporation providing resources to its employees following a disaster, the private sector plays an important role in response efforts. Some businesses also have contractual relationships with the public sector to provide response operations after a disaster. Throughout the years, the public, private, and nonprofit sectors have built collaborative and contractual relationships with one another in an effort to respond to disasters and emergencies as quickly and efficiently as possible. Public–private partnerships have become commonplace in developing emergency response plans.

One of the latest trends in emergency and disaster response is the privatization of these operations. Though public–private contractual partnerships existed before 2005, Hurricane Katrina served as the catalyst to further explore these partnerships. Localities, states, and even the federal government now have contracts with the private sector to provide a wide array of services following disasters and everyday emergencies. The greater geographic scope of the private sector can aid it in mobilizing and sharing resources. However, this generally only holds true for large corporations; smaller businesses and corporations often face the same challenges as the government. The size and scale of the disaster is an important indicator of how the private sector can best respond. The privatization of emergency response has proven beneficial in many disasters, including Hurricane Sandy. Members of the private sector are now common in emergency response planning discussions, and many are even present at emergency response command centers during drills and actual events. This chapter explores both the role of the private sector in emergency response and the privatization of emergency response operations.

HISTORY OF EMERGENCY RESPONSE IN THE UNITED STATES

Before government involvement following an emergency or disaster, private citizens and businesses had no choice but to respond to these events on their own. It was not long after the founding of the United States that the first piece of disaster-relief legislation was passed at the federal level. In 1803, a Congressional Act was passed to provide financial assistance to a New Hampshire town devastated by fire (Federal Emergency Management Agency [FEMA], 2014a). Despite efforts from firefighters in the town, the fire spread rapidly from building to building. Townspeople joined in the efforts by forming a bucket brigade to pass water to firefighters; however, they were unable to reach the tops of buildings, causing the near destruction of the town. Following the New Hampshire fire, and up until the 1930s, the federal government fostered an ad hoc approach to emergency management and response. During this time period, the U.S. Congress passed more than one hundred ad hoc pieces of legislation in response to hurricanes, earthquakes, floods, and other natural disasters (FEMA, 2014a). These pieces of legislation were typically only passed following a large-scale event, or events that captured the attention of the public and/or media; there was no systematic process.

From the 1930s to the early 1960s, the country's focus was on the Great Depression, the Cold War, and civil defense; few disasters occurred that required federal legislation. A series of storms, hurricanes, and earthquakes struck all corners of the country, increasing the need for a federal agency that addressed emergency management as a whole. The Ash Wednesday Storm in 1962 devastated more than 620 miles of shoreline on the East Coast, producing more than $300 million in damages (FEMA, 2014a). Hurricanes Betsy and Camille caused hundreds of millions of dollars in damage and claimed the lives of hundreds along the Gulf Coast. During this time, coordination between the government, nonprofits, and the private sector was nonexistent, resulting in slow response times from each entity. Like the disasters of the past, the response to these storms was ad hoc legislation to provide relief to stricken areas. The financial burden placed on the government following Hurricanes Betsy and Camille spurred a discussion about the creation of a program aimed at providing insurance for disaster-prone areas; subsequently, the National Flood Insurance Act of 1968 was passed and the National Flood Insurance Program (NFIP) was created. The private insurance industry was also greatly affected by these storms. Insurance companies paid out millions of dollars in claims, nearly bankrupting some companies.

The passage of the legislation coupled with the creation of the NFIP continued to call attention to the need to center emergency management and response duties into one agency. The private sector pushed for standards as well. Businesses of all sizes needed and wanted the government to create a specific set of standards regarding all aspects of emergency management. Since the private sector was absorbing the costs from disasters, the need for change was pressing. In the early 1970s, five different federal agencies bore responsibility for responding to disasters. Disaster response and recovery became the responsibility of the Department of Housing and Urban Development, and the Federal Disaster Assistance Administration (FDAA) was created. The FDAA was charged with responding to disasters and providing temporary housing and aid to disaster victims. The FDAA played an important role in disaster recovery throughout the 1960s as well. Although emergency management was now centralized under one federal department, emergency response responsibilities were scattered and unclear at the state and local levels. In 1979, President Jimmy Carter responded to the growing need to consolidate emergency management responsibilities into one agency. He signed an executive order creating the FEMA; its director would report directly to the president.

By the end of the 1980s, just a decade after being created, FEMA was in trouble due to slow responses to Hurricane Hugo and the Loma Prieta Earthquake in the Bay Area of California. The early 1990s were no better for the agency. In 1992, within months of each other, Hurricane Andrew struck Florida and Louisiana, and Hurricane Iniki struck Hawaii (FEMA Training Course, n.d., a). The agency's failure to respond was witnessed by Americans across the entire country as major news organizations documented the crisis (FEMA Training Course, n.d., a). FEMA's image changed drastically with the election of President Bill Clinton. James Lee Witt, President Clinton's choice for FEMA director, made several changes to the agency that proved effective in the agency's response to the disasters during his administration. Among these changes was Witt's emphasis on the value of local partnerships, including collaboration with the private sector.

The unprecedented terrorist attacks on September 11, 2001, changed the country's emergency management focus to terrorism preparedness. The response to the attacks, however, was effective at the local, state, and federal levels. The Department of Homeland Security absorbed FEMA following the attacks, and the agency once again experienced major changes. FEMA and the nation's focus were now on terrorism, and few major disasters occurred in the few years following the attacks. A focus on terrorism resulted in the transfer of funds of many FEMA projects and programs to other terrorism-related programs. States and localities were given military-grade equipment to enhance efforts in fighting terrorism. FEMA was left underfunded, leaving the agency little room to achieve its mission. This proved costly just a few years later when, in late August 2005, Hurricane Katrina formed off the coast of Florida. The storm passed over Florida causing minimal damage; however, as it entered the Gulf of Mexico, the storm grew into a category 5 hurricane. On August 29, Hurricane Katrina made landfall near the Louisiana–Mississippi border as a strong category 3 storm. The storm overwhelmed state and local officials, and many communities were completely destroyed. Mayor Ray Nagin's decision to delay a mandatory evacuation order for New Orleans worsened the effects of the storm; local officials only expected a few thousand residents to stay in the city, yet tens of thousands were left stranded. The city had no plan in place to provide food, shelter, or water to that many people, resulting in a chaotic

109

and dangerous situation for stranded residents. FEMA's poor response to the storm was heavily criticized, putting the agency in jeopardy once again. Many were quick to point out that the underfunding of the agency was in large part to blame for the poor response, but this did not satisfy the masses. The slow response spawned a discussion among emergency management and elected officials about the need to privatize many facets of the emergency response process.

These discussions turned to actions as federal, state, and local emergency management officials began to partner with the private sector. These public–private partnerships can be seen in all four phases of emergency management, especially response. In late October 2012, Hurricane Sandy formed in the tropics and eventually became one of the largest Atlantic storms on record affecting 24 states. Much of the response to the storm was carried out through contracts with the private sector, and dozens of private sector companies donated a variety of relief items (United States Chamber of Commerce Foundation, 2013). Contracts across the region were activated. Hospitals deployed ambulances to agreed upon sites, and private sector responders installed and operated generators. Though response was slow in areas, efforts by both FEMA and the private sector were deemed an overall success. The trend toward privatization of many facets of emergency response is growing at each level of government, and both the public and private sectors have recognized many benefits of this trend.

STRUCTURE OF EMERGENCY RESPONSE

The structure of emergency response differs at each level of government (Table 5.1). Each level has its own responsibilities, policies, and emergency response methods. The adage within the emergency management community of "all emergencies are local" remains true, yet major disasters typically overwhelm local emergency response capabilities. Each level of government relies on one another during major disasters for information, support, and financial resources. The National Response Framework (NRF) provides guidelines and principles that direct each level of government on how to best respond to an emergency. The private sector has played an increasing role in each level of response. This section will explore the structure of local, state, regional, and federal emergency response and how the private and public sectors work together during emergencies.

110

Table 5.1 Structure of Emergency Response in the United States

	Federal	Regional	State	Local
Actors	President of the United States, national FEMA administrator, Congress	Regional FEMA administrator, regional planning coordinators	Governor, state emergency management office, agency/department heads	Jurisdictional chief executives, local emergency manager, agency/department heads
Responsibilities	Emergency/Major Disaster Declarations, coordination of response operations, approve federal aid and relief response operations	Coordinate with other states/localities, ensure continuity and effectiveness of response, ensure regional plan is being carried out	Declare statewide emergency, activate statewide emergency response plan, coordinate communications between cities and communities, provide information to the public	Activate local emergency response plans, mandatory evacuation orders, provide information to the public, coordinate local emergency response
Private sector role	Perform contracted emergency response activities, share best practices	Share best practices, provide resources following a disaster (contract or voluntary)	Coordinate with state emergency management office, perform contracted emergency response activities, share best practices	Coordinate with local emergency manager/ agency, perform contracted emergency response activities

Local Level

The most important level of emergency response is at the local level. The NRF provides the basic framework for local emergency response, and outlines the responsibilities for jurisdictional chief executives, emergency managers, and other local officials. Responsibility for immediate response to a disaster lies with local officials, emergency management officials, private citizens, and local first responders. These individuals are familiar with the community and generally know where help may be needed first in order to perform potentially life-saving operations. Jurisdictional chief executives are responsible for the public safety and welfare of the people of their jurisdiction (FEMA, 2013a). The decisions they make, along with policies and other priorities, often determine how well a community will do immediately following a disaster. It is essential for these individuals to understand their responsibilities as decision makers in the emergency management and response domain. They must also provide information to the public while directing response activities as well. When a disaster overwhelms the capabilities of local emergency response teams, the jurisdictional chief executive is responsible for reaching out to other jurisdictions, and often the state governor.

The emergency manager works with chief elected and appointed officials to establish unified objectives regarding the jurisdiction's emergency plans and activities (FEMA, 2013a). During a disaster, the emergency manager activates the local emergency response plan and advises the jurisdictional chief executive and other relevant local officials. Other duties include coordinating the response of nongovernmental organizations, private sector entities, and local first responders, and ensuring operations are executed as smoothly as possible. The local emergency manager also, for example, remits information to state-level emergency managers so they can be prepared to take any necessary action.

The private sector may play a large and important role at the local response level. Private sector entities include large, medium, and small businesses; commerce, private cultural and educational institutions; and industry, as well as public–private partnerships that have been established specifically for emergency management purposes (FEMA, 2013a). Local governments often contract private businesses to provide aid immediately following a disaster. Local private businesses can quickly provide resources without communities waiting on resources to be delivered from out of state or out of the region. Within hours of a disaster, the private sector can set up stations for distribution of food, water, and other necessities. While these businesses are dependent on delivery of resources as well, they can provide immediate and efficient response. Local contractors can quickly provide cranes and other equipment to aid in tree and debris removal so local infrastructure can be restored as quickly as possible. The privatization of response operations is not limited to large-scale disasters. A substantial percentage of emergency medical services responders are private companies that have contracts with both state-run and private hospitals. Although not as great in number, many cities have also contracted out fire-fighting response operations to private companies.

The private sector also voluntarily provides resources following major disasters. Hundreds of private companies pledged food, water, and financial resources following Hurricane Sandy. Some private businesses respond to disasters by opening back up as quickly as possible following a disaster. Waffle House has become famous for opening its doors sometimes just hours after a disaster. In fact, FEMA unofficially uses the *Waffle House Index* to judge the extent of damage to a community following a disaster; the menu is the indicator (Bauerlein, 2011). "If you get there and the Waffle House is closed?," FEMA administrator Craig Fugate has said. "That's really bad. That's where you go to work." (Bauerlein, 2011). Businesses that are quick to reopen can help provide a sense of normalcy to residents affected by a disaster.

State Level

Many disasters affect more than communities; they affect an entire state. Each state has its own emergency response plan that a variety of actors help create. When communities are overwhelmed by a disaster, they turn to statewide officials for help, including the governor. The governor coordinates state resources and provides the strategic guidance for response to all types of incidents (FEMA, 2013a). The governor also declares states of emergency, activates state emergency response plans, and requests federal assistance if he or she sees fit. Another responsibility is to effectively communicate to the public the actions that are being taken to respond to the disaster. This is critical immediately following a disaster, as there is typically a lot of chaos and confusion; the governor can help dispel fear and confusion through regular communication with the public. Often the governor will deploy the state's National Guard to assist in rescue and recovery operations, distribution of basic necessities, and removal of debris from roadways.

All states have laws mandating the establishment of a state emergency management agency, as well as the emergency plans coordinated by that agency (FEMA, 2013a). Therefore, each state has an office or agency in charge of emergency management; a director or manager heads each state organization. The director or manager is responsible for making sure the state is prepared to respond to disasters, and is in regular contact with local emergency managers following a disaster. This individual may also provide assistance and guidance to the governor, and often helps coordinate response operations between nongovernmental organizations and the private sector. National Guard members have expertise in critical areas, such as emergency medical response; communications; logistics; search and rescue; civil engineering; chemical, biological, radiological, and nuclear response and planning; and decontamination (FEMA, 2013a). The National Guard can also provide support to local police forces to ensure the safety of storm victims and, in some cases, to bring civility to chaotic situations.

The private sector plays a role in emergency response similar to the local level but at a larger scale. Many states have statewide contracts with the private sector to respond to emergencies. Large corporations like Wal-Mart, Home Depot, Lowes, and Anheuser-Busch have plans that enable them to set up distribution centers in communities and rural areas across an affected state. Because these corporations are found in communities across the country, response time is minimal and the recovery phase can begin more quickly. Most states have one, if not more, business alliance that specifically deals with emergency management and response. Louisiana has the Louisiana Business Emergency Operations Center (LABEOC), designed to keep businesses across the state informed following a disaster. Serving as an annex of the state's emergency operations center, the LABEOC facilitates communication with the state's major economic-driver industries, as well as owners and operators of critical infrastructures and key resources, to enhance Louisiana's emergency management efforts (LABEOC, 2014). Missouri has an active Business Emergency Operations Center; it played a large role in the search and rescue efforts following the EF-5 tornado that struck Joplin, Missouri, in 2011. Its emergency plan was activated directly after the tornado, resulting in businesses immediately responding. Sprint provided emergency workers with headsets to help workers communicate with one another. Coca-Cola has a distribution plant in Joplin, so the company was quickly able to provide water and juice to emergency workers and victims of the tornado.

Regional Level

Natural disasters like hurricanes and severe winter storms rarely affect just one state; often, an entire region of the country is affected. States across the country have formed partnerships with one another to coordinate swift and effective responses to disasters. FEMA has ten regional offices that are able to respond to disasters when necessary. In larger-scale incidents, these regional and field offices may provide the initial response assets with additional support being provided from other department and agency offices across the nation (FEMA, 2013a). Back-to-back disasters can overwhelm even the most efficient FEMA operations. For example, Hurricane Isaac recovery in Louisiana was impeded by the outflow of FEMA staff and private contractors to Hurricane Sandy–stricken areas in the northeastern United States. Each regional office is headed by a regional administrator who runs emergency response coordination activities following a disaster. Each regional office also has a private sector liaison that acts as an intermediary on behalf of the private sector. The liaison communicates the needs of the private sector and informs FEMA of best practices in communicating with the private sector in emergency response situations.

Interstate regional partnerships are common as well. Through these partnerships, communities and emergency officials can easily share critical information during emergency response scenarios. Many regions routinely engage in emergency response training scenarios to ensure effective coordination in actual disaster situations. The Ready Hampton Roads program in Virginia and North Carolina is a public awareness program aimed at encouraging citizens to effectively prepare for a disaster. The program also identifies relevant emergency response activities, including feeding and sheltering disaster victims. Its main objective is to promote the interjurisdictional and interagency coordination of emergency management issues and foster emergency preparedness in the Hampton Roads area (Hampton Roads Regional Catastrophic Planning Team Mass Care and Shelter Findings Report, 2014).

The Emergency Management Assistance Compact (EMAC), established in 1996, is a program that facilitates the sharing of aid between states following a man-made or natural disaster. EMAC is the first national disaster relief compact since the Civil Defense and Disaster Compact of 1950 to be ratified by Congress (Emergency Management Assistance Compact, n.d., a). The agreement allows the rapid movement of resources and aid during a governor-declared state of emergency from one state to another.

Once the conditions for providing assistance to a requesting state have been set, the terms constitute a legally binding contractual agreement that makes affected states responsible for reimbursement (Emergency Management Assistance Compact, n.d., b). EMAC streamlines and simplifies any questions regarding liability about reimbursement and provides relevant actors an easily readable legal document. The agreements are the public answer to the issue of insufficient local resources; when EMAC is successful, there is less reliance on the private sector.

Many large and/or disaster-prone states have been broken down by region by their own state's emergency management agency. California, for example, is divided into coastal, inland, and southern regions (FEMA, 2013b). Each region is responsible for coordination of counties and communities within that region as well as coordinating with other regions. Following the active hurricane seasons of 2004 and 2005, Florida conducted statewide evacuation studies and developed a regional evacuation plan for the state. Many states also have regional planning commissions that are in charge of a variety of activities, including emergency response. Large metropolitan areas often have their own regional planning commissions as well. Many large metropolitan areas are also a part of the Urban Areas Security Initiative (UASI). UASI program funds address the unique planning, organization, equipment, training, and exercise needs of high-threat, high-density urban areas, and assists them in building an enhanced and sustainable capacity to prevent, protect against, mitigate, respond to, and recover from acts of terrorism (FEMA, 2006).

Federal Level

The federal government responds to emergencies and disasters only in unique circumstances. A governor may determine, after consulting with local government officials, that the recovery appears to be beyond the combined resources of both the state and local governments and that federal assistance may be needed (FEMA, 2014b). The process for requesting federal emergency response assistance is set forth by the Robert T. Stafford Disaster Relief and Emergency Assistance Act (Stafford Act). The governor of the state requesting assistance must (FEMA, 2014b)

- Certify that the severity and magnitude of the disaster exceed state and local capabilities
- Certify that federal assistance is necessary to supplement the efforts and available resources of the state and local governments,

disaster relief organizations, and compensation by insurance for disaster-related losses
• Confirm execution of the state's emergency plan
• Certify adherence to cost-sharing requirements

This information, along with other criteria such as damage assessments and level of imminent threats to public health, determine whether the president will make a major disaster declaration (FEMA, 2014b). A governor must then submit a written request to the regional FEMA administrator who will then submit the request to the president. The Stafford Act allows the president to move federal aid and resources into the stricken area once a declaration is made. The president may also issue an emergency declaration before a disaster. This allows resources to be activated in advance of an emergency in order to mitigate the effects of a disaster and to prevent a possible catastrophic event. Such deployments of significant federal assets would occur in anticipation of or following catastrophic incidents involving chemical, biological, radiological, nuclear, or high-yield explosive weapons of mass destruction; large-magnitude earthquakes; or other incidents affecting heavily populated areas (FEMA, 2014c).

FEMA has created a number of public–private partnerships at the federal level and has created a private sector division within the agency. The division seeks to partner with small, medium, and large businesses as well as national corporations. Since the private sector often responds to disasters and emergencies in its own way, it shares best practices with relevant emergency response actors at the federal level. Through public–private collaboration, the government and the private sector can (FEMA, 2015)

• Enhance situational awareness
• Access more resources and capabilities
• Improve coordination
• Create more resilient communities and increase jurisdictional capacity to prevent, protect against, respond to, and recover from major incidents
• Maintain strong relationships built on mutual understanding

Nongovernmental Organizations

Nongovernmental organizations (NGOs) often play a large role in emergency response. NGOs are nonprofit entities with an association that is based on interests of its members, individuals, or institutions and that is not created by government, but may work cooperatively with government (FEMA, 2013b). Most states and local jurisdictions have partnerships with a variety of NGOs to aid in response operations; NGOs can be either faith-based or secular. Following a disaster, some NGOs operate on their own without coordinating with *official* emergency response efforts; their response efforts are generally of a smaller scale. Sometimes, NGOs coordinate with each other within the Voluntary Organizations Active in Disaster (VOAD) system. VOAD is the primary point of contact for voluntary organization in the National Response Coordination Center (at FEMA headquarters), a signatory to the National Response Plan, and an Emergency Support Function partner of many other federal agencies as delineated in the National Disaster Recovery Framework (National Voluntary Organizations Active in Disaster, 2014). NGOs can perform a number of activities and provide a number of essential services following a disaster including

- Provide shelter for displaced residents
- Provide food and water for citizens and first responders
- Provide psychological services
- Aid in pet/animal rescue
- Provide medical services
- Aid in disaster assessments

Perhaps the best-known and most recognizable NGO in emergency response is the American Red Cross. The Red Cross received a Congressional charter in 1900 to perform disaster relief services, and the organization now has 2 million volunteers and locations across the United States (American Red Cross, 2014). They have partnerships with emergency management officials at the local, state, regional, and federal levels of response operations. The Red Cross also partners with the Salvation Army in local jurisdictions regularly. The Salvation Army is also officially recognized by each level of government to provide relief immediately following a disaster. They provide food, shelter, cleanup supplies, and aid in emergency communications. Both the Red Cross and the Salvation Army use the National Incident Management System (NIMS) as a template for their emergency response operations. Both organizations are also important in the ongoing recovery of communities after disasters. NIMS provides a consistent template enabling federal, state, tribal, and local governments, the private sector, and nongovernmental organizations to work together to prepare for, prevent, respond to, recover from, and mitigate the effects of incidents regardless of cause, size, location, or complexity (FEMA, 2011). NIMS uses and provides best practices in order to achieve a collaborative and effective response to an emergency or disaster.

Private Sector

The private sector responds to emergencies and disasters in numerous ways. Private sector entities provide response resources (donated or compensated) during an incident—including specialized teams, essential services, equipment, and advanced technologies—through local public–private emergency plans or mutual aid and assistance agreements or in response to requests from government and nongovernmental–volunteer initiatives (FEMA, 2013a). Privatization of emergency response is becoming more commonplace due to the supply chain capabilities of the private sector. In large disasters, the private sector may also be able to meet surge capacity demands that cannot be met by government entities or NGOs.

Companies like Wal-Mart and Home Depot provide relief to their employees following a disaster, taking the burden off government entities. Other businesses simply volunteer their resources in emergency response situations. Stewart, Kolluru, and Smith (2009) state, "… some private sector firms have responded as part of a government contract, while others responded because they have vested interest in the impact area through physical assets, suppliers, customers, and/or corporate values of social responsibility." Following Hurricane Katrina, Acadian Ambulance performed contractual duties but went beyond the realm of their contracts. They rescued stranded residents and provided medical care to citizens across the state of Louisiana when they were not legally bound to do so; the first responders felt it was the right thing to do. Local private sector response can be valuable due to the proximity to a disaster. Local businesses can provide resources and relief within hours of a disaster when NGOs and government entities may not be able to access affected areas. These businesses can also respond by opening as soon as possible following a disaster to help an affected community or population begin to return to normalcy as quickly as possible.

The private sector owns 80% of the nation's critical infrastructure; its response capabilities are critical to an affected community. The roles of preparedness and mitigation are important so that businesses can respond to a disaster as quickly as possible. Companies that are contracted by the government to perform emergency response operations must ensure that their response capabilities can meet demand. Since the private sector is contracted in large part due to its greater supply chain capabilities, businesses often partner with each other in creating emergency response plans in order to enhance response operations. Collaboration among the public and private sectors along with NGOs is essential in disaster response.

LEGISLATION GUIDING EMERGENCY RESPONSE

Local Emergency Operations Plan

A local emergency operations plan (LEOP) is a document that describes the roles and responsibilities to be performed by various actors following an emergency situation. LEOPs are required by law and are important because local governments are the first to respond following an emergency. In accordance with the national all-hazards approach to emergency management, LEOPs address a number of emergencies including wildfires, terrorist attacks, and floods. While each plan is specific according to locality, FEMA suggests that each LEOP address the following (FEMA, 1996):

- Set forth lines of authority and organizational relationships, and shows how all actions will be coordinated
- Describe how people and property will be protected in emergencies and disasters
- Assign responsibility to organizations and individuals for carrying out specific actions at projected times and places in an emergency that exceeds the capability or routine responsibility of any one agency
- Identify personnel, equipment, facilities, supplies, and other resources available—within the jurisdiction or by agreement with other jurisdictions—for use during response and recovery operations

A comprehensive LEOP contains maps of the locality and a checklist to be referred to during and after an emergency. The checklist will contain local actors from the public, private, and nonprofit sectors that are expected to respond to emergencies. Local coordinators of a wide variety of services (health and medical, mass care, evacuation, animal welfare) should be identified along with their responsibilities. The LEOP should also contain areas for emergency response personnel to record what time-specific actions were performed as well as areas for comments regarding the success or failure of each action taken. Since the private sector is playing an increasing role in emergency response, businesses and corporations are often directly referred to in LEOPs. Often these businesses will have a representative at the local emergency operations center in order to coordinate with the public and nonprofit sectors.

Not every emergency or disaster is due to natural causes. Many are man-made and contained within the private sector; accordingly, corporations that produce chemicals, refine petroleum products, and/ or process food must have their own emergency operations plans. In April 2010, the Deepwater Horizon oil drilling rig owned by British Petroleum (BP) exploded, leading to the worst oil spill in U.S. history. BP quickly put its own emergency response plan into place in order to mitigate the effects of the explosion and the spill. The meticulously created document contains dozens of maps, several checklists, and names of coordinators for hundreds of actionable items. The size and scope of the disaster forced government and nonprofit sector involvement, leading to an unprecedented coordinated response lasting months. Despite the relatively quick response to the spill, there are inherent problems with an at-fault company or corporation leading response efforts. BP was accused of not being forthright with the actual amount of oil spilling from the deepwater well; this may have resulted in a scaled-down response to what was eventually classified as the worst environmental disaster in U.S. history.

Memorandums of Understanding

Important to coordinating and clarifying emergency response activities, memorandums of understanding (MOUs) between the public, nonprofit, and private sectors are a simple way to establish a clear process of responding to emergencies. MOUs are common in every phase of emergency management but are especially important during the response phase because they provide emergency management officials a quick and easily readable legal document on who is responsible to carry out specific duties. Public–private, public–nonprofit, and private–nonprofit MOUs are all common at each level of government. The nonprofit organization Collaborating Agencies Responding to Disasters (CARD), based in Oakland, California, was created following the Loma Prieta earthquake in 1989 and has created a template for organizations to use when creating an MOU (CARD, n.d.). They suggest including (Florida State University, 2013)

- *A purpose*: An MOU should clearly articulate the desired outcome of entering the agreement.
- *Mission statements*: An MOU should include a brief description of the respective organizations and their fundamental mission.
- *Activation protocols*: Clearly define the situations under which the MOU will be activated and the individuals with the authority to activate it.
- *Response procedures and obligations*: What is going to be done? Who is going to do it? Who pays for what?
- *Financial relations*: If the MOU includes a fee for service arrangement or other financial obligations, a method for determining financial payments should be clearly established.

CARD has also outlined common resources to be secured with an MOU, including volunteers, expertise, specialized equipment, food and water, sheltering space, and alternate office space (Florida State University, 2013).

Public–private sector MOU partnerships are common in every state. California has MOUs with a number of private corporations that provide a variety of goods and services. The state has MOUs with Wal-Mart, Target, and Home Depot that allow for fast and efficient delivery of supplies and resources to disaster-stricken areas (California Office of Emergency Services, 2015a). In 2008, the California Grocers Association was one of the first in the private sector to partner with the state's office of emergency services. The agreement allows for a representative of the association to be present in an emergency command center during and after a disaster. The agreement is designed to expedite the delivery of food and water to disaster-stricken areas (California Grocers Association, 2014). The state's Office of Emergency Services also has an MOU with Bank of America to provide mobile ATMs and banking centers to communities affected by a disaster (California Office of Emergency Services, 2015b). Home Depot also has an MOU with a number of coastal states in which the corporation allows FEMA to give presentations and hazard mitigation tips to residents of the area. Many states also have MOUs with the American Red Cross. The Red Cross is considered a private nonprofit, placing it in both the private and nonprofit sectors. Oregon's MOU with the Red Cross provides a detailed narrative of what is expected of each party involved during emergency response operations. For emergency workers and people returning to their homes, the American Red Cross mobilizes emergency response vehicles from which disaster workers distribute food, water, and essential cleanup items that might not be immediately available in the community (Memorandum of Understanding between the American Red Cross and the State of Oregon, 2013).

Mutual Aid Agreements

Mutual aid agreements (MAAs) and other types of assistance agreements facilitate the rapid sharing of emergency aid and resources among governments and organizations at all levels (Association of State and Territorial Health Officials, 2011). These agreements are considered to be an important part of the NIMS because they provide guidance to the public, private, and nonprofit sectors in developing emergency response plans. They can be written as legal statutes or can be somewhat informal as long as each party is aware of their responsibility in the agreement. The U.S. Department of Homeland Security has identified, in accordance with NIMS guidelines, some elements that an MAA should include (Association of State and Territorial Health Officials, 2011):

- Definitions of key terms
- Procedures for requesting and receiving aid
- Roles and responsibilities of individual parties
- Relationships to other MAAs
- Protocols for interoperable communications
- Provisions to update and terminate the agreement

Public–private MAAs are common. Among the most common of these MAAs is airports entering into agreements with a variety of private sector organizations. In Alaska, for example, the coastal city of Sitka is a popular cruise ship destination so the local airport entered into an MAA with a cruise line in case of emergency. Midway and O'Hare International Airports, operated by the city of Chicago, each have public–private MAAs as well. In the case of severe storms, wind, or lightning, private cargo companies and airlines have permission to use city-owned buildings for shelter (Airport Cooperative Research Program, 2013). Agreements within the private sector are also common in disaster response scenarios. Many privately owned hospitals have MAAs with each other. Hospitals are a common example of this. During disaster response scenarios, hospitals can share equipment, supplies, personnel, and can aid in patient transfers. MAAs ultimately help ensure that the public, private, and nonprofit sectors respond efficiently and effectively following a disaster.

BENEFITS AND LIMITATIONS
OF PRIVATIZING EMERGENCY RESPONSE

The literature in new public management suggests that privatization of government services creates a more effective and efficient delivery system of public goods and services. However, it must always be remembered that public service criteria for success extend well beyond effectiveness and efficiency. Responsiveness, fairness, representativeness, equity, accountability, and many other criteria must also be considered when providing a public service. Many factors have pushed government officials to contract with the private sector, including resource availability, cost of goods, and the modern rebirth of the *small government* movement. There are, no doubt, many benefits to privatizing many services; however, there are most certainly inherent limitations as well. This section will explore the benefits and limitations of privatizing emergency and disaster response.

Benefits

Large-scale disasters during the last two decades have highlighted the fact that the government alone cannot effectively respond to disasters and emergencies. Hurricane Katrina was a painful reminder of this fact. Since then, emergency management officials across the country have begun to privatize many emergency response activities and have forged partnerships with the private sector to help alleviate suffering following a disaster. The country's latest push toward smaller government seems to have played a role as well. The general public's resentment toward bureaucracy and red tape is especially high following a large-scale disaster. Procedural requirements do indeed impede efficient disaster response, thus worsening already chaotic situations. Privatization can certainly alleviate this problem as the private sector can immediately respond to a situation without having to go through an entire bureaucratic process.

Limited resource availability has also pushed governments to contract with the private sector to supply goods and services governments otherwise cannot afford to provide, especially in the context of supply of goods and services for emergency and disaster response (Egan, 2010). States and localities simply may not have enough food or water for victims of disasters. Furthermore, critical infrastructure may be damaged, entirely isolating an area in serious need of resources and aid. Hurricane Katrina was a devastating example of this, as tens of thousands of people went days without food or water. Another benefit of privatization is the private sector's supply chain capabilities. To put it simply, the private sector knows where goods are stored, who has them, the best practices for transporting them, and has the connections for locating them quickly. It is important for the government, in turn, to trust the private sector's capabilities and to quickly mobilize resources to clear roads to increase efficient delivery of goods.

Another benefit of public–private contract partnerships is the private sector's expertise in a variety of disciplines. Communications failures are common following a large-scale disaster, creating an absence of Internet and telephone capabilities. Individuals and firms with technological expertise can alleviate communications breakdowns by providing advice and assistance in creating mobile and wireless communications systems vital in the hours after a disaster. Engineering and construction firms can also provide expertise in response operations. Engineering firms can provide technical knowledge regarding structural damage and/or structural integrity during search and rescue operations. Construction firms may provide specialized equipment and expertise to quickly remove debris from roadways to enhance response times. Finally, government may contract with the private sector to provide logistical know-how. Logistics competence, the capacity to manage the movement of materials quickly, efficiently, and securely is consistently an important need in disaster response and recovery effort, and it is one that many private sector organizations have developed to support their primary business (Statler, Burgi, & Raisch, 2008). Efficient movement of large shipments of goods and resources is invaluable during emergency response operations.

Politicization of disasters has become commonplace following a disaster. Finger pointing and the political blame-game by emergency management and elected officials occur at the local, state, and regional levels. Hurricane Katrina serves as yet another example. Mayor Ray Nagin of New Orleans, and Louisiana Governor Kathleen Blanco engaged in a very bitter and public battle about who was to blame for slow response times. Many officials eventually placed blame on FEMA and President George W. Bush. This sort of political theater only worsens the situation and takes the focus off of the actual victims of the disaster. Contracting with the private sector may mitigate this problem. Private consultants generally have the advantage of being less subject to the politics of local communities and states and may be better able to develop unbiased plans and recommendations (FEMA Training Course, n.d., b) Reducing the role of the government in response activities leaves little room for politicization and finger pointing.

Limitations/Obstacles

Public–private contractual partnerships continue to be hampered by a number of obstacles. One such obstacle is the cultural divide that exists between the public and private sectors. The two sectors have historically regarded each other with a high level of distrust. The private sector often views the public sector as a regulatory entity that oversteps its boundaries; the public sector often views the private sector's profit-driven motivations as suspect. The remedy for this is for each sector to build trust through continued partnerships and collaboration at each level of government. Indeed, the private sector's inherent goal of profit can be seen as a limitation. Should businesses and corporations profit from the suffering that comes along with disasters? Some would answer absolutely not, while others may argue that the efficiency of the private sector in providing goods helps alleviate suffering. Governments must therefore carefully choose services to privatize as to uphold their contracts with the communities they serve—to protect citizens from harm and to protect basic human rights.

America's economy is based on free-market capitalism, meaning the public at large is vulnerable to the whims of the market. Large-scale disasters can decrease the availability of goods, in turn increasing their cost. Gas prices may skyrocket, increasing the transportations costs for a business. Therefore, businesses that have contracted with governments may have to charge more for the goods negating the goal of cost-efficiency. The contract must be honored regardless of cost to provide citizens with life-saving resources. Along this same thread is the issue of the contract itself. Major disasters may make it difficult, if not impossible, for businesses to uphold their legal and contractual obligations. Mandatory evacuations could force employees out of the disaster-stricken areas; conditions may become extremely dangerous, causing the same outcome. Even if employees are able to stay, they may become overwhelmed at the size and severity of the disaster themselves, making it difficult for them to act as *first responders*. When a business is unable to uphold its legal obligations following a disaster, there is risk for a cascade of ramifications. Since the government was relying on the services of the business, it will most likely not be able to pick up the slack of the missing goods or resources. The problem goes both ways. In some instances, government entities may be so overwhelmed (again, see Hurricane Katrina) that they may be unable to make timely decisions to deploy private sector contractual responsibilities. Thus, the business is at risk of losing money, and valuable goods may go unused. Additionally, two or more major disasters that occur within a short amount of time of each other may limit the capacity of the private sector to respond, even under contract. Governments and businesses should take great care in crafting contracts to mitigate against lawsuits and wasted resources in the event of any of these situations.

Just as privatization of disaster response can reduce political finger pointing, it may also create long-term issues for elected officials and the public at large. Government employees want to avoid the appearance of giving *preferential treatment* to any one company, as such *favoritism*, it seems, might jeopardize careers (Statler et al., 2008). The decade following Hurricane Katrina has seen dozens of elected officials in New Orleans and Louisiana convicted of taking bribes in exchange for awarding disaster response and recovery contracts. The trials have cost Louisiana taxpayers hundreds of thousands of dollars and have caused trust in government to plummet. Although regulations and laws are in place to prevent these activities, limited oversight about how contracts are awarded is largely to blame for this problem. Elected officials and emergency managers should make the process of awarding contracts public knowledge to rebuild citizen trust and to provide transparency. Privatization may also encourage elected officials and emergency management officials to place blame on the private sector in the case of a poor response. Taking ownership of poor coordination and response is important for government transparency and citizen trust in government.

SUMMARY

The evolution of emergency response operations in the United States has been extensive in recent decades. From the creation of the NFIP to the creation of FEMA, many different actors have assumed roles in these operations. As this chapter has explained, the private sector has played an increasingly more important role. Businesses and large corporations donate a variety of resources, including volunteers, expertise, food, and water. Many businesses now have legal contracts with governments to provide response operations the public sector used to provide. Collaboration among the public, private, and nonprofit sectors is commonplace and provides a variety of benefits for each sector. LEOPs, MOU, and MAAs provide legal guidelines for these contractual partnerships. Each level of government (local, state, regional, and federal) is responsible for emergency response operations, but the responsibilities differ according to level. The private sector plays its own role at each level. Privatization of emergency response has inherent benefits and limitations. Utilizing the private sector can save tax dollars, support the government in providing resources and by providing expertise, and decrease politicization of disasters. On the other hand, privatization can lead to legal issues and, in some instances, the private sector itself may be overwhelmed following a disaster, leaving citizens at greater risk. We suggest that, while the private sector plays an important and often irreplaceable role in disasters, the ultimate responsibility for community safety and responsibility rests with the government. The government can never abrogate its responsibility to its citizens in ensuring public safety and security.

CHAPTER QUESTIONS

1. What types of emergencies or disasters have occurred in your community? Was the response effective?
2. What are some businesses or companies in your community that could help respond to an emergency?
3. Describe the various roles the private sector can play during emergency response operations. Give some examples.
4. What types of legislation provide guidance to creating public–private partnerships?
5. Discuss the benefits and limitations of privatizing emergency response.

REFERENCES

Airport Cooperative Research Program. (2013). Model mutual aid agreements for airports. Retrieved from: http://onlinepubs.trb.org/onlinepubs/acrp/acrp_syn_045.pdf. Accessed July 10, 2015.

American Red Cross. (2014). Our history. Retrieved from: http://www.redcross.org/about-us/history. Accessed July 10, 2015.

Association of State and Territorial Health Officials. (2011). Mutual aid and assistance agreements fact sheet. Retrieved from: http://www.astho.org/Programs/Preparedness/Public-Health-Emergency-Law/Emergency-Authority-and-Immunity-Toolkit/Mutual-Aid-and-Assistance-Agreements-Fact-Sheet/. Accessed July 10, 2015.

Bauerlein, V. (2011). How to measure a storm's fury one breakfast at a time. *Wall Street Journal*. Retrieved from: http://online.wsj.com/news/articles/SB10001424053111904716604576542460736605364. Accessed July 10, 2015.

Busch, N.E. & Givens, A.D. (2012). Public-Private Partnerships in Homeland Security: Opportunities and Challenges. Homeland Security Affairs 8, Article 18. Retrieved from: https://www.hsaj.org/articles/233. Accessed July 29, 2015.

California Grocers Association. (2014). Emergency management. Retrieved from: http://www.cagrocers.com/about/emergency-management/. Accessed July 10, 2015.

California Office of Emergency Services. (2015a). Memorandums of understanding. Retrieved from: http://www.caloes.ca.gov/cal-oes-divisions/hazard -mitigation/hazard-mitigation-planning/public-private-partnerships. Accessed July 10, 2015.

California Office of Emergency Services. (2015b). Regional operations. Retrieved from: http://www.caloes.ca.gov/for-governments-tribal/response/regional -operations. Accessed July 10, 2015.

Collaborating Agencies Responding to Disasters (CARD). (n.d.). Partnering for strength: MOUs, getting your relationships in print. Retrieved from: http:// hurricanes.ii.fsu.edu/docs/mou_workshop.pdf. Accessed July 10, 2015.

Egan, M.J. (2010). Private goods and services contracts: Increased emergency response capacity or increased vulnerability? *International Journal of Production Economics, 126*(1), 46–56.

Emergency Management Assistance Compact. (n.d., a). An analysis of EMAC capabilities for private sector and volunteer resource coordination. Retrieved from: http://www.emacweb.org/index.php/mutualaidresources/emac -library/12/private-sector-deployments-through-emac/277-emac-private -sector-and-volunteer-resources-analysis/file. Accessed July 10, 2015.

Emergency Management Assistance Compact. (n.d., b). What is EMAC? Retrieved from: http://www.emacweb.org/index.php/learnaboutemac/what-is-emac. Accessed July 10, 2015.

Federal Emergency Management Agency (FEMA). (1996). Guide for all-hazard emergency operations planning. Retrieved from: http://www.fema.gov /pdf/plan/slg101.pdf. Accessed July 10, 2015.

Federal Emergency Management Agency (FEMA). (2006). NIMS fact sheet. Retrieved from: http://www.fema.gov/media-library-data/20130726-1824-25045-8645 /nims_implementation_for_nongovernmental_organizations_2006.pdf. Accessed July 10, 2015.

Federal Emergency Management Agency (FEMA). (2011). National Incident Management System Training Program. Retrieved from: http://www.fema .gov/pdf/emergency/nims/nims_training_program.pdf. Accessed July 10, 2015.

Federal Emergency Management Agency (FEMA). (2013a). National response framework. Retrieved from: http://www.fema.gov/media-library-data /20130726-1914-25045-1246/final_national_response_framework_20130501 .pdf. Accessed July 10, 2015.

Federal Emergency Management Agency (FEMA). (2013b). FY 2013 Homeland Security Grant Program. Retrieved from: https://www.fema.gov/fy-2013 -homeland-security-grant-program. Accessed July 10, 2015.

Federal Emergency Management Agency (FEMA). (2014a). About the agency. Retrieved from: http://www.fema.gov/about-agency. Accessed July 10, 2015.

Federal Emergency Management Agency (FEMA). (2014b). Declaration process fact sheet. Retrieved from: http://www.fema.gov/declaration-process-fact -sheet. Accessed July 10, 2015.

Federal Emergency Management Agency (FEMA). (2014c). Homeland Security Grant Program. Retrieved from: https://www.fema.gov/fy-2013-homeland -security-grant-program-hsgp-0. Accessed July 10, 2015.

Federal Emergency Management Agency (FEMA). (2015). Public-Private Partner- ships. Retrieved from: https://www.fema.gov/public-private-partnerships. Accessed July 10, 2015.

Federal Emergency Management Agency (FEMA). (n.d., a). Course title: Incident management and NIMS. Retrieved from: http://www.training.fema .gov/hiedu/docs/nimsc2/nims%20-%20session%202%20-%20local,%20 state%20and%20fed%20em%20structures%20and%20systems%20-%20final .doc. Accessed July 10, 2015.

Federal Emergency Management Agency (FEMA). (n.d., b). Course title: Public administration and emergency management. Retrieved from: http://training .fema.gov/hiedu/docs/paem/pa&em_session_5a[1].doc. Accessed July 10, 2015.

Florida State University. (2013). Hurricane preparedness and response for Florida public libraries. Retrieved from: http://hurricanes.ii.fsu.edu/. Accessed July 10, 2015.

Hampton Roads Regional Catastrophic Planning Team Mass Care and Shelter Findings Report. (2014). Retrieved from: https://www.llis.dhs.gov/sites /default/files/RCPGP%20National%20Report%202014.pdf. Accessed July 10, 2015.

Louisiana Business Emergency Operations Center (LABEOC). (2014). Retrieved from: http://www.ofi.state.la.us/LABEOC.pdf. Accessed July 10, 2015.

Memorandum of Understanding between the American Red Cross and the State of Oregon. (2013). Retrieved from: http://www.oregon.gov/OMD/OEM /docs/library/mou_oem_arc.pdf. Accessed July 10, 2015.

National Voluntary Organizations Active in Disaster (2014). Who we are. Retrieved from: http://www.nvoad.org/about-us/our-history/. Accessed July 10, 2015.

Statler, M., Burgi, P. & Raisch, B. (2008). Mobilising corporate resources to disasters: A comparative analysis of major initiatives. *International Journal of Technology, Policy and Management, 8*(4), 359–382.

Stewart, G.T., Kolluru, R. & Smith, M. (2009). Leveraging public–private partner- ships to improve community resilience in times of disaster. *International Journal of Physical Distribution & Logistics Management, 39*(5), 343–364.

United States Chamber of Commerce Foundation. (2012). Hurricane Sandy— Corporate aid tracker. Retrieved from: http://www.uschamberfoundation .org/site-page/hurricane-sandy-corporate-aid-tracker. Accessed July 10, 2015.

6

Recovery and Rebuilding with the Private and Public Sectors

Melissa Wilkins

Contents

Learning Objective

- The reader will understand the important role of the private sector in recovery efforts. Several important case studies are presented to illustrate real-world, post-disaster examples.

INTRODUCTION

On a national level, most people first think of the Federal Emergency Management Agency, or FEMA, as the lead administrator during a disaster response. The agency was initially created in the late seventies in order to centralize disaster management in one organization. Before this shift in procedures, functions were carried out in a different structure. FEMA became a household name during the aftermath of Hurricane Katrina in New Orleans as the face of what many considered to be an underwhelming and, at times, incompetent response to the disaster. On a local level, debris removal, lack of available funding, and locating transitional housing were just a few of the major challenges New Orleans faced after Hurricane Katrina. These challenges proved to be greater than what the local government and the Department of Housing and Urban Development could accomplish without the help of the private sector and federal assistance.

Despite being under greater scrutiny, FEMA received higher marks for its efforts in the recovery after Superstorm Sandy. Although the damage sustained after Katrina was more extensive, Sandy was the most expensive natural disaster since Katrina. There was a need for a more direct approach with massive improvements to policies and procedures made available by valuable lessons from the aftermath of Katrina. FEMA handled Sandy's recovery more efficiently.

Within FEMA's structure is the National Planning Frameworks, which identifies the roles and functions that individuals, nonprofit organizations, the private sector, nongovernmental organizations, governments, and communities explicitly serve as part of a recovery process. These guidelines have been established by the parent agency of FEMA, the Department of Homeland Security (DHS). This structure shows an implicit understanding of the imperative nature of cooperation and communication between the previously mentioned entities to provide planning and solutions that prevent and mitigate problems. Within FEMA's framework is an understanding that the private sector must play a large role in both the planning and preparedness before a disaster and the recovery process after one.

The goal of emergency management in recovery is to provide the most efficient service to a government's constituency both before and after a disaster. This includes both man-made and natural disasters. However, it is the aftermath of a disaster that often defines the efficacy of a governing body's response to an event. At this stage, the time for planning has past and there is only room for a course of action that will repair any harmful effects. The scrutiny that comes with that response mandates that the recovery effort be of the highest levels of efficiency, speed, safety, and cost-effectiveness. Other necessary attributes that vendors, both internal and external, must be able to provide is immediacy of availability, versatility of planning and material options, and specificity of expertise of the task at hand. Disaster recovery necessitates collaboration between private and public entities to achieve the most effective results. Choosing to contract services to a private vendor is not an opportunity for governing bodies to relinquish responsibility, but rather it is an opportunity to seek the best strategy to meet recovery expectations. In times of need, governing agencies have to make quick decisions to accomplish both long- and short-term goals. Ensuring medical needs are met, transportation, shelter, and basic necessities are just a few of the areas of concern on a more temporary basis. Decisions on a larger scale, including fire and law enforcement, clearing debris from major road ways, mold remediation of residential and commercial buildings, hazardous waste disposal, repairing power and utility lines, and figuring out alternative means of public transportation, are issues that can take much longer to solve. The assistance from private agencies can help improve conditions quicker with less convenience to the community.

A strong advantage of outsourcing to private vendors is the luxury of ending the service contract at the end of the disaster recovery or after a specified time, a task that is much murkier when dealing with internal government resources. Although outsourcing services and forming new partnerships could contribute to a hollow state environment, the primary concern for agencies during a disaster response should be finding fast, effective, and efficient ways to promote a sense of urgency during recovery efforts. The quality of services and the flexibility offered by the privatization of services and contracts will be viewed as an advantage in better serving the community. However, there may also be disadvantages from the use of professionals with little to no knowledge of the affected area. Officials also have to allow for fluctuating weather demands depending on the location of the governing municipality. Some areas may be vulnerable to snow and ice, while others must deal with heavy rainfall. In such events as flooding or snowstorms, private agencies are better equipped with manpower, expertise, and equipment. Innovation is also another benefit to privatizing services as companies often stay current with new trends, improved solutions, and new methods in providing lower costs (New Jersey Privatization Task Force Report, 2010). Incidents like the September 11, 2001, terrorist attacks; Hurricanes Katrina and Isaac; Superstorm Sandy; and BP oil spill are just a few events that called for outside assistance from the private and public sectors to produce better recovery results. This chapter will identify the role and importance of private entities in disaster management strategies and explore incidents where established relationships between the government entities and the private and public sectors have helped produce better and faster results. The recovery process develops outward—starting locally to address immediate concerns and those concerns that are manageable with the existing resources in place, and then extending beyond to state and federal levels. The ultimate responsibility of contracting restoration, debris removal, and reconstruction companies almost entirely will fall on local governments from a jurisdictional standpoint. Larger government agencies are and should be brought in only as a last resort, as they bring with them greater costs and more bureaucracy that must be managed.

PUBLIC WORKS AND INFRASTRUCTURE RECOVERY EFFORTS

Government officials are often left with the aftermath of such natural disasters as fire, tornadoes, hurricanes, floods, or man-made events like acts of terrorism that can create both short and long-term impediments on the road to recovery. Because debris removal can become a challenge after any disaster, governing agencies are encouraged to have a debris removal plan in place within the overall emergency management plan that is readily available when called upon. According to FEMA, areas with an efficient debris removal plan have a faster recovery rate in restoring services to the public while keeping communities safe (Public Assistance Debris Management Guide, 2007). Having an effective plan in place can also help prevent unexpected emergency costs, decrease recovery costs, and help residents have a greater awareness of what to expect after a disaster. Officials in Sandusky, Ohio, were unprepared to handle several issues with debris removal after a tornado ripped through the area in 1992. Without a proper plan in place, recovery efforts took almost three months to clear approximately 600 tons of waste. Their challenges included, but were not limited to, communicating concise instructions and separating green waste from regular debris (Environmental Protection Agency [EPA], 2012).

Minnesota Bridge Collapse in August 2007

This is a catastrophe of historic proportions for Minnesota. We are doing everything we can to make sure we respond as quickly as we can to this emergency.

Tim Pawlenty
Governor of Minnesota

On August 1, 2007, governing officials responded to the collapse of an eight-lane bridge along I-35 in Minnesota during rush-hour traffic. According to reports, the bridge crumbled and broke in half, leaving eight people dead and several injured. The incident directly affected travelers and neighboring areas as officials had to remove remaining vehicles and school buses with passengers from the bridge and recover crushed vehicles from beneath the bridge that had fallen into the Mississippi River. Given the nature of the incident, officials were immediately concerned with emergency search and rescue efforts. Those efforts were slowed considerably by the continuing search efforts for survivors in the river while having to simultaneously clear rubble and bridge remnants out of the way (Kimball & Williamson, 2007).

There was also a direct concern with air pollution and water contamination as particles from the collapse were released both airborne and into the river. The emergency required responding representatives from the Minnesota Department of Transportation, Minnesota Pollution Control Agency, and Mississippi Watershed Management Organization. These agencies quickly began the recovery process. Included in those efforts were clearing, testing, and monitoring mitigation to help protect workers, residents, and the Mississippi River (PB Works, n.d.).

Despite the DHS ruling terrorism out as a cause for the crumbling of the bridge, the cause of the collapse was unknown given that the bridge had passed inspections in 2005 and 2006. Local officials said before the incident that lane resurfacing and guardrail improvements were among the minor repairs the bridge underwent shortly before the tragedy (Kimball &

Williamson, 2007). Two days after the bridge collapsed, Minnesota officials made the decision to delegate a portion of the recovery process out by contacting a private agency, allotting $15 million to implement a debris removal plan (PB Works, n.d.).

According to the contract between the private agency and area officials, the vendor's job would revolve primarily around demolition and clearing of debris. The private contractor committed to providing labor, equipment, and materials needed to complete the job, while also agreeing to complete the project by December 3, 2007. A provision was also included within the emergency contract that gave state officials the authority to decrease the overall payment if the project exceeded the agreed upon timeline of approximately four months, or if the results did not meet the expectations of the project engineer or commissioner (State of Minnesota Department of Transportation, 2007).

In the end, the company carried out this piece of the recovery plan by coordinating duties to approximately twenty different subcontractors on local, state, and federal levels. Fourteen thousand tons of steel and cement remnants and several cars from the river were removed during the project. With an explicit detailed plan of sixty crewmembers in action, the contractor was able to complete the project in less time and without going over the budgeted project price. The company was given a target schedule of four months but finished in only two and a half months and at a cost of only $8 million, almost half of the budgeted amount (PB Works, n.d.). The Minnesota Bridge tragedy and the cleanup and recovery process that ensured is a clear example of the efficiencies and effectiveness a private vendor can bring to disaster mitigation. Within a few days of the incident, the local government took an aggressive approach to secure an agreement with the contracting company and began immediately working to make improvements. Area officials were then able to focus their much-needed attention to other areas. In the end, the contractor completed the project both ahead of schedule and under budget.

Twin Span Bridge Collapse

On August 28, 2005, Hurricane Katrina crashed into southeast Louisiana, causing mass destruction as one of the five deadliest hurricanes in U.S. history. Approximately 80% of New Orleans flooded. Approximately 1600 people died, and more than a million residents were forced to evacuate from their homes. The amount of flooded homes reached into the thousands, with many more homes requiring demolition or intense reconstruction.

With assistance provided by FEMA, the Louisiana Road Home program funded the costs of demolition or repairs to more than 20,000 homes in the amount of $13.4 billon statewide. Additional funding was also appropriated by FEMA through a Hazard Mitigation Grant program (Keegan, 2009).

While $108 billion dollars in property damage was incurred, a successful recovery for the city would include partnerships with the Orleans Levee Board, U.S. Army Corps of Engineers, FEMA, members of the New Orleans Emergency Management Team, and several nonprofit agencies. It would be a long road to recovery for the 800,000 displaced residents and property owners, but city officials were focused and committed to restoring the Crescent City. New Orleans showed great resilience in the immediate aftermath of Hurricane Katrina. During the declared state of emergency, New Orleans Mayor Ray Nagin and his administration focused on ways to recover various parts of New Orleans, and to provide safety and emergency care, food, and shelter those who were unable to adhere to the mandatory evacuation order. The city also bore the responsibility of recovering the bodies of those lost in the storm. Of the many repairs and construction projects needed to rebuild New Orleans, the reconstruction of the collapsed I-10 Twin Span Bridge over Lake Pontchartrain was of utmost importance as it was a major transportation artery in and out of the city to the east. Although small portions of the bridge were not damaged, the six-mile bridge suffered a tremendous amount of damage that included 64 missing spans or bridge pieces and 473 total pieces that separated from both the east and westbound bridges (Gautreau, 2007).

The weight of each span was 255 tons, which only added an additional challenge to restoring the bridge. Because of the nature of the emergency, resources were expedited. Less than two weeks after Hurricane Katrina, state officials outsourced this project to a local firm for the bidding price of $31 million dollars. That price included removing debris, a new design, equipment, labor, and materials and a target completion date of 120 days. As earlier stated, the company worked diligently to complete the project seventeen days ahead of schedule with savings greater than the initial projected cost. The total completion cost of the project was $30,964,255. The bridge featured a wider and taller design and constructed to handle strong hurricane winds and intense surges (Lee & Hall, 2011).

Official Debris Locations

The recovery process after any disaster includes locating specific places to properly dispose of debris as well as locating places that can be used for landfill purposes as mandated by the Resource Conservation and Recovery Act. The Act addresses the proper disposal of the different types of waste, including both hazardous and other solid wastes as well as landfill disposal. Under this Act, the state must find locations that meet regulations put in place by the EPA. The systematic cleanup after Hurricane Katrina laid the groundwork for the Water Resources Development Act of 2007. The U.S. Government Accountability Office under the Act addressed certain activities and processes related to debris removal and disposal as it related to environmental issues at the Gentilly Landfill in New Orleans.

Outside of more traditional debris removal likes trees, wood, and steel, Louisiana officials had to turn to private contractors to assist with the disposal of hazardous waste, rotten food from commercial developments, abandoned boats and cars, and more. Area officials were dealing with debris as a direct effect of the hurricane and the debris from the levee breaking, which dramatically increased the amount of flooding in homes, businesses, and developments. According to the U.S. Army Corps of Engineers (Corps), 36 million pounds of spoiled meat and other foods had to be properly disposed after Hurricane Katrina. Because 350,000 cars and 60,000 vessels used for fishing and other recreational activities were damaged, abandoned, or destroyed, officials were left with the task of disposing those items as well. There was also a need to assist with debris removal from private property for residents and business owners who were forced to remove white goods like freezers, refrigerators, and other appliances as well as electronic waste that required a special disposal process. To help with the separation process of debris items like recyclables, vegetative waste, hazardous materials, and more, officials outsourced to a local company that could handle the entire coordination. Some items could be burned or buried while a large portion of debris could be recycled in some way (Luther, 2008).

WASTEWATER TREATMENT

In addition to worrying about proper debris disposal, New Orleans officials also had to handle recovery efforts of sewage or wastewater treatment after the hurricane. As stated earlier, 80% of the city was under water for up to three weeks in some areas. With nearly the entirety of New Orleans being below sea level, the challenge of draining the city was even more daunting. As a matter of public health, this was not a task city officials were prepared to handle. Because the damage was so catastrophic, some felt the Sewage and Water Board of New Orleans would not be fully restored for at least a year. To ensure the safety of residential water, it was imperative that the city outsource to a private company that not only had the experience and resources available, but also had the resources and knowledge to stay within EPA regulations. Because of a great partnership that was already established between the company that won the bid and the City of New Orleans, the transition was simple and the private company knew how to step in and assist. The decision was cost-effective and helped officials provide high-quality service. The private company served as the primary water source for the city, working with resources around the world to stay within the EPA deadline of sixty days to provide and maintain a high level of sewage and water treatment that included safe drinking water to residents. Between two facilities, the company treated 142 million gallons of water a day. The company met all requirements with a savings of $6 million to the city. Donations of $1.6 million were also given by the private company to continue the rebuilding process (New Orleans Wastewater Facilities, n.d.).

EMERGENCY RECOVERY EFFORTS
THROUGH STRONG PARTNERSHIPS

The private sector, from the Fortune 500 companies to your local grocery store, is an essential member of the team ... Growing strong working relationships between emergency managers and the private sector is a good business decision for everyone—it helps us better serve survivor, rebuild our communities and boost local economies.

Craig Fugate
Federal Emergency Management Agency Administrator

Governing agencies, nonprofits, and public and private entities must exhibit a high degree of resilience to achieve meaningful and lasting results. Partnerships between both private and public agencies is the growing trend, as these partnerships have proven to help areas and communities recover with effective planning due to shared resources from both parts. Federal officials see the potential and advantages of partnerships and encourage government agencies to include private and public agencies in disaster management policies (Busch & Givens). Outreach efforts positively influenced Joplin, Missouri, during one of the deadliest tornadoes in the state's history.

Joplin, Missouri, Tornado in May 2011

Emergency medical needs cannot be predicted during the recovery phase after any disaster. The same can also be said for necessities like food, water, and shelter. Governing agencies are responsible for their constituents before, during, and after a disaster. Providing effective and timely services during that period can become an extremely difficult task. Through strong partnerships between governing agencies and both public and private groups, more needs are met in the advancement of the recovery process of areas in need. An emergency left one city and community in despair after a disastrous tornado depleted much of the area, affecting 7500 homes and 50 businesses. Thanks to strong partnerships with nongovernmental organizations, the community of Joplin, Missouri, was able to recover faster.

It was total devastation in my view. I just couldn't believe what I saw.

Jay Nixon
Governor of Missouri

The city of Joplin, Missouri, was largely an unknown municipality nationwide before May 22, 2011. However, the afternoon of that day brought an EF-5 tornado and catastrophic destruction to the town. The immense devastation proved to be more than the small city could handle, as approximately 158 lost their lives, an additional 1150 were injured, and more than 8000 structures were destroyed. With 30% of Joplin in ruins, officials had to act fast to get emergency services to injured residents, coordinate search efforts to locate those who were missing, and find a way to implement rapid recovery services. Two major retailers, Home Depot and Wal-Mart, contributed 1 million dollars each to help the recovery process. Additionally, Delta Airlines flew in approximately 200 volunteers from Georgia to aid the recovery effort. Assistance also arrived in the form of cell phones and plans for emergency workers from Sprint, and drinks and food from both Coca-Cola and Chick-fil-A.

Several development partners were instrumental in working with area officials and with the Joplin City Council to help with infrastructure, residential, and commercial construction projects. In an effort to quickly restore the area, city council members teamed up with a Texas-based development firm that had a plan to attract approximately $1 billion in private investment opportunities. The private agency had experience in working with other government entities to help disaster-stricken areas recover. The private agency assisted local governments in Texas in the cities of Waco and Amarillo with recovery efforts after the nation's eleventh deadliest tornado since 1953 left 114 dead and destroyed structures, buildings, and major developments. Joplin, Missouri, would be the third project of its kind the company would take on. The firm was willing to financially commit to the project without requiring any upfront fees in addition to also committing to hiring local construction companies to help the local economy recover, and working with the Joplin Chamber of Commerce, the City Council, and the residents throughout the road to recovery (Woodin, 2012). The Joplin tornado disaster served as a showcase of how public and private companies can come together to assist with the short-term needs of a community. This relief gives governing agencies an opportunity to focus more on accomplishing long-term goals of recovery.

FEMA released a postscript study of the response to the 2011 tornado that ripped through Joplin, revealing that a multitude of instances of anticipated partnership with the private sector as well as several examples of private sector initiative were unanticipated. In the case of the latter, each scenario proved to be vital to the efficacy of the response and recovery. A directive called the Whole Community Approach was applied in the Joplin response that mandated that any type of disaster would require the use of all available resources and that they should be coordinated in a cooperative manner. One specific example FEMA found in the study was the benefit that communicating a response not only using traditional means like press conferences, press releases, and news alerts but also on private sector social media outlets like Facebook and Twitter was essential to the recovery.

Several locally operated and private businesses assisted with the overall recovery efforts of the city. On a local level, the Facebook page served as an in-depth source for residents to obtain critical information about shelters, volunteer centers, government assistance, and more. It also was used as a marketing tool to convey Joplin's recovery progress to the rest of the country. This attracted a larger response in donations and attention nationwide. Members of the Chamber of Commerce and Joplin city officials also used Facebook to post responses to questions posed by residents at a town hall meeting held the night before. The availability of social media to provide those answers at all times provided a service that traditional government communications simply could not provide.

While the Joplin tornado affected a small community, Superstorm Sandy devastated an enormous area of the eastern coast of the United States. However, unlike the disaster that Sandy is often compared with—Hurricane Katrina—the response was much more engaging and collaborative with the private sector. While the overall response to Sandy was not considered a complete success, most would consider it a vast improvement to that of Katrina seven years prior. Planning and preparedness beforehand made the coordinating efforts between FEMA and the private sector much more smoother and effective, immediately after the storm hit. The agency's private sector division had already established relationships with area businesses, universities, industry associations, and chambers of commerce. One specific example was the dissemination of the FEMA electronic newsletter by area businesses. The information in the newsletters reached a vast population that likely would not have seen the newsletter otherwise. Out of this public–private partnership also came recommendations that reached as high as President Obama's desk as part of his Hurricane Sandy Rebuilding Task Force.

Way of Life Threatened

Ensuring the safety of the community is a huge portion of recovery planning for governing agencies. Since the private sector is in control of about 85% of the nation's critical infrastructure that include power plants and electrical substations, strong partnerships between the private sector, public companies, and government offices are detrimental to providing the best public safety. Entities had to work together during a critical incident in the Gulf of Mexico that quickly became a matter of homeland security.

Deep Water Horizon Incident, Gulf of Mexico

Owing to extreme safety concerns and a matter of homeland security, government agencies were forced to step in to assist with the largest marine oil spill in the history of the petroleum industry. On April 20, 2010, an explosion claimed the lives of eleven individuals in the Gulf of Mexico and posed a health scare for many coastal residents, tourists, animals, and several environments. This highly critical accident was soon referred to as the BP oil spill. Despite the initial explosion, oil continued to leak into the ocean for almost ninety days with little signs of improvement as recovery and cleanup efforts were continuous. Although the oil spill affected coastal areas including beaches and wetlands, estuary areas were a huge concern as further water contamination also affected animals, habitats, and different forms of wildlife.

An estimated 210 million gallons of oil was dispersed into the ocean, and the government was at the mercy of the private sector in trying to stop the leak after the government failed at several attempts to control the oil from spreading further into the ocean or to stop the leak altogether. As time passed, the problem grew worse. According to the after action report, the government was unsuccessful simply because it did not have the expertise. The private sector, however, had the right equipment, skilled personnel, and an effective strategy to properly manage and control the situation. A report after the incident confirmed that the lack of strong relationships between the private and government was a disservice as a lot of time was spent on trying to solve the problem within a government agency. The oil spill required intense and rapid recovery efforts to combat the situation. Existing partnerships before the oil spill would have expedited results to a faster recovery rate. More succinct channels of communication, even those on a tangential basis, among the primary parties involved—BP, Transocean, and even state and regional regulators and disaster recovery—might have provided the necessary oversight to predict and prevent the mechanical and staffing issues involved in the accident. Much of the analysis in the aftermath of this particular disaster showed that simple and easily implemented changes, while more costly, would likely have prevented the explosion.

Relationships with Public, Nonprofit, and Private Sectors

As stated earlier, the private sector is in control of 85% of the nation's critical infrastructure. Those areas include chemical, commercial facilities, critical manufacturing, dams, emergency services, and nuclear reactors, materials, and waste. The Office of Infrastructure Protection (OIP), under the DHS, is responsible for making sure that all parties have the correct information, policies, and protocols in place for day-to-day operations. In the event of an emergency involving these areas of infrastructure, a thoroughly maintained protocol of the aforementioned areas is critical.

Proactive Recovery Planning

In light of disaster situations, officials are becoming proactive in better preparing for emergency and extending plans to include those of the private sector. There is no denying that the use of private agencies has caused problems in disaster recovery in the past; however, when examined from a larger perspective, the benefits greatly outweigh the negative. It becomes incumbent upon those in charge of managing the recovery to utilize and optimize the resources of both the private and public sector in conjunction so that the desired outcome can be reached. Governor Chris Christy of New Jersey created a task force to not only help the community rebuild but to also assess internal policies and procedure to find areas of savings that could be added to additional emergency funding. Superstorm Sandy experienced high numbers of recovery damage attached to high dollar recovery amounts just like recovery efforts after other disasters like Hurricanes Katrina and Isaac, the BP oil spill in the Gulf, the 911 terrorist attacks, and the Minnesota Bridge collapse. Although federal funding was approved to help these areas, each governing agency were responsible for finding alternative sources to recover, as the amount of federal dollars was not enough to cover the entire recovery costs.

Superstorm Sandy Task Force

Hurricane Sandy affected the East Coast as a category 3 hurricane on October 29, 2012, devastating the New York metropolitan and surrounded areas. As a result of the hurricane, approximately 160 people were killed, 700,000 homes were destroyed, and thousands of businesses were not operational and forced to close. In the nation's history, Hurricane Sandy is the second costliest hurricane and the largest storm to affect the east coast. The recovery process would be a daunting task for officials who had to prioritize different elements that included public safety, supporting local business, helping local displaced residents recover, recovering the major infrastructure needs, and many other city aspects. Sand from area beaches had washed upon roads and major travel ways, along with homes, rivers, and coastal islands, damaging waterways and habitats. Officials had to figure out how to recover areas and solve problems unique to the coastal areas.

To help the area recover and rebuild faster, President Obama signed an Executive Order to create the Hurricane Sandy Rebuilding Task Force. The task force included officials, residents, and members of the private and public sector who all had the same goal in mind to effectively restore the coastal region after Sandy and create an action plan in the event of another emergency. Critical infrastructure categories like hospital care, transit systems, water treatment, public health, and sanitation were just a few of the aspects covered by the task force. Keeping refineries, industries, railway and waterway transportation, and businesses in full operations was also a concern for members. After six months of research, an effective rebuilding strategy was created that included the best practices and most efficient ways to rebuild after Sandy. An established plan for future emergencies and key players was also developed that helped strengthen partnerships with the private sector and nongovernment agencies (Hurricane Sandy Rebuilding, 2013).

Bring New Orleans Back

The damage to New Orleans and surrounding areas after Hurricane Katrina was not limited to just infrastructure. Several programs like the Road Home made it possible for the community to pick up the pieces and begin to rebuild. Residents needed more than a home to return to because the quality of life for many people was lost. Trying to obtain medical care had become a major challenge, along with having basic necessities like food and water. The transit system was down, which disabled a lot of residents who needed transportation to and from work, medical appointments, stores, and more. City officials also needed to configure a flood and storm water protection plan since a large portion of the Crescent City was vulnerable with the existing break in the levee system. These roadblocks were just a few of the challenges the city faced. The City of New Orleans created a nonprofit agency after Hurricane Katrina to help recover, rebuild, and plan for future natural disasters. Bring New Orleans Back, created by Mayor Ray Nagin's administration, focused on assisting with the many infrastructure and medical care needs of the city with the help of the private sector (National Association of Community Health Centers Inc., 2006).

The aftermath and subsequent criticism of the response to Hurricane Katrina prompted the formation of the Post-Katrina Emergency Management Reform Act of 2006. This Act demanded a greater level of cooperation and partnership with the private sector, and FEMA was specifically targeted as an agency that was to participate. Part of that cooperation involves partnering with it in advance of a recovery to make the response more immediate and efficient. FEMA has a private sector division whose responsibilities primarily involve coordination with commercial NGOs. Within that department is the Private Sector Representative (PSR) program. These partnerships occur on a ninety-day rotational basis and have brought on board the expertise of companies like Target, Verizon, Wal-Mart, Big Lots, and Citigroup, among others. These representatives help FEMA not only on the local level with more targeted initiatives, but also serve as an integral partner on large national projects. The aim is simply to improve emergency management and to use any tools that are available. The PSR serves fewer than two sets of circumstances.

When the National Response Coordination Center (NRCC) is activated, the PSR works specifically to "communicate, coordinate, and collaborate between public and private stakeholders to fulfill various objectives that support and contribute to the overall response and recovery during an event" (FEMA, 2015). The NRCC activates when the threat of an impending disaster will happen soon or during the aftermath of an unforeseen event. FEMA delegates out responsibilities during NRCC activation to also include

- Serving as a key channel of communication between FEMA and the private sector
- Supporting situational awareness of disaster impacts and recovery within the private sector
- Coordinating with other relevant emergency supporting functions and infrastructure liaisons in support of private sector recovery efforts

When the NRCC is not activated, the PSRs collaborate on longer-term goals by "… seeking and sharing information with the private sector on preparedness planning, training, exercising, and mitigation activities" (FEMA, 2015).

CASE STUDY   The National Flood Insurance Program's Impact on Lousiana's River Parishes

Congress created the National Flood Insurance Program (NFIP) in 1968. It enables property owners to purchase insurance from the government against losses from flooding. Close to 6 million homes in all fifty states participate in the NFIP program. In 2012, Congress passed the Biggert–Waters Flood Insurance Reform Act of 2012 (BW-12). In the spring of 2013, Greater New Orleans Inc. (GNO Inc.), led by Director Michael Hecht, along with Louisiana Parish Presidents and key legislators, created the Coalition for Sustainable Flood Insurance (CSFI).

The coalition identified three major problems with BW-12:

1. Phase-out of grandfathering
2. Incomplete mapping
3. Questionable calculations

St. James Parish President Timothy P. Roussel joined the coalition, along with the other River Parish Presidents since BW-12 would have a direct impact on the residents of the three parishes. President Roussel stated, "Congress passed the Biggert–Waters Act of 2012 as it was included in the Transportation Bill, along with other meaningful instruments such as the Restore Act, which caused unintentional consequences on homeowners across the United States. In 364 days from the time we started to champion this cause, we achieved a presidential signature on an Act of Congress. In this day and age, having the dysfunctional congress that exists, is a lot to be said and I am proud of the accomplishment" (Roussel, 2014).

While CSFI supported a financially stable National Flood Insurance Program that balances premium affordability with financial solvency, it needed to address drastic and unintended increases to NFIP rates for home and business owners. The coalition grew to include more than twenty parishes in Louisiana, more than twenty other states in the United States, and other national associations such as bankers, realtors, homebuilders, chambers of commerce, and other alliances. Originally, the Biggert–Waters Act of 2012 was supposed to gradually phase out subsidized rates for about 20% of property owners—half would pay 25% more per year while the rest moved to the full cost for flood insurance upon the purchase of an older property. However, FEMA did not issue the new rates for fifteen months, allowing many to buy the property before they could be warned of a retroactive rate increase. Others saw wildly inaccurate rate quotes well above the intended 25% increases that did not stand up to expert scrutiny. Most of these insurance rating discrepancies appeared to be the result of confusion caused by the implementation of BW-12.

Throughout 2013, CSFI met with key members of FEMA, Louisiana Congressional Delegation, and state, local, and business leaders to address the concerns. In May 2013, the coalition organized a delegation to meet in Washington, DC, to address critical issues with NFIP and FEMA preliminary maps. On March 13, 2014, Congress amended the 2012 Biggert–Waters law with the *Homeowner Flood Insurance Affordability Act*, HR 3370, by an overwhelming 306–91 bipartisan majority. President Obama signed this milestone legislation into law on March 21, 2014. The law repeals and modifies certain provisions of BW-12 and makes additional program changes not covered by the Act. The Louisiana federal delegation, which included local parish presidents, and elected officials from across the country have all acted with notable teamwork to help fix flood insurance. Some of the provisions of the Act are

- Repeals FEMA's authority to raise flood insurance rates at the time of property sale.
- Returns to allowing buyers to assume the seller's current rates so the rate stays/transfers with the property, not the owner.
- Restores grandfathering so properties built and maintained to code in one flood zone are not rated in a higher cost zone, simply because FEMA corrects the misrating on a later flood map.
- Caps premium increases at 18% annually for new properties or 25% for the older ones.
- Refunds premiums paid by property owners in excess of rates under these amendments.

The River Parish Presidents still have work to do; the U.S. Army Corps of Engineers has initiated the process to develop a programmatic agreement for the West Shore Lake Pontchartrain Hurricane and Storm Damage Risk Reduction Study (WSLP). In 2012, Hurricane Isaac reinforced the need for a risk reduction study. This resulted in the West Shore Lake Pontchartrain Hurricane and Storm Damage Risk Reduction Study Integrated Draft Feasibility Report and Environmental Impact Statement released in August 2013 (Rousell, 2014).

SUMMARY

Disaster recovery presents challenges that are often unprecedented to a community or municipality. Government officials, community leaders, and the business community are forced to quickly address problems that require solutions with a high degree of immediacy. Electric power outages, street clearing, and tree and limb removal are some of the initial duties the government must accomplish in order to progress with the longer-term recovery goals. Reestablishing infrastructure is essential for citizens and businesses alike to return to normalcy. The goals, timelines, and what they entail vary from person to person, constituency to constituency, and from business to business. For some, it is simply having power restored to a home. For others, it is a complicated process of insurance payments and government assistance needed to rebuild a business that may have been wiped away. With so many variables in play, utilizing the private sector has proven to be essential in expediting recovery at all levels. The flexibility and specialized resources the private sector is able to uniquely provide makes it a necessary component as a collaborator and partner with municipalities in the overall recovery process. The essential nature of the private sector in the days and weeks following any disaster are proven both systematically and organically.

CHAPTER QUESTIONS

True or False

1. The private sector is in control of a large portion of the nation's critical infrastructure. Those areas include chemical, commercial facilities, critical manufacturing, dams, emergency services, and nuclear reactors, materials, and waste.
2. The OIP, under the DHS, is responsible for the private sector.
3. During the Deep Water Horizon BP oil spill incident in the Gulf, oil continued to leak for almost eighty days.
4. After a deadly tornado ripped through Joplin, Missouri, a Texas-based development firm created a private investment package that would attract approximately $1 billion in private opportunities.
5. According to the U.S. Army Corps of Engineers (Corps), 34 million pounds of spoiled meat and other foods had to be properly disposed of after Hurricane Katrina.
6. The I-10 Twin Span Bridge Collapse was a major project outsourced to a private agency after Hurricane Katrina. The company managed to complete the project two weeks and three days ahead of schedule at a lower price than the original bid.
7. Government officials are trained and expected to handle the aftermath of a disaster like tornadoes, hurricanes, and floods but not fires and police-related safety issues.
8. In 1994, Sandusky, Ohio, officials did not have an effective plan in place for debris removal. As a result, it took three months to remove 700 tons of waste.
9. The City of New Orleans is just above sea level.
10. The sector stepped in after Hurricane Katrina to assist with wastewater treatment. This cost-effective decision resulted in savings of $4.8 million.

REFERENCES

Busch, N. & Givens, A. Public-Private Partnerships in Homeland Security: Opportunities and Challenges. The Journal of the NPS Center for Homeland Defense and Security VIII.508 (2012). *Homeland Security Affairs.* Retrieved from: https://www.hsaj.org/articles/233 (accessed August 11, 2015).

Environmental Protection Agency. (2012). Planning for disaster debris. Available from: http://www.epa.gov/waste/conserve/imr/cdm/pubs/disaster.htm (accessed August 3, 2014).

FEMA. (2015). Private Sector Representative Inside FEMA. Retrieved from: http://www.fema.gov/private-sector/90-day-private-sector-representative -program#wcm-survey-target-id (accessed July 10, 2015).

FEMA. (2013). Progress Report: Hurricane Sandy Recovery_One Year Later. Retrieved from http://www.fema.gov/media-library-data/1387208905270 -ce9650055aa2fbfbcde79d2d8c6b73e/11-14-2013-PROGRESS+REPORT _HURRICANE+SANDY+RECOVERY+ONE+YEAR+LATER.pdf (accessed July 10, 2015).

Gautreau, G. (2007). I-10 Twin Spans repair. *Louisiana Transportation Engineering Conference.* Baton Rouge, LA. Lecture. Available from: http://www.ltrc.lsu.edu /tec_07/presentations/repairs-web.pdf (accessed July 10, 2015).

Keegan, N. (2009). The Louisiana Road Home Program: Federal Aid for State Disaster Housing Assistance Programs Analyst in American Federalism and Emergency Management Policy. Congressional Research Service. https:// www.hsdl.org/?view&did=714345 (accessed August 28, 2014).

Kimball, J. & Williamson, K. (2007). Interstate bridge collapses into Mississippi River in Minneapolis. *Washington Post.* Available from: http:// www.washingtonposts.com/wp-dyn/content/article/2007/08/01/AR 2007080102072_2.html (accessed August 2, 2014).

Lee, L. & Hall, B. (2011). I-10 Twin Span Bridge. Louisiana's Recovery 1.75. *U.S. Department of Transportation Federal Highway Administration.* Available from: https://www.fhwa.dot.gov/publications/publicroads/11julaug/05.cfm (accessed August 5, 2014).

Luther, L. (2008). Disaster debris removal after Hurricane Katrina. *CRS Report for Congress.* Congressional Research Service. Available from: http://congres sionalresearch.com/RL33477/document.php?study=Disaster+Debris+Rem oval+After+Hurricane+Katrina+Status+and+Associated+Issues (accessed August 26, 2014).

National Association of Community Health Centers, Inc. (2006). Legacy of a Disaster: Health Centers and Hurricane Katrina-One Year Later.

New Jersey Privatization Task Force Report. (2010). City of New Jersey. Available from: http://www.nj.gov/governor/news/reports/pdf/2010709_NJ_Privatiza tion_Task_Force_Final_Report_(May_2010).pdf (accessed September 1, 2014).

New Orleans Wastewater Facilities. (n.d.). *National Council for Public Private Partnerships.* Available from: http://www.ncppp.org/resources/case-studies /waterwastewater-infrastructure/new-orleans-wastewater-facilities/ (accessed August 31, 2014).

PB Works. (n.d.). Environmental. I-35W bridge collapse. Available from: http://35wbridge.pbworks.com/w/page/900694/Environmental (accessed August 3, 2014).

Public Assistance Debris Management Guide. (2007). *Federal Emergency Management Agency.* Available from: http://www.fema.gov/pdf/government/grant/pa /demagde.pdf (accessed August 3, 2014).

Roussel, T.P. (2014). West Shore Lake Pontchartrain Hurricane and Storm Damage Risk Study. Personal Interview.

State of Minnesota Department of Transportation. (2007). Emergency contract: State highway construction and maintenance projects. Available from: http://www.dot.state.mn.us/i35wbridge/contracts/bolander/bolander .pdf (accessed August 1, 2014).

Woodin, D. (2012). Texas firm could guide Joplin's tornado recovery. *Joplin Globe.* Available from: http://www.joplinglobe.com/local/x1940320988/Texas -firm-could-guide-Joplin-s-tornado-recovery &cd=1&hl=en&ct=clnk&gl=us (accessed August 12, 2014).

7

Hazard Mitigation

Alessandra Jerolleman

Contents

Learning Objectives

- To understand the creation of the private industry of hazard mitigation, and the ways in which it has worked with all levels of governments.
- To describe the history of the creation of federal hazard mitigation programs and their implementation.

INTRODUCTION

This chapter is based on the dissertation by Jerolleman (2013) that analyzed the role of the private sector in the creation and implementation of federal hazard mitigation programs. The dissertation utilized a mixed-method approach consisting of semistructured interviews, a review of primary sources, and various coding and analysis strategies. Interview respondents were selected through a snowball sample and asked directly about the role of the private sector, including the decision to use private actors and about the results from this decision. Interview respondents are cited anonymously throughout this chapter.

OVERVIEW OF HAZARD MITIGATION

Disaster mitigation activities in the United States are primarily funded by the federal government through both grant funds made available immediately following natural disasters and through yearly grant programs. Local governments may choose to provide mitigation funds at any given time, and individuals may elect to undertake self-protective behavior, but they ordinarily do not (Kunreuther, 2006). As a result of the Disaster Mitigation Act of 2000 (DMA, 2000), one of the prerequisites for local governments receiving federal aid when a disaster strikes is that they have a written hazard mitigation plan in place. Local governments often use contractors for this work due to a lack of local resources (manpower or expertise), particularly after a disaster when local expertise is in short supply. Data from a recent study of mitigation plans in California show that at least 50% of local hazard mitigation plans involve the use of consultants (Schwab, 2010).

Another mitigation domain where private sector contractors are heavily involved is in the immediate aftermath of a large natural disaster, when an affected state is faced with the need to significantly increase staffing levels of their Homeland Security and Emergency Preparedness depart-ments* in order to manage the recovery process. States often use private contractors to administer hazard mitigation efforts and recovery activi-ties, such as (1) supplying the large amount of manpower needed to take care of the Public Assistance (PA) process, (2) making disaster payments to the affected area to rebuild the public infrastructure, and (3) providing technical support to affected counties in order to take advantage of the mitigation opportunities available within this public rebuilding process (Respondent 25).

Definitions of Hazard Mitigation

To discuss hazard mitigation as an activity and as a business sector, it is necessary to spend some time looking at the range of definitions that are currently available. The particular components of these definitions, which are emphasized by particular programs or actors, have an impact on the outcomes of the activities. Neither the Stafford Act nor DMA 2000 provides a distinct definition for hazard mitigation. For the purposes of this book, hazard mitigation is defined as the effort to reduce personal, societal, and governmental impacts from natural disasters by reducing the risk to people, to property, and to infrastructure before hazards occur. However, it is useful to begin with a broader look at the different defini-tions within the literature of natural hazard mitigation. These definitions share certain characteristics but are sufficiently diverse as to direct aca-demic inquiry and policy action in multiple directions. In particular, only some of the definitions consider the social elements of mitigation while other definitions focus solely on changes to physical structures. All defi-nitions begin with the premise that mitigation constitutes an action that leads to risk reduction. However, this action, which can be voluntary or required, can take on many different forms and can be carried out by a variety of agents. The government and individual roles in hazard mitiga-tion vary by the definition used.

According to the Federal Emergency Management Agency (FEMA), whose definition is primarily applicable for grant-making purposes, haz-ard mitigation involves a "sustained action taken to reduce or eliminate

---

* Some states, such as Louisiana, may elect to establish Recovery Authorities, but the vast majority of mitigation funds available during recovery flow through the Federal Emergency Management Agency and therefore homeland security agencies. The second most commonly used funding source flows through the Department of Housing and Urban Development.

long-term risk to human life and property from natural hazards" (FEMA, 2006: 1). This particular conceptualization leads to an understanding of mitigation as an ongoing process. Mileti's (1999) discussion of sustainable hazard mitigation also assumes a process, one that consists of policies and activities.

Godschalk, Beatley, Berke, Brower, & Kaiser (1999) describe mitigation in terms of an action taken before a disaster, implying that mitigation is finite and must occur at a particular point in time, i.e., before the occurrence of a natural hazard. This definition emphasizes the ideal timing for best protection and purposefully deemphasizes the greatest *window of opportunity* for mitigation that is opened by the occurrence of a disaster (Godschalk et al., 1999). Other definitions are much broader, calling for any action (Interagency, 1994). Furthermore, various states also provide their interpretations of the federal definition of mitigation. For example, in Pennsylvania, mitigation is explained as follows: "Hazard mitigation means reducing, eliminating, redirecting, or avoiding the effects of ... hazards" (PEMA, 2012).

The wide range of definitions of hazard mitigation suggests that there is a great deal of complexity involved in this activity. There is much that is unique about natural hazard mitigation in the United States as compared to other types of services that are typically considered in the privatization literature, such as wholesale take-over of prisons and schools. The characteristics of mitigation influence the way in which the private sector's involvement has evolved. Before federal involvement in mitigation, there were a few state-level efforts in place, some utilizing private and academic partners, but overall, early hazard mitigation consisted of activities that certain landowners (and later homeowners) undertook of their own initiatives. For example, landowners constructed many of the original levees in the United States. In other words, the levees were privately built (Colten, 2006). Owners have mitigated risks to their homes over time, and some literature exists on this effort (Laska, 1991). Hazard mitigation had its genesis as a federally funded activity at a time of increasing privatization of government activities, a movement that gained strength in the United States in the 1980s and that was carried over through the 1990s and beyond (Henig, 1989–1990). An outcome of this timing is that hazard mitigation may be the only federally required activity that is a government activity designed largely by the private sector for almost complete private sector implementation.[*]

---

[*] The literature does not appear to contain references to any similar scenarios in the creation and implementation of other federal programs.

This chapter is based largely on two phases of interviews that were conducted as part of doctoral research into the role of the private sector in the creation and implementation of hazard mitigation policies in the United States (Jerolleman, 2013). The interviews were focused on the evolution of hazard mitigation and on the role of the private sector over two time periods, before the passage of DMA 2000 and afterward. Overall, twenty-eight individuals with a wide range of experience across multiple roles were interviewed. Primary sources were also obtained where possible and as identified by the interviews.

Historical Overview of Hazard Mitigation before the Disaster Mitigation Act of 2000

To adequately chart the evolution of federal government involvement in hazard mitigation, it is necessary to begin by looking at the federal government's involvement in disaster recovery. The federal government has been involved in disaster recovery as far back as at least the early 1900s, but this involvement was isolated to particular events, and there was little to no involvement in hazard mitigation efforts. Early efforts at hazard mitigation were either undertaken by individuals or by corporations for their own protection or were driven by economic considerations and/or the insurance industry. An excellent example of this followed the Great Chicago Fire of 1871 when pressure from the private sector led to the adoption of fire codes by the public sector in many parts of the city.

More extensive federal involvement with hazard mitigation, although still driven by disaster events, began with flood-protection efforts. These efforts focused solely on structural mitigation projects following a series of flood disasters. Beginning in 1917 and culminating in 1944, Congress passed a series of Federal Flood Control Acts; they led to the federal government taking on the costs of constructing structural mitigation projects such as dams and levees and to giving the U.S. Army Corps of Engineers (USACE) a major role in disaster recovery efforts (Federal, 1996). During this time period, disaster recovery efforts were piecemeal, were not associated with any particular federal agency (despite the growing role of the USACE following floods), and were dependent on congressional or presidential action. For example, Congress provided some disaster recovery funds for a series of significant floods, including the 1927 flood. It is unclear the extent to which the federal government utilized private contractors in these early efforts (if they were utilized at all); however, private sector entities do appear to have been actors in some of these efforts.

For example, many of the early USACE studies utilized local engineers (Respondent 3).

In 1950, this piecemeal approach changed when disaster relief for victims of flooding was made into official policy with the passage of the Federal Disaster Act (Federal, 1996). This legislation occurred in a period of continuously increasing floodplain occupancy and of a growing belief among individuals and local governments that the federal government would step in and offer assistance once an area had flooded (Wright, 2000). The national culture of disaster recovery (and hazard mitigation efforts by extension) shifted away from the model of 1871 in which individuals and corporations occupied the primary role without government involvement. By the 1960s, the increase in federal expenditures on disasters coupled with the increasing number of individuals at risk had institutionalized the costs to the federal government and set the stage for additional federal legislation to be put in place, as described further below.

Throughout this time period, the USACE often remained the primary federal agency involved in disaster recovery. It also began to create Reconnaissance Reports for communities with significant flood problems. These reports followed a systematic method of taking a basic look at the flood problem, looking at alternatives, and determining if a flood control project could be done. In many cases, these reports indicated that structural projects would not be an option, and they helped to shift the focus to smaller projects that the states and communities could do. This was a driver for local planning efforts in Illinois (Respondent 2). However, the reports themselves focused on large flood control projects. Their influence on local efforts depended very much on local officials who could choose to use them as a means to spur local action. Over time, the USACE moved away from doing those reports; their focus shifted to more exact planning for much larger projects.

National Flood Insurance Program

As described above, the growing federal role in and increasing expenses related to flood recovery set the stage for the creation of the National Flood Insurance Program (NFIP) in 1968, which was the first significant public sector involvement in mitigation before a disaster (Respondent 1). Earlier efforts had focused primarily on disaster recovery and not on the incorporation of mitigation, much less mitigation outside of the recovery context. The NFIP made flood insurance available to homeowners in participating communities, something that private insurers were not able to offer due to the high level of risk and to the challenges of maintaining a sufficiently diverse portfolio to diversify that risk (Federal Interagency Floodplain Management Task Force, 1996). The private insurers simply could not provide flood insurance policies at a low enough premium for a sufficient number of policies to be purchased. Although many respondents did not consider the NFIP to be an example of a federal mitigation initiative, it was in fact created in part to reduce losses to the federal government following floods (Respondent 1). Initially, the insurance component was managed by a consortium of insurance companies known as the National Flood Insurance Association (NFIA). These companies "were used to hazard mitigation, had grown up with the accepted concepts of reducing risks, reducing consequences, through zoning and building codes" (Respondent 1). This partnership model between government and private insurers allowed for greater ease of arbitration and brought together the expertise of companies and individuals who were trained in reducing risks and consequences. The insurance industry, as illustrated by the Great Chicago Fire, had long been a driver of risk-reduction efforts (Respondent 1).

However, some within the Department of Housing and Urban Development (HUD), which was then responsible for disaster response, were concerned at a lack of transparency in the process of determining damages, feeling that HUD was simply being billed for damages without transparency in the claims process (Respondent 2). The role of private insurers was reduced in 1978 when the decision was made to shift away from the use of the private sector and to the use of the federal government to manage the NFIP. However, the private insurers were later reengaged through the Write Your Own (WYO) program under President Reagan and eventually managed more than 90% of all policies, but did not assume the risk (Respondent 2). There was a concern that the insurance industry was making too much money and that the system had been designed to place greater costs on the government than on the private insurers (Respondent 1). Unfortunately, detailed records regarding flood insurance policies at this time are not available; it is unclear if there was indeed any impropriety (Respondent 2). This is particularly interesting considering the fact that the federal government entered into the insurance market specifically because private sector insurers did not consider it economically viable to offer flood insurance at rates that homeowners could afford. This shift had several negative consequences for both the federal government and for policyholders. Some respondents argue that the focus on insurance as a driver of risk reduction was lost at this time

(Respondent 1). Private companies are still responsible for wind coverage, leading to challenges in disasters such as hurricanes where flooding and winds occur simultaneously. This has often resulted in battles over which damages are caused by wind or by water (flooding). These battles are difficult to resolve without the partnership of coverage within the same entity, despite the fact that insurance companies are still involved through the WYO program. Whereas initially the need to reduce costs (profit motive) drove hazard mitigation, it now drives insurance companies to declare that flooding has caused damages (including more recent court battles regarding the distinction between wind-driven rain and other sources of water damage) and are therefore not their responsibilities (Respondent 1). This results in harm to the policyholders because they must await resolution of this conflict to receive their insurance award to begin rebuilding.

It is also interesting to note that the mandatory purchase requirement, which requires borrowers who are purchasing a home within a mapped flood zone to purchase insurance, has been consistently ruled by the courts to represent protection of lenders and not just of homeowners (ASFPM, 2010). This is particularly relevant because the protection of the lenders helps ensure the continued availability of home loans within the floodplain and potentially contributes to the further development of the floodplain. This, in some ways, supports the arguments that the NFIP has promoted development of the floodplain by both subsidizing insurance and requiring its purchase when a mortgage is secured.

During this same time period of growing federal involvement, and beginning in 1973, HUD was given authority over disaster relief and recovery, which it retained until the formation of FEMA in 1979. The Federal Disaster Assistance Administration (FDAA), a subset of HUD, was responsible for disaster operations and utilized disaster reservists* in addition to some full-time staff in its response efforts. Once FEMA was created, it continued that policy of utilizing reservists to increase capacity following a disaster. The reservists served the same function as private sector contractors, supplementing existing federal staff when additional resources were needed. The reservist model is, in some ways, an alternative to direct, private sector involvement, which is also utilized by FEMA. Some of these reservists spent years responding to a variety of disasters and began to ask "Why are we putting this back the same way? Is this a

---

* Individuals who were called upon following a disaster to serve as temporary employees.

nonefficient use of government funds? Isn't there a better solution? Haven't we been in this town before? Haven't we fixed this bridge before? What are the costs?" (Respondent 12). Although FEMA officially recognized mitigation as one of the four phases of emergency management, it was pretty much treated as "just an idea in the mind of a number of researchers" (Respondent 14). Initially, mitigation was considered to primarily consist of building codes and construction standards (both of which are controlled locally); perhaps this was due to the earlier role played by HUD. There was little to no money associated with mitigation at this time. Although federal expenditures on recovery had increased dramatically, the NFIP, with its flood mapping program and the requirement for local flood ordinances that reflected the flood map risk, was still the significant federal mitigation effort outside of isolated actions by reservists and others (Respondent 14). In fact, the effectiveness of the NFIP as a risk reduction measure, or even as a means of reducing government expenditure in disasters, has been called into question. Although the NFIP did require that certain regulations be met, it also had the adverse effect of increasing federal expenditures through the payment of claims to homeowners who built their homes in high-risk areas.

Blizzard of 1978

HUD did lead an extensive mitigation effort following the *Blizzard of 1978* along the New England coast. Following the blizzard, the substantial damage requirements of the NFIP were enforced for the first time, showcasing the role of the NFIP in promoting hazard mitigation during recovery when utilized in this fashion (an example of the power of street-level bureaucracy and individual discretion). Substantial damage requirements are triggered when a structure is considered to be more than 50% damaged. In cases of total destruction, it is clear that substantial damage has taken place, but there is a greater amount of subjectivity when damages are moderate or not clearly visible from the exterior of a property. In many instances, local officials underdesignate the number of substantially damaged properties in an effort to alleviate the potential regulatory burden on homeowners. However, this only serves to promote their continued high risk. HUD employees chose to actively enforce and promote substantial damage requirements, in part by showcasing the value of hazard mitigation.

An additional resource from the NFIP was Section 1362, referred to as the 1362 Program. It allowed for the buyout of properties. This was part of one of the first concerted federal efforts at post-disaster hazard mitigation. The recovery effort included the compilation of the first post-disaster hazard mitigation report, and it marked the first real organized effort to integrate HUD's flood insurance program into disaster relief efforts. Mitigation efforts in New England were driven by committed HUD staff and were supported by state leadership (Respondent 1). They included elevation of homes on a voluntary basis, wet flood proofing,* dry flood proofing,† and other innovations. The Small Business Administration (SBA) took on a role as well, paying out disaster loans that, for the first time (following the intervention of the Lieutenant Governor of Massachusetts and the Speaker of the U.S. House of Representatives), included hazard mitigation elements. The interest of the Lieutenant Governor in promoting hazard mitigation was a key driver of the efforts that followed and illustrates the extent to which one individual can have a significant impact (Respondent 1). In fact, individual action and community desire for change appear to have been far more of a driver than was the existence of federal policies, although it can be argued that the existence of federal programs was a key resource to this effort (Respondent 2, Respondent 8).

Just as there were in New England in 1978, over the course of the 1980s and early 1990s there were isolated efforts at hazard mitigation across the nation. These efforts were dependent on having a committed individual in a leadership position such as the Federal Coordinating Officer (FCO), on the knowledge or interest in mitigation of the disaster reservists responding, or on having a state that was already progressive in that regard; however, hazard mitigation at this time could be described as a *guerilla* effort (Respondent 1) by some dedicated FCOs and others within FEMA and in certain states; it "had a lot to do with personal leadership and personal values" (Respondent 1). When hazard mitigation was undertaken, it was done quietly to avoid controversy or push back by agencies—another example of street-level bureaucracy at work. The philosophy among those who promoted mitigation was to avoid documentation and to use public assistance and other funding sources, such as SBA, as creatively as possible to do what needed to be done. However, in cases where state government was very supportive, such as in Massachusetts in 1978, a great deal could be accomplished. Unfortunately, as late as 1990, the mantra

---

* Wet flood proofing is the use of materials that can survive brief inundation and other mechanisms to minimize damages when water does enter a structure.
† Dry flood proofing is the use of sealants, short walls, and other mechanisms to prevent water from entering a structure.

remained "restore to pre-disaster conditions" (Respondent 1). Through the early 1990s, more and more like-minded people began pushing for hazard mitigation, and it gained greater acceptance.

In addition to these isolated efforts, there were changes at the federal level that helped set the stage for increasing hazard mitigation. One of these changes, in the early 1980s, was the formation of the Flood Hazard Mitigation Task Force as a result of a 1980 Office of Management and Budget (OMB) directive that all federal disaster assistance programs incorporate mitigation (Respondent 6). The task force was composed of twelve federal agencies that provide technical assistance for nonstructural measures during the recovery phase, and its goal was to ensure that personnel would be available to search for obstacles to mitigation in current policies and to participate in post-disaster teams (Wright, 2000). As a result of this OMB directive, interagency teams were convened by a mitigation officer following a disaster; they created hazard mitigation reports, also called fifteen-day reports. This team would include representatives from USACE, SBA, National Weather Service, and others. It was given fifteen days to identify ways in which existing programs could be used for hazard mitigation and to identify opportunities. The teams also created a ninety-day follow up report.

Many respondents saw these teams as excellent mechanisms for fostering collaboration among federal agencies, for promoting coordination between the state and federal efforts (and occasionally the local), and for focusing on mitigation. Much like the role of committed individuals, the institutionalized creation of collaborative groups, which could function as performance regimes, resulted in a great many successes; however, these groups were more effective in some regions than others, depending greatly on their implementation. In some cases, the twelve federal agencies would send different representatives to each meeting or would send individuals who only had knowledge of their own program, not of the range of programs offered by their agency (Respondent 12). Although the various federal agencies, such as the Department of Agriculture, all had or were developing relevant programs for funding and technical assistance, these programs were not always utilized or brought to the attention of the teams. This conundrum remains a challenge today. The wide range of programs available is not widely known, and there are various challenges to face in making the guidelines work with each other, a problem that has only been exacerbated by the now long history of program implementation and resulting bureaucracy. The Coastal Barrier Resources Act of 1972, which prohibited the expenditure of federal resources on undeveloped barrier coastal islands (denying flood insurance and disaster assistance to anyone who developed those areas), was a key tool as well.

Federal Emergency Management Agency

FEMA Region VIII* was one region that quickly saw the value of mitigation. It took steps to convene the team outside of disasters and to identify the most appropriate individuals from the agencies represented. The team in Region VIII was headed by FEMA reservists, many of whom had come out of graduate programs at the University of Colorado and were focused on floodplain management; as previously described, other regions also utilized reservists and followed the model set by Region VIII. This key role for reservists remained in place until the regions began to hire full-time mitigation employees. Between 1980 and 1982, the team in Region VIII wrote the first standard operating procedures for a hazard mitigation team. It also served as a leader in mitigation planning. By 1986, Region VIII had statewide multihazard mitigation plans and mitigation officers in every state (Respondent 12).

Around this same time, FEMA created the first all-hazard pre-disaster mitigation grant program, the Hazard Mitigation Assistance Program (HMA). In its first year, the program provided $18,000 grants to each region. It was created in response to a request from Region VIII for funding to conduct a study to assist a local community in Colorado with creation of a local stormwater management district. At the time of the request, FEMA headquarters had some funding that could be made available but had to ensure its equitable distribution across regions. As a result, the one-time funding request became the responsibility of the HMA and was made available across the nation (Respondent 12).

In the late 1980s, as FEMA began to create mitigation offices and positions, some reservists who had been active in previous post-disaster mitigation efforts were unable to secure the positions due to federal hiring criteria (e.g., the requirement to provide preference to veterans and former federal employees). Many of these reservists went on to work for the private sector, either as individual consultants or in positions with the larger firms, continuing their existing model of periodic engagement with FEMA. As FEMA staff members who were engaged in mitigation retired in the mid- to late 1990s, many also moved into private sector positions (Respondent 12).

---

* FEMA Region VIII includes the following states: Colorado, Montana, North Dakota, South Dakota, Utah, and Wyoming.

The interagency team process remained in place until the 1990s and allowed FCOs who wanted to promote hazard mitigation to pull together broad coalitions. The absence of dedicated funds sparked creativity and forced many agencies to bring resources to the table (Respondent 14). Over time, the various federal agencies developed technical assistance and funding programs. This played a key role in the response to future disasters. Some of these programs had begun as early as the 1970s and 1980s. The Department of the Interior, which houses the U.S. Fish and Wildlife Service and the U.S. Geological Survey, had twenty-six programs with which the interagency teams actively worked. Another resource was the 1988 Upton Jones Amendment to the NFIP. It allowed for the relocation of coastal properties at risk of imminent collapse, without having to wait for the properties to actually collapse or be significantly damaged. This allowed the NFIP to spend less on relocation than the cost of a full insurance claim. Projects funded during this time were done with comprehensive packages of funds from various agencies and the affected states. In Illinois, for example, FEMA funds were used to purchase insured buildings. HUD funds were used to purchase those structures where the property owners met income requirements, and state funds covered the rest.

An important piece of legislation in the late 1980s was the Robert T. Stafford Disaster Relief and Emergency Assistance Amendments of 1988. The stated reasons for the amendment are as follows: (1) because disasters often cause loss of life, human suffering, loss of income, and property loss and damage, and (2) because disasters often disrupt the normal functioning of governments and communities, and adversely affect individuals and families with great severity; special measures, designed to assist the efforts of the affected states in expediting the rendering of aid, assistance, and emergency services, and the reconstruction and rehabilitation of devastated areas, are necessary (Stafford Act Section, 101). It is worth noting that these reasons are premised upon the assumption that federal aid will be provided to affected states.

The stated intent of the Stafford Act is as follows: "It is the intent of the Congress, by this Act, to provide an orderly and continuing means of assistance by the Federal Government to State and local governments in carrying out their responsibilities to alleviate the suffering and damage that result from such disasters by doing the following: (1) revising and broadening the scope of existing disaster relief programs; (2) encouraging the development of comprehensive disaster preparedness and assistance plans, programs, capabilities, and organizations by the states and by local governments; (3) achieving greater coordination and responsiveness of disaster preparedness and relief programs; (4) encouraging individuals, states, and local governments to protect themselves by obtaining insurance coverage to supplement or replace governmental assistance; (5) encouraging hazard mitigation measures to reduce losses from disasters, including development of land use and construction regulations; and (6) providing federal assistance programs for both public and private losses sustained in disasters" (Stafford Act, Section 101).

The specific language utilized within the Stafford Act is particularly interesting. Item number (4) specifically cites insurance coverage as a means for supplementing or replacing governmental assistance, despite the fact that the NFIP is heavily federally subsidized. Also, item (5) specifically describes the encouragement of land use and construction regulations both of which are largely outside the purview of the federal programs. Although federal mitigation dollars can be used for projects such as acquisitions, which remove existing properties from the hazard area, land use has not been the focus of the vast majority of programs that have followed. In fact, it is worth noting that acquisitions of existing properties are not an example of utilizing land use constraints to prevent at-risk development; instead, they remove existing development that has experienced a certain degree of loss.

Overall, the Stafford Act made changes to existing relief programs to increase mitigation and to encourage acquisitions. The inclusion of management costs within the Stafford Act funding allowed states to play a larger role in the management of funds and mitigation projects, but it also opened the door for some of the recovery contracts in place today. The act was intended to guide rebuilding toward nonhazard areas, thereby reducing future exposure to risk following reconstruction (Wright, 2000). It also created the PA program that allowed for the incorporation of hazard mitigation into the repair and replacement of damaged elements of public buildings and infrastructure. The federal government was becoming aware that simply rebuilding in a hazard-prone zone might lead to the need for additional federal aid in the future but was limited in its ability to promote or demand local change.

Hazard mitigation plans following a presidentially declared disaster were required under Section 409 of the Stafford Act. Within the guidance documents, FEMA specifically mentioned land use and construction practices as components of successful hazard mitigation efforts. The 409 guidance also recommended that local plans be developed for areas with repetitive events and/or extensive damage from a particular event. The guidance described existing hazard identification and capability assessment studies that had been completed for every county in the 1980s. Although this guidance helped to set the stage for the later guidance under DMA 2000, the concept of a nationally maintained database of hazard identification and capability assessment studies was not a part of the conversation at that time.

Section 404 of the Stafford Act created the Hazard Mitigation Grant Program (HMGP). It allowed for hazard mitigation projects following a declared disaster. Originally, up to 10% of the monies allocated to recovery could be used for mitigation, a number that was raised to 15% following the 1993 flooding and was subsequently reduced to 7.5% when the amount of pre-disaster mitigation funds available were increased (Hinshaw, 2006). The goal of this program was to reduce future suffering and damage by reducing future losses. Initially, under Section 404, there was a 50/50 cost share, and few communities took advantage of the available funds. This was changed to 75/25 following the 1993 floods, with the federal contribution being the 75%. Perhaps the most important effect of this Act was that it made FEMA formally responsible for implementing hazard mitigation. Previously, hazard mitigation had not been considered a key role of any one agency, or even of the federal government, despite the creation of the NFIP and the role in response being played by several agencies such as the USACE. The assignation of that responsibility to a particular federal agency indicated a sea change in the federal emphasis on hazard mitigation and a tremendous shift from the days of guerilla FCOs finding ways to make hazard mitigation work. Additionally, states were encouraged to begin creating hazard mitigation plans and were able to receive assistance from the ten regional FEMA offices to do so (Godschalk et al., 1999).

As the range of federal hazard mitigation programs expanded in the 1980s, the corresponding private sector organizational infrastructure expanded as well. Large engineering firms had become involved in the floodplain mapping program under the NFIP, and many other small industries, such as home elevation, were growing in response to greater demand for their services following the release of federal funding for these activities. Regional and local firms became involved in mitigation efforts within their geographic areas, and individual consultants established themselves, often as they left public sector employment. Large firms, which were not yet ready to build hazard mitigation product lines, turned to these few consultants to bring the needed expertise as they sought to enter into the developing mitigation marketplace (Respondent 12). While initial private sector involvement in hazard mitigation was focused heavily on protecting private sector assets and interests, the newly emerging mitigation marketplace established hazard mitigation services as a product line (Respondent 12). Private sector firms, particularly the national and international firms, continued their own efforts to protect their assets under the umbrella of risk management.

Several programs were created in the 1990s to promote hazard mitigation. These included (1) the creation of the Community Rating System (CRS); (2) the addition of Increased Cost of Compliance (ICC) to the NFIP as a result of hearings in 1990–1991; and (3) the Pre-disaster Mitigation Program (see the following subsections for descriptions). These programs illustrate a growing federal role in hazard mitigation through local and state incentives, grant programs, and mandates. At the same time, these new programs, with the accompanying regulations, began creating a greater need for expertise in the public sector to handle grants management. The new programs also created a greater need for review capabilities at the federal and (occasionally) state levels (Respondent 1). The 1993 Midwest floods were a key event during this time period; existing programs were expanded, and others were created, after which FEMA played a significantly increased role in mitigation efforts (FEMA 1990). The need for grants management and administration assistance further expanded the private sector mitigation marketplace.

Community Rating System

One of the programs in place before the 1993 floods was the CRS; it was implemented by FEMA in 1990 but was discussed as far back as the mid 1980s as a way to reward communities that exceeded the minimum regulatory standards for floodplain management (including risk reduction through ordinances) as set forth by the NFIP. The CRS is administered by the Insurance Services Office (ISO), a private firm that has many other federal and state clients looking to identify and to mitigate risk. ISO initially participated as a stakeholder in the first CRS task force, created in 1987. ISO was invited to participate in the task force because of its expertise in rating communities for fire. Other stakeholders with experience in risk reduction were included, such as representatives from the Association of State Floodplain Managers (ASFPM).

The primary goal of the program was to encourage communities to practice comprehensive floodplain management. Participating communities are rewarded through a system of lowered insurance premiums (Wright, 2000). The CRS included a planning component and recognized the key role of a comprehensive planning process. It was eventually used as one of the models for the development of federal hazard mitigation planning guidance. The management model of the CRS is quite interesting; FEMA appears to maintain a significant level of involvement with ISO, in addition to utilizing individual contractors, in more of a partnership model than is traditionally the case for federal contracts. In fact, ISO does not actually have a contract with FEMA. Instead, there is an *arrangement* in place modeled after the WYO system, which allows FEMA to pay for "rate-making assistance" (Respondent 2). At the time in which ISO was approached by FEMA to assist with the creation of the CRS, there was a great deal of distrust between the insurance industry and the federal government; it had only been a few years since the NFIA had been removed from their role with the NFIP due to HUD's concerns regarding transparency. Although ISO worked closely with FEMA as a stakeholder, there was concern about entering into a contract with the federal government; however, FEMA recognized that ISO had ratemaking expertise and that it was uniquely qualified to assist with the creation of a program such as the CRS. To secure the participation of ISO, which explicitly did not want a federal contract (and all of the complications they involve), FEMA worked with a group of WYO insurance companies to fund the assistance by ISO, because the WYO had an existing arrangement with FEMA that did not involve a specific contract. The partnership model that exists between ISO and FEMA appears to be a function of the commitment of ISO to risk reduction, of the continued involvement by the same individuals from the creation of the CRS up until the present day, and of the relationships that have been established. It is unclear whether the contracting mechanism utilized has had any real impact on the outcomes (Respondent 2). It is interesting to note that the lack of an actual contract means that components such as nondiscrimination are not explicitly required. This arrangement stands as an interesting, seemingly productive form of public–private implementation of a new (at the time), innovative concept. That it has remained functioning in a form similar to how it was conceived for over 30 years makes it worthy of continued attention.

In 1991, Disaster Assistance Employees received the very first formal hazard mitigation training. This training, building upon the successful mitigation efforts of the 1980s (in which those contractors had been involved), was developed by FEMA with the assistance of some individual contractors. As previously described, FEMA reservists had been involved in mitigation efforts for some time, but there was no formal mechanism in place to promote or to teach hazard mitigation. Some regions had very committed reservists who were knowledgeable, and others did not. The implementation of this training led to the brief norm of FEMA having a cadre of people in place who understood mitigation, who could easily become temporary full-time employees following a disaster, and who could help implement hazard mitigation following a disaster. FEMA, much like the states, could not sustain a large enough disaster recovery and mitigation staff to be prepared for the eventuality of a major disaster. Utilizing a cadre of individuals who could be hired as needed reduced FEMA's normal operating costs. To this day, FEMA utilizes reservists. These reservists often function as private contractors, still known as disaster assistance employees (DAEs), and occasionally increase FEMA's staff through standing contracts with the larger firms.

This cadre was in place at the time of the 1993 Midwest flooding, often considered a turning point in national policy regarding mitigation because it led to a national policy shift toward relocating families outside of the floodplain (National Wildlife Federation [NWF], 1997). The flooding, which affected more than 80,000 buildings in nine states, contributed to the growing realization that structural flood control measures alone were insufficient, thus resulting in the Hazard Mitigation and Relocation Assistance Act of 1993 (NWF, 1997).

At the time, there was a federal administration in office that was very supportive of mitigation, and a great deal of money was made available. Various federal agencies worked together to fund the buyouts by combining multiple funding programs. However, some argue that the sheer amount of money and the challenge of managing it made planning less of a priority than "just lining up all of the qualified properties" (Respondent 2). This is cited as marking a post-disaster shift away from looking at ways to make the programs work together for solutions and a shift toward justifying the expenditure of money (Respondent 2). "If there is a lot of money, your job is to get rid of it because you won't get that money again if you don't spend it" (Respondent 2). The need to spend the money quickly, and the fear of losing the funds if the local expertise to manage the grants was not in place, is a key component to appreciating the future involvement of the private sector. There was a need to be able to bring in experts who would not be kept on staff between disasters, and there were funds available to pay for them when a disaster occurred.

Although many respondents questioned the quality of the projects and the challenges of the process that was taking place, mitigation had become publicly accepted (Respondent 3, Respondent 5). In particular, relocation was clearly taken seriously at the federal level, and mitigation was shown to be a federal priority, both during the 1993 floods and over the following years. However, the challenges of issuing regulations for mitigation funds were tremendous. FEMA, as an organization, was conservative in its definition of mitigation, focusing almost exclusively on construction, on buyouts, and on relocations (Respondent 14). At the same time, there was external pressure to emphasize Emergency Operations Center (EOC) operations, communications systems, and generators. Also, there were real, local funding needs for response equipment that communities and states were trying to fit into the mitigation process, because federal funding was directed toward hazard mitigation.

Also in 1993, the FEMA Mitigation Division was established to manage the NFIP and mitigation programs. Its goal was to create safer communities and to reduce disaster losses (Mitigation, 2006). However the Mitigation Division had very little staff until 1995 when, as part of the continuing effort to encourage mitigation, FEMA published the National Mitigation Strategy. Its primary goal was to find the means by which to change the public's attitude toward and awareness of risk (Hinshaw, 2006). A secondary goal of the strategy was to provide resources to communities to encourage mitigation (CPCU, 2001). The National Mitigation Strategy marked a turning point at FEMA because the Mitigation Directorate became a major business segment for the organization and a major business line for its contractors. As the federal government further institutionalized mitigation funding mechanisms, the corresponding private sector grew to meet the needs of the marketplace.

Increased federal efforts to promote pre-disaster mitigation continued in 1997 when Section 203 of the Stafford Act authorized the Pre-Disaster Mitigation Grant (PDM) (ASFPM, 2006; FEMA, 1990). PDM came about as part of an effort to do more pre-disaster mitigation to reduce the impacts and costs of recovery. It was heavily lobbied for by organizations such as the National Emergency Management Association (NEMA), an organization formed in 1974 by state directors of emergency management; they sought to share information and to work together. NEMA represented state directors who relied heavily on federal funding for their emergency management activities and has continued to lobby strongly for maintaining existing grant programs. As part of its passage, there was a compromise in which the percentage of disaster funding allocated to HMGP was reduced; this was due to the underlying assumption that spending money on hazard mitigation before an event would have a greater return than if spent following an event. Unfortunately, this premise does not take into account the impacts of continued development into at-risk areas. Nor does it take into account the possibility for some mitigation efforts, such as flood

171

control or insurance, to potentially lead to increased development. Ray Burby (2006) has described this as a "safe development paradox" in that through its efforts to make hazardous areas safer, the federal government has increased the potential for property damage and catastrophic loss in those areas. It is important to note that this marked both a shift away from post-disaster mitigation funding and a shift away from a flood-heavy focus toward an all-hazard approach, which later characterized mitigation planning. This new approach was influenced by recent disasters that were not flood based (such as the Northridge earthquake), as well as by frequent localized weather events such as tornadoes.

Project Impact

Project Impact was also introduced by FEMA in 1997 as a pilot program under PDM and as part of the broader push to increase mitigation at the local level. It was a community-based program that used a four-step approach to creating disaster-resistant communities: building community partnerships, assessing risks, prioritizing needs, and finally, building community support and communicating findings. Unlike many other FEMA programs that responded once damages occurred, the focus of Project Impact was on prevention. It was promoting the all-hazards approach previously discussed. All of these changes were consistent with the strategy being implemented through PDM. However, it was very unique in many ways.

Project Impact was developed from the concept that the community itself could define its needs and identify solutions to its problems, a perspective that is missing from most current programs, despite the fact that the most successful examples of mitigation all included significant community involvement, desire for change, and engagement. The program was led internally at FEMA by an individual who had a background in sociology and political science, both of which informed the program design. Project Impact was designed on the basis of three principles: that mitigation is primarily a local issue, that local private sector participation is essential, and that mitigation requires a long-term commitment. This is a very different view of private sector participation in which the private sector is viewed as a part of the community with a vested interest in the protection of its employees, customers, and property. Despite being found to be a cost-effective program and representing significant government savings by reducing losses, Project Impact has since been terminated (Multihazard, 2005) largely due to a change in political administrations (Respondent 8). Project Impact was closely associated with FEMA

Director James Lee Witt, as well as with President Bill Clinton. As such, it was quickly terminated when a new administration of the opposing party came into power (Respondent 17).

In the first two years of Project Impact, there were seven pilots, each of which was given $1 million for its projects. The following year, each state was given $500,000, and in the one following that, communities were given $250,000. Eventually, communities became participants without federal funding, indicating that the program itself was seen as valuable by participants. This notion of seeding community efforts was a key component of the project. It worked so well in some communities that community members maintained the efforts after the program was defunded entirely (Respondent 27). The challenge was how to allow communities to be creative while maintaining federal requirements. Another challenge was how to avoid just creating *grant experts*, instead creating mitigation experts within local communities (Respondent 15). As was previously described, the expansion of federal mitigation programs had generated an expertise in grant applications because of the sheer amount of effort required to locally manage the funds (eventually this would lead to the use of contractors following disasters as programs became more complex), not necessarily in hazard mitigation. Additionally, the communities had to meet a lot of requirements for the right to participate; this placed a burden on their limited resources. An annual conference was used to promote peer mentoring and to allow the communities to talk with each other. There was also an element of linking practitioners and researchers.

With the exception of Project Impact, the preceding discussion on private sector participation has largely focused on the private sector's role as a vendor of services. However, the private sector remained involved throughout the 1990s, not just through contracting mechanisms but also by being a partner in education and outreach efforts. Following Hurricane Andrew, FEMA, Home Depot, and the American Red Cross worked together to create videos and brochures that educated homeowners on basic mitigation measures (such as the use of hurricane clips). This outreach increased the visibility of these companies and marketed mitigation products. The private sector also turned to hazard mitigation for the protection of its own assets as a means to promote business continuity, a business practice that has grown, creating its own industry of consultants to private sector firms. The various federal disaster assistance programs that had been developed did not provide much (if any) assistance to affected business owners (Respondent 12). In fact, it is possible that the lack of federal assistance for private firms actually spurred the development of in-house expertise in order to minimize losses post-disaster. It is interesting to note that a similar development of in-house expertise developed in some states but not among the majority. Likely the difference was that the cost of the damage was absorbed by the federal government, not the case for businesses.

In addition to the growing federal role, many state governments were becoming involved in hazard mitigation as early as the 1970s. These states all had significant risks, primarily from flooding and seismic events, and all took steps to reduce their vulnerabilities. This was mostly done through comprehensive planning mechanisms, with several states including a requirement in their state planning legislation that hazards be addressed. This requirement was known as a safety element. In 1972, California, a state concerned particularly with the risk of significant earthquakes, was one of the first to do so when the state legislature passed the Seismic Safety Studies Zones Act (Respondent 17). In the 1980s and 1990s, some cities in the state were also looking at recovery and reconstruction plans, which were first tested following the Northridge Earthquake in 1994.

A 1985 report on state activity found that Maryland had funded 14 watershed studies to identify flood-prone areas and possible mitigation measures (Wright, 2000). A similar study in 1989 found that Minnesota had established a grant to assist with homeowner mitigation (Wright, 2000). Other states, such as Florida, required a flood control and coastal management element. There were many other such isolated efforts at risk reduction taking place around the nation.

In addition to the requiring of safety elements (which were specific components of comprehensive plans and were not focused on hazard mitigation efforts), other states, such as Illinois, had actively been doing mitigation planning (as far back as the early 1980s) as part of an effort to reduce flood losses. In Illinois, this effort was driven by the Office of Water Resources. Projects were funded through the use of FEMA 1362 funds as well as through state funds. The projects were pretty much all acquisitions, due in part to the fact that Illinois had authority to purchase any floodplain lands it wanted. The projects were always preceded by mitigation plans that framed the problem, estimated funds, and included redevelopment concerns. The earliest of these plans were completed at the very end of the 1970s and beginning of the 1980s and were focused on small communities. They were prepared primarily by employees at the Division of Water Resources Emergency Services and Disaster Agency, working in partnership with federal agencies, other state departments, and with local actors. The planning process that was initially followed involved direct work with homeowners and efforts to identify individual actions that could be taken in frequently flooded areas. They often described development regulations, floodplain management, stormwater regulations, zoning, and land use (i.e., Illinois Department of Transportation, Division of Water Resources, 1979, 1983, 1985a,b, 1986).

The state eventually provided a template for these plans, in order to ensure consistency as state staff retired (Respondent 4). Through its early efforts, the state realized that, without these plans, acquisitions resulted in checkerboard effects and that communities had to have a plan for the use of the vacant lands as well as the funds to maintain them. Although many communities preferred structural flood control projects, the mitigation planning process showed that there were no economical projects for some areas, and that buyouts were appropriate.

The state of Illinois conducted annual program reviews throughout the 1980s in order to track the success of these local mitigation efforts. In some cases, these reviews were conducted by contractors or university staff. Recommendations included that the mitigation plans should ensure implementation of projects identified and that mitigation plans should be a condition of any assistance (Illinois Department of Transportation, Division of Water Resources, 1985). At times, these state successes influenced future federal policy.

The successes in Illinois influenced the USACE's later thinking on acquisitions, in which communities would need to show a greater amount of planning for how that land would be used. Even when the 1362 funds faded, Illinois continued funding acquisitions and began including funding in the state budget (up to $5 million for 1993). This funding then became a match when the flood of 1993 triggered a tremendous amount of federal funding for mitigation. The increased funding shifted mitigation away from something that had just been done in a few small towns to something that was a statewide effort.

Florida Local Mitigation Strategy

Another state that had begun doing hazard mitigation planning before DMA 2000 was Florida. The Coastal Management Element in Florida Comprehensive Plans was a requirement by 1975. It required that coastal jurisdictions address post-disaster recovery. However, in the mid-1990s, Florida launched its Local Mitigation Strategy (LMS) Program (Florida, 1997). This was a statewide initiative that required the development of local mitigation plans done on a countywide, multijurisdictional basis.

This effort was born out of a realization that Washington was questioning the fact that disaster costs continued to increase despite the expenditures of the mitigation programs. It was also born out of the desire of the then Florida Emergency Management Division's director who wanted to simplify grant review at the state level. It is worth noting that the focus of the program was, at least in part, on being prepared to apply for federal mitigation funds, described within the guidance as *intergovernmental coordination* and a *funding and recovery* (Florida, 1997). This focus on simplifying grants administration does not necessarily lead to the state focusing on the important question of what areas could benefit from the greatest risk-reduction efforts, nor does it easily take into account solutions such as land use and regulations (which do not easily fit into a *project*). The planning steps required for the LMS were essentially the same as those later developed for DMA 2000; the primary goal being the identification and prioritization of eligible projects—perhaps one of the reasons why DMA 2000 has not succeeded at comprehensive risk reduction. The focus on *eligible* projects is particularly problematic because it forces an emphasis on those project types that can be funded through grants, not necessarily on the best solutions to the risk identified.

In Florida, many of the early LMS plans were heavily driven by emergency management and did not involve local planners nor pay sufficient attention to land use (Respondent 21), a fact that may have influenced the project focus described above. However, the guidebook created by Florida did mention code enforcement and responsible development as part of risk reduction. It is worth noting that a sample Scope of Work, providing a template for a fixed fee contract for the development of the LMS plans, was provided as a template with the guidance (Florida, 1997). This indicates an early assumption that contract mechanisms would be utilized by at least some communities. DMA 2000 drew upon some of the lessons learned in Florida and actually reciprocally influenced the Florida plans being that it required that planning and land use be addressed.

North Carolina Hazard Mitigation Planning

Another state that designed a local hazard mitigation planning initiative was North Carolina. It had greater focus on integration into local, comprehensive planning than was the case in Florida (Florida, 1997; North Carolina, Division of Emergency Management, 2000). Although the Florida guidance did mention land use, the various guidance documents created by North Carolina went into much greater detail on the importance of land use, zoning, integration with development plans, and sustainable development (North Carolina Division of Emergency Management, 1998a,b, 2003). The value of including hazard mitigation as a component of comprehensive planning is reinforced by the literature (Burby, 2006) but outside the purview of an emergency management agency. This is a different focus from the expenditure of federal funds, although federal funding was certainly a consideration in North Carolina's efforts as well. The state of North Carolina worked closely with the University of North Carolina's urban planning department and had access to the documents created in Florida and to the staff that had been previously working in Florida.

North Carolina published three documents as part of its voluntary mitigation planning initiative. The first of these was a Hazard Mitigation Plan Workbook to assist local communities. It included a worksheet that walked community members through the process of creating a plan, while emphasizing land use and zoning. The second was a manual that highlighted the uniqueness of each different community, described the possibility of including the mitigation plan as part of the comprehensive plan, and suggested planning for post-disaster redevelopment. It went into more detail and included technical guidance on risk assessments and other elements. Finally, there was a third document, a Tools and Techniques Manual, referred to as an *encyclopedia*. It included information on regulatory tools such as development regulations, on basic planning tools such as transferring development rights, and on capital improvements and structural mitigation projects. The Tools and Techniques Manual considered potential impacts to low-income residents, political challenges, and included a strong focus on plan integration. Although there is some discussion of these components within the DMA 2000 guidance, it is nowhere near as much of a focus as in the North Carolina documents.

The state of Ohio began a hazard mitigation planning project when DMA 2000 passed but before federal guidance was available. The state wanted to have a head start and was able to do mitigation plans in fifteen communities that had recently flooded (Respondent 10). Ohio created a mitigation planning guidebook that also preceded the DMA guidance.

HISTORIC ROLE OF THE PUBLIC SECTOR, PRIVATE SECTOR, AND ACADEMIA

As described in the previous section, early public sector involvement in hazard mitigation was often driven by demand from private industry or

177

insurance interests. This demand resulted in some of the first fire codes at the state level, and similarly in federal guidelines for airport safety, among other examples (Respondent 1). Public sector involvement through policies, regulations, and other actions take place at the federal, state, and local levels (although the preceding section focused primarily on federal actions). The public sector role in hazard mitigation varies across the various levels of government, across the various communities and states, between day-to-day activities and post-disaster efforts, and also by type and magnitude of a disaster event.

In terms of federal involvement, and as shown previously, institutionalized involvement stemmed from growing public expenditure in disaster response and recovery that was primarily related to flooding. At the federal level, early public investments in risk reduction were structural projects related to flood control. Creation of the NFIP in 1968 marked not only the first significant federal mitigation program (though its emphasis was on land use and flood reduction), but it also increased the costs to the federal government from damages to insured properties. As a result, the NFIP provided an increased incentive for the federal government to promote hazard mitigation as a means of reducing its expenditures on claims.

Although some have argued that the NFIP was actually more of a mechanism to allow for floodplain development than it was a true deterrent, the challenges faced by the NFIP in remaining solvent (particularly once the initial public–private partnership was dissolved) spurred a great many of the federal grant programs and efforts. The institutionalization of disaster response funding, through the Disaster Relief Act of 1974 and later through the Stafford Act amendment in 1988, had a similar impact. It increased the response costs consistently born by the federal government through Individual Assistance and PA, leading to a need to defray costs with upfront measures.

This model of valuing hazard mitigation primarily for its potential impact on future costs (aka an investment now to reduce cost later) is not so different from the early impetus for private sector efforts at mitigation. In a sense, it illustrates the public sector behaving in a similar fashion to that of the private sector, a behavior that was sought after through the New Public Management (NPM) movement. It is also worth noting that mitigation, which is focused on reducing expenditures and not necessarily on reducing risk and vulnerability, can have the unintended consequence of failing to assist the most vulnerable within a community. The public hazard mitigation programs and policies that exist at this time are largely focused on individual structures and provide the greatest assistance to those homeowners (not renters) who have insured structures and who experience frequent losses. It is therefore critical to ask whether the goal of mitigation programs is solely the reduction of federal expenditures or the reduction of community vulnerability. Current mitigation practices do not appear to consider the overall vulnerability of the community, including the need to take into account those who are most at risk within it. This is particularly troubling because public sector provision of services is seen by much of the literature as a means of improving equity (Chamberlin & Jackson, 1987). Although DMA 2000 mitigation planning guidance does require some level of vulnerability analysis and consideration of vulnerable populations, this is not reflected within the FEMA grant programs (FEMA 2011, 2013). Essentially, in the case of hazard mitigation, it is unclear that equity was a clear goal of the public sector.

The notion that federal mitigation programs are geared primarily toward the reduction of federal expenditures, particularly those related to the NFIP, is supported by the comments of several state and local informants. At the state and local levels, several informants reported that they faced challenges in attempting to incorporate mitigation strategies that went beyond structure-by-structure solutions or that did not fall under the purview of federal grant programs. It is unclear, given the data available, whether states would have been more able or willing to utilize self-funded mechanisms for risk reduction, as a select few have and do, without the existence of federal funding and the assumption that funding hazard mitigation is a federal responsibility. This question is key to understanding the actual impacts of the federal mitigation efforts on local mitigation outcomes. If the states and communities that have been successful would have been equally successful without the federal programs, then the primary outcome may have been the growth of an industry. On the other hand, if communities engaged in hazard mitigation that would otherwise not have, then the outcome may have been risk reduction at the local level.

The measures emphasized by the NFIP, and therefore by many of the mitigation programs, are geared at floodplains that are already developed or are pending development (Respondent 11). In fact, it can be argued that insurance is more a tool for reducing the risk to existing buildings than it is for the preservation of open space or for the promotion of safe development and building practices. One respondent reported a meeting in which the then administrator of the NFIP stated that it was not appropriate to incentivize communities against development because "a good risk is better than no risk at all" (Respondent 11). Although land use is a local decision, federal regulations and funding programs can push communities toward floodplain development and push them away from other approaches that would achieve risk reduction. As Mileti and Peek (2001) described, the inability of the United States to reduce disaster losses is clearly a consequence of development patterns and attitudes toward the natural environment.

Only one short-lived public program sought to promote public–private partnerships in support of holistic and whole-community mitigation efforts: Project Impact. Researchers such as Kunreuther (2006) have found that public–private partnerships can serve to promote individual mitigation actions. The program focused on reward mechanisms instead of on compliance enforcement and was geared toward local consensus around solutions to identified problems. The model for this program was based on collaboration and partnership among many community actors, including the private sector. Another interesting component of the program was its design to be both responsive to local needs and to remain within the bounds of federal government regulations. This was constantly a challenge. This challenge appears to be present in all federal efforts to promote hazard mitigation, leading to the question of whether the federal government can truly effect positive, risk-reducing, local change. It is interesting to note that Project Impact was designed without the use of consultants and instead represented more of a joint effort between FEMA and participating communities, a further example of the use of partnerships, in this case between levels of government. This included ensuring that federal dollars were well spent while still giving communities the freedom to be creative so that they could focus on using the funds and not on becoming *grant experts*.

Many respondents cited the Project Impact model as a successful means of encouraging local action and fostering hazard mitigation. The challenge of keeping the focus on mitigation itself and not on grants management is one that exists in all the federally funded programs and one that no other program seems to have handled as well. In fact, the focus on federal grants is a key downfall of the mitigation planning efforts. However, not all Project Impact communities were successful. As with all the mitigation efforts, the local communities had a strong role to play in the success of the program. Those communities that had the capacity to be innovative and inclusive were far more successful. Each community structured its Project Impact program in a different way. Some were informal, but others were structured. Some of the least wealthy communities, which could be assumed to have the lowest capacity, were the most successful. However, a key component appears to have been a local advocate, partnership development including collaboration with the private sector, citizen associations, nongovernmental organizations, academia, and the involvement of elected officials (a key indicator of political support). The program eventually funded local coordinators because doing so was seen as a key component of success. The model of private sector involvement, which Project Impact utilized, was partnership based. For example, "we had one community that had a bank as a partner to the committee, and on one of the first meetings they had they said, wait a second you guys, you're just looking at us because you want to make available low-interest loans for mitigation, but what you are not looking at is we have financial management capabilities that our people can help you guys organize if you use our skills; don't just look at us as a bank" (Respondent 15). The Project Impact communities also worked with state and federal agencies as partners and were able to access technical skills for risk assessments and other difficult components (Respondent 15). This model is particularly interesting because the federal government filled the technical assistance role now filled primarily by contractors. No other program successfully institutionalized public and private sector collaboration in quite this way.

The Project Impact model was quite different from the DMA 2000 mitigation planning model that followed it (described in Chapter 5) in that it fostered collaboration and not simply the identification of projects. It also sought to build local capacity and to spur local action, in some cases perhaps setting the stage for the creation of local performance regimes in which broad coalitions could come together in support of a common goal of risk reduction. The Project Impact model managed in many cases to successfully navigate the challenge of creating a centralized approach without being insensitive to local particulars, a challenge described by Turgerson (2005). Under Project Impact, public and private sectors worked together in a collaborative model and not simply as contractors.

The private sector role in hazard mitigation, as described in the preceding section, has been quite varied, ranging from the collaborative model described above to one in which public entities purchase services in the marketplace. The insurance industry is a key example of a private sector industry, which has been, and remains, an advocate of specific risk-reduction efforts as insurers seek to protect their investments by requiring protective and preventative measures such as sprinklers as a prerequisite to providing insurance. In some ways, the insurance industry has even served as a model for public programs. However, the application of this model to federal programs has raised some key challenges regarding equity, as previously described. Even when programs have been authorized or mandated by the government, private industry has still played a significant role in the design of the programs (either as a model or as the designer) and often in their implementation at all levels of government. This may largely be due to the fact that the ideological climate of the late 1980s and early 1990s was marked by a strong preference for privatization with little discussion around the make-or-buy decision (Cohen & Eimicke, 2008). In fact, private industry initially managed the insurance components of the NFIP through a consortium of insurers (Respondent 1). Although some federal staff expressed concern about the ways risk was shared between insurers and the federal agencies, at least one respondent recalled the private sector role as leading to a far better arbitration process for issues such as wind versus water. Later efforts to involve the insurance industry were limited primarily to the WYO, which focuses solely on the sale of policies and the limited engagement of ISO through the CRS.

At the local level, the private sector has a long history of involvement in floodplain management and projects. Local engineers worked with groups such as USACE on local projects and studies. These local firms had strong relationships, and often, "when it became a planning effort, they put their engineers into the planning or hired planners" (Respondent 2). This shifting role is described further in Chapter 5.

The development community, although it does not typically consider itself a part of the mitigation industry, also plays a key role in either preventing or encouraging the adoption of safer construction practices that reduce risk and vulnerability. However, it has not been a key partner in the many federal efforts and has often opposed efforts to promote stricter building codes and land use requirements. In fact, development decisions play a key role in increasing risk at the local level (Freudenburg, 2008). It is worth noting that the National Association of Development Associations was present at the DMA 2000 Listening Sessions.

Academic institutions have also played a significant role in several public initiatives, at times providing a similar type of expertise to that provided by the private sector. It is unclear whether academic institutions have followed a model that is different from that of the private sector or if they have been any more successful at building capacity. Academic partners played a larger role before the growth of the private hazard mitigation industry and were quite active in several of the efforts that pre-dated DMA 2000, such as efforts in North Carolina. In some communities, representatives from the academic community who were also residents were able to step up and serve as the local drivers of the process.

One example of a university professor who spearheaded a local planning process was in the town of Campsville, Illinois, where Northwestern University had an archeological dig. The archeologists and other experts became very active in the local planning process and served as a resource to the community (Respondent 2). This planning effort preceded DMA 2000.

Universities were also used as contractors to states. North Carolina contracted with the University of North Carolina's planning school for its state-run hazard mitigation planning effort, which was described in the previous section. University contractors put together all of the guidance materials, documents that are still described as some of the best guidance available (Respondent 3). The guidance that they created included a Hazard Mitigation Plan Workbook to assist local communities that lacked a lot of capability. A second component of the guidance was a Mitigation Plan Manual that went into greater technical detail on components such as the risk assessment.

WHAT ROLES SHOULD THE VARIOUS SECTORS PLAY?

The preceding discussion leads to the question of what role the various sectors are most suited to play in risk reduction (Forrer et al., 2010). At the most basic level, there is a debate regarding whether the private sector is better suited to the promotion of hazard mitigation and provision of such services for the government (part of the broader debate around privatization and whether the private sector is more efficient) or whether the government is better suited to provide such services in a fair and equitable manner. This debate takes place primarily within the public administration literature, but does not appear to have been given much consideration during this time period. There is a further distinction in this discussion between levels of government and the various types of firms that act in the private sector. Even among those actors who feel that a government role is necessary, the extent of private involvement that they advocate can range from harnessing private industry through contracting mechanisms to partnership models that make use of the expertise housed within the private market to complete local control with little to no private involvement, except as in Project Impact, as a co-equal member of the community. Perhaps a more important consideration is the scale of the effort, with many respondents suggesting that locally driven efforts are far more effective, regardless of the implementing sector.

This debate does not appear to have significantly influenced early hazard mitigation efforts. This may be due to the political and ideological climate in which private contracting had been, and in many ways continues to be, an accepted norm for the public sector. A recent report found that using contractors, as opposed to direct hiring by the federal government, can add up to 1.6 times the cost per position and that government is failing to get market prices (Project, 2011). Despite these findings, the overall climate remains in favor of using private contractors for a wide range of services. The decision to use the private sector for hazard mitigation may also be due to the long history of private involvement and to the fact that the public programs were designed in part to reflect the private models of investing now to reduce future costs, often under pressure from private industry, and shared a similar goal to that of private efforts: the reduction of government costs. However, hazard mitigation, as an activity, does not really meet the elements that the literature would suggest make a service appropriate for privatization. Hazard mitigation is characterized by infrequent purchases, a lack of adequate information by government actors with which to compare providers, insufficient competition at the federal level, and a high cost (life safety) in the case of mistakes (Chamberlin & Jackson, 1987). In fact, in many ways, hazard mitigation as an industry exhibits some of the characteristics of market failure described previously (Bozeman, 2007).

During the time period covered by this section, there has been, within the public sector, the constant challenge of determining which agencies should be in charge of mitigation efforts. There has also been the challenge of determining which levels of government ought to provide guidance or regulation and just how much guidance should be provided. The majority of the federal hazard mitigation programs defer to the authority of the states, and their success is dependent on a wide range of local actors. Additionally, even if hazard mitigation is best suited to public sector provision, there is a real question regarding the capacity of the public sector to provide it. Consistent reductions in budgets, in staffing cuts, and in the inability to pay competitive wages create a situation in which the prerequisite expertise is not always available within the public sector when it is needed episodically (Frederickson & Frederickson, 2007).

Creation and Early Implementation
of the Disaster Mitigation Act of 2000

FEMA had been looking at local planning efforts, as described above, as far back as 1979, with the NSF study on land use planning previously mentioned, and had been requiring state hazard mitigation plans for some. The deliberations around mitigation planning included having individuals who had been active in the early mitigation plans in Illinois testify before a House Committee from 1989 to 1991, along with other groups such as NEMA and ASFPM, as described previously. Their testimony focused on the need for money to get plans and projects funded (Respondent 2). These hearings laid the groundwork for creation of Flood Mitigation Assistance (FMA), ICC, and other efforts in the 1990s, which were described previously. Although these hearings helped set the stage for passage of DMA 2000 and for FEMA efforts to promote hazard mitigation planning, they had the unintended consequence of focusing discussion on the need for funding above the need for collaboration and local engagement (both of which are clearly identified as important by the literature).

The Congressional Record, for both the House and Senate, shows that discussion regarding DMA 2000 (H.R. 707) focused primarily on reducing the impacts to people and property from natural disasters (Congressional Record, 1999b). Various senators and congressional representatives shared statistics regarding disaster losses in their particular states and described the inability of insurance to fully cover the needs of people. They cited the support of agencies such as FEMA, NEMA, ASFPM, the National League of Cities, and the American Red Cross as well as potential savings to the federal budget of up to $109 million over the first five years (Congressional Record, 1999a, H965). The conversation in the Senate, in particular, referenced "months working closely with FEMA, the States, local communities, and other stakeholders" in the development of the bill. Congressman Oberstar stated that, "The cost of the Federal, state, and local response to disaster has been going up incrementally and, in the last few years, almost explosively with the number of disaster and the greater intensity of disasters we are seeing" (Congressional Record, 1999a, H966). The need for public–private partnerships was also described as key to effective mitigation. The congressmen who spoke in favor of the bill were from states that had experienced a recent disaster, such as California and Florida.

Beyond the legislative efforts, FEMA headquarters staff members were aware of hazard mitigation programs in states such as North Carolina and Florida and were engaging in dialogue with some individuals involved in the local initiatives. This dialogue included listening sessions and at least some awareness of what the local guidance materials were. However, actual federal mitigation planning guidance was created by a hired consulting firm: United Research Services Corporation (URS). URS was established in 1951 as a commercial research group in the physical and engineering sciences. By the early 2000s, URS had expanded through various acquisitions and began focusing on architectural and engineering practices as well. One of these acquisitions, EG&G Technical Services, was a long-time provider of technical support to the Departments of Defense and Homeland Security. This acquisition positioned URS as one of the primary U.S. federal services contractors (URS, 2015).

The hazard mitigation planning program was created at a time when the private sector played an increasing role in the implementation of many federal programs. Within FEMA, there were already many existing contractual relationships with engineering firms, particularly ones that involved working on floodplain mapping. There were also many existing contractual relationships with firms that were assisting with the HMGP (application review for technical components such as the risk assessment), and they were well positioned to simply add a product line (Respondent 3). These firms already had offices established in Washington, DC, to pursue just these kinds of contracts. Given the existing relationships that these companies had with FEMA and given the prevailing climate of using private sector contractors, they were tapped early on in FEMA's hazard mitigation efforts and were able to leverage that involvement to obtain hazard mitigation work locally.

The decision to hire a contractor—instead of creating the guidance in-house or in partnership with the states that had already undertaken these efforts—appears to stem from the habitual reliance on contractors. The NFIP, as one example, relies heavily on contractors for flood insurance mapping. Greenhorne, O'Mara, Dewberry & Nealon (Dewberry) is one example of a national corporation that has served as a key HUD/FEMA contractor since the 1970s. Dewberry began in the late 1950s in Arlington, Virginia, as an engineering firm involved in development of the beltway suburbs. Dewberry's involvement with flood insurance mapping began in the 1970s and marked the beginning of significant contracts with HUD and FEMA. Dewberry, much like URS, later became active in hazard mitigation planning.

Creation of the Guidance for DMA 2000

URS, which was described previously, was hired by FEMA in the fall of 1999 to develop hazard mitigation planning guidance (which eventually became the guidance for DMA 2000). URS utilized several other beltway firms as subcontractors for the effort. Firms such as URS drew upon staff with a range of experience levels and had a great deal more engineering expertise than planning expertise; many actually had to hire planners and then educate them in hazard mitigation (Respondent 5). As the federal programs helped to create a mitigation industry, firms such as URS would go on to use their existing networks in states where they had offices to pursue local hazard mitigation work or acquire local engineering firms in order to do.

URS staff members were tasked to create what are now referred to as the state and local mitigation planning how-to-guides, without access to any draft materials (Respondent 5) but with the understanding that federal regulations were forthcoming. This situation resulted in what one respondent described as a "psyzchophrenic approach" in which the guidance documents were created as if there would be no law, while those creating it knew the regulations were being enacted, but even those within the public sector could not necessarily participate in that process (Respondent 5). There appears to have been a disconnect between the efforts to draft the law and corresponding regulations and the effort to create the guidance. In fact, there are a series of mitigation planning guidebooks, referred to as the How To Guides, as well as a much shorter mitigation planning guidance document, referred to as The Blue Book. The How To Guides were developed as part of a FEMA push for consistency and improved quality in mitigation plans across the United States and not intended to serve as a the programmatic guidance for DMA 2000. These were separate from the efforts to enact a law such as DMA 2000, which was driven primarily by other divisions (departments) within the agency (Respondent 5). Although there had been some isolated state initiatives, and states themselves had plans, there was no overall guidance from the federal government before this effort.

The URS team was asked to look at the CRS process as a model, but not to mimic it; FEMA wanted communities to be able to choose to do both at the same time (Respondent 5). It is unclear why a separate process was generated when existing models were in place for a planning process that already existed and had similar goals, although they were focused solely on flooding. In addition to the question of how to set up the process, there was also a great deal of debate within FEMA over how to structure the guidance documents themselves, and eventually the vision for the guidance was that there would be core documents and additional resources for specific topics (Respondent 5). Although DMA 2000 was about to become law, the guides were not supposed to be the handbook for DMA 2000. In fact, the consultant team was repeatedly instructed to ensure that they were not creating DMA 2000 guidance, a fact that puzzled many of them (Respondent 5).

That handbook was created later and was referred to as the *Blue Book*. It focused more on how to make a plan that passed the minimum standards set forth by the regulations; it was essentially a compliance manual. This emphasis on writing a plan to meet a standard, as opposed to creating one that emphasizes the value of the entire planning process, has often been cited as one of the greatest failures of the program (Respondent 20). Although the focus on meeting the minimum requirement could stem from the initial decisions regarding the structure of the guidance, it is unclear if this was due to the contractor or to a lack of internal coordination within FEMA itself. Additionally, the broader historical context regarding the growing role of technical expertise through a focus on mechanisms such as benefit–cost analysis and risk assessment (Fischer, 2005), may have influenced the perception that local communities were unable to manage the process without the help of a detailed process and technical assistance.

It is also interesting to note that the How To Guides were developed with local planners, and not emergency managers, in mind (Respondent 5). Many at FEMA saw the local planners as key to the hazard mitigation effort, but were faced with the challenge that FEMA funds would go through emergency management departments. It is unclear if the disconnect between intended and actual audience was taken into account, but it certainly added to the challenges faced by local emergency managers seeking to develop these plans.

The consultants involved in developing the guidance in addition to the FEMA staff seem to have operated from the assumption that many local communities would elect to use contractors for the writing of their plans (Respondent 5). Although the federal model had been to use contractors, many local planning efforts such as those in Illinois, which predated DMA 2000, had barely relied on contractors at all. More recent models, such as the LMS in Florida, had seen greater contractor involvement. Many of the models relied on technical assistance from the state or other sources (Respondent 3). In fact, risk-assessment guidance was the first area of focus because it was expected to be the most difficult, with training sessions conducted in each region (Respondent 8). This existing model was far less dependent on private sector infrastructure than the developers of the guidance appear to have assumed. However, the capabilities of the states to support a national expansion of mitigation planning was limited outside of those states that already had efforts in place. In many ways, it appears as though the process and guidance were made more complicated than was necessary (Respondent 5).

Whether this had anything to do with the assumption that communities might hire contractors to do their plans is unclear. However, the decision to deviate from the CRS framework, by modifying the planning process while still using it as a model, is particularly important to examine, as there was existing capacity in some areas for CRS planning.*

When DMA 2000 became law, the corresponding guidance documents were still in the process of being created, and some states chose to begin their mitigation planning efforts without the formal guidance. Other communities took much longer to become interested in mitigation planning, despite the consequences of not participating, i.e., the inability to access federal mitigation funds and some components of federal disaster assistance. However, many communities had been submitting applications for planning grants before the release of the guidance, and some received funding before the guidance being released (Respondent 10).

As communities began issuing requests for proposals to complete their mitigation plans, the same firms that were actively working on the guidance for FEMA were actively preparing to bid on the planning work. There was minimal discussion at FEMA about whether there might be a conflict of interest, and firms such as URS were given the green light to go after the projects (Respondent 5). This set a precedent for the other major national firms that had existing contracts with FEMA and DHS to also expand into the local mitigation realm. The firms that were active in creation of the guidance or that were already doing similar work in other states had a tremendous advantage over local firms. These same firms were also contracted by FEMA regions for plan–review assistance, and they could point to their involvement in the creation of the guidance, something local firms could not claim (Respondent 5).

One respondent described the situation as follows:

> There was no perceived conflict of interest in that and that's how I think a lot of those planning projects, especially the larger ones, went to the big firms. They could point to the fact that they were involved with crafting the guidance and then they built the track record of doing so many mitigation plans in other portions of the country. Then they could point to how many approved plans they have; that became a very strong qualification for them even over some of the smaller, perhaps more appropriate planning firms, who really knew the communities in some cases, to develop the mitigation plans. Again some of those firms [who ranged in size] may not have the prerequisite [*sic* local] expertise. (Respondent 3)

---

* The most current guidance from FEMA build upon the initial guidance, but includes no substantive changes as the regulations have not been altered. Instead, some areas of interpretation are clarified (FEMA, 2011, 2013).

Overall, the rollout of DMA 2000 was a more drawn out process than FEMA had desired. The program design was aggressive, broad, and complex, a fact that made speedy implementation a challenge (Respondent 5). The passage of DMA 2000 helped to create a market for private sector planning that soon extended even beyond those initial engineering firms. One consultant described the process as

> the time when local governments and states were ramping up to develop a lot of these local mitigation plans, grant funds were being provided from FEMA through the states, and there were a lot of RFPs out there... it was a good time, and it was really the heyday if you were in the private sector to find work, to find willing clients to hire you to help them with local mitigation planning. (Respondent 3)

As the quote illustrates, following DMA 2000, a great deal of money became available for planning, and it became worthwhile for the companies to create in-house expertise. Private sector firms had isolated expertise in certain states and had used that staff as a base for pursuing hazard mitigation planning work. Suddenly, communities that had not wanted hazard mitigation were interested because money was available, and firms were quick to pursue what appeared to be regular work.

The private sector boom described above resulted in the creation of a large hazard mitigation industry, not just at the national level but also at the local and regional levels. More recently, the private sector market has shifted because there are fewer local communities looking for consultants to assist with their hazard mitigation planning efforts and because the amount of money made available for these efforts has declined (Respondent 3). Some states had initially set funding levels quite low, below $20,000 for regional hazard mitigation plans, but many had allowed much larger grants of over $100,000 for a single-county hazard mitigation plan and later reduced the grants to below $50,000 (Respondents 3, 5, and 20). Large urban areas, particularly those funding hazard mitigation plans through PDM, are often still able to secure large grants for mitigation planning efforts. However, this is the exception to the trend. The larger firms are often unable to take on the work for the amount of money available, unless they happen to have a local office. This has made smaller, more nimble firms, far more competitive. A lot of independent consultants have left firms where they did the mitigation plans and now can do the work for a lot less (Respondent 3). The large, national firms remain the primary recipients of federal mitigation contracts (including mapping initiatives, disaster response, and hazard mitigation plan review) through standing contract mechanisms such as the Hazard Mitigation Technical Assistance Program (HMTAP), and have expanded their operations into disaster recovery as they have withdrawn from local planning.

One significant initiative in recent years (beginning in FY 2009) has been the Risk Mapping, Assessment, and Planning (Risk MAP) effort. Risk MAP replaced the earlier Map Mod program, which began in 2004 as an effort to digitize flood maps. The transition to Risk MAP was an attempt to better integrate the mapping with the planning. FEMA has contracted with several major mapping firms to improve the availability of quality risk data, to increase public awareness regarding risk, and to support hazard mitigation planning. Risk MAP is structured as several different contracts, including one for Program Management that includes coordination among all contractors. Risk MAP and the previous map-modernization initiative undertaken by FEMA have been the primary federal contracts for the major firms involved in hazard mitigation. It is worth noting that these firms work together in many different ways through these types of contracts. The relationships range from partnerships to direct supervision, even to serving as the source for accountability as exemplified by the Project Management contract. These efforts carry far higher profit margins than local mitigation planning work, with the 2011 Customer and Data Services contract alone worth over $125,000,000, and they allow for very close relationships between the major firms. It could be argued that this has an impact on the true level of competition as these firms interact with each other in myriad ways across the various levels of government.

As the disaster recovery programs have become institutionalized and as a record of previous interpretations of the regulations has come into existence, they have lost some of their initial flexibility, as recent interpretations are limited to what has previously been accepted. The increased bureaucracy tied to these programs, including the complexity of the guidance and previous interpretations, now requires a greater amount of experience and historical knowledge than was previously required. There was greater flexibility when the mitigation staff involved in a particular disaster response consisted of only ten to fifteen people, as was the case until the mid-1990s. The smaller teams were able to work closely on issues and to be flexible in the application of regulations (Respondent 6). Joint field offices now house tremendous cadres of DAEs and full-time FEMA employees. As one former public employee stated,

> When the program first began we thought it was a good idea we could do it and we could get grants to do those projects that we thought were a good idea. We didn't have to really navigate through a lot of the obstacles that sort of impede the effectiveness of the hazard mitigation program today. (Respondent 14)

Components such as the cost–benefit analysis and the historic preservation requirement have also made the process far more complex than it initially was (Respondent 14), another factor leading to increased contracting at the state level. Additionally, HUD and FEMA employees who undertook the initial rogue mitigation efforts are largely retired and are now employed by the private sector. Their experience, obtained through contracting with a large firm, provides states with their own private sector cadre of sorts. These contractors, former FEMA and HUD employees, assist the states with appealing the decisions of current FEMA and HUD employees. Often, these contractors have a greater level of institutional knowledge than existing federal staff regarding the historic interpretation of the various programs, including interpretations used in other regions. They are able to show previous interpretations of guidance, including previously allowable uses of funds, in order to win appeals.

Another factor is that the amount of money available now means that funding decisions are not based on a strategic approach (Respondent 2). In other words, there is a drive to spend the money available as quickly as possible, without engaging in a robust planning process and often without drawing upon the existing hazard mitigation plan. Instead, the large sums of money available become politicized and get used in local political agendas, often in support of local growth machines. Hazard mitigation plans are required, but there is no clear linkage between the contents of the plan and what gets funded. In fact, very different actors are often involved in the initial planning effort as opposed to the *spending effort* that follows a disaster. Additional, local control over how funds are spent might lead to more strategic approaches even when a community's strategy does not fit cleanly into a grant program (Respondent 14).

PUBLIC SECTOR, PRIVATE, AND OTHER ROLES

As a public program, hazard mitigation planning has the potential to focus on real solutions and to take a holistic approach that engages the whole community. This section describes in greater detail the roles played by the public, private, and other sectors during the time period described above. It also details some of the concerns and challenges regarding the quality and success of mitigation efforts. Although hazard mitigation planning is federally mandated, the success of this planning depends heavily upon local implementation, including the range of actors involved and whether the plan will remain a priority following a disaster. With the exception of federal grants, which are often the primary consideration in the identification of projects, more effective solutions, such as land use, fall within the purview of the state or locality. Even consultants describe the more effective mitigation planning efforts as those that have strong local leadership, buy-in, and involvement (Respondents 3 and 21).

When asked for examples of *very good local plans,* respondents cited those plans in which "the motivation for doing plans was not FEMA money, it was to help solve the question of what to do we do to solve our flood problems, we've got angry citizens, we've been flooded, we need to show them that we're doing something" (Respondent 2). In these instances, residents were clamoring for change, and community staff were looking for answers. One respondent described a needed combination of political support and technical expertise (either from a consultant or in-house). Although a consultant can play a role in this type of successful plan, the respondent noted that it is necessary to keep the planner around to ensure that there is implementation. In essence, the involvement of consistent local actors and collaboration across the community appears to have more of an impact than does which sector is in charge.

However, despite the great potential for the use of mitigation planning, some locals describe DMA 2000 planning as focused on implementing a grant program and not as a planning philosophy. "There is this assumption that everything will be, every mitigation action should be done through a FEMA grant program and you're going to hire more or less a certain set of contractors to do that" (Respondent 20). This appears to be borne out by the policy of only looking at natural hazards (as FEMA funds and authority only apply there). In some cases, consultants and FEMA regions explicitly prevented communities from including other hazards in their plans, despite the fact that many planning efforts now include man-made hazards (Respondent 20).

In terms of hazard mitigation planning, and as described previously, the federal government relied heavily on contractors for both the creation of the programs and their implementation. FEMA uses its HMTAP mechanism to readily access contractors for plan review and following a disaster. There were voices within FEMA, during the creation of the mitigation planning guidance, calling for the process to be simple enough that "Joe the Barber could do it on the back of an envelope because he's had his shop here, he's lived here, he knows what's going to happen" (Respondent 8). Some of the authors of the guidance have noted that it was simply a lot of information to put into one set of documents. This suggests that the challenges are inherent to the process and are not a function of private sector involvement in the drafting of legislation. FEMA's office of Legislative Affairs actively sought to promote mitigation with legislators, particularly following disasters (Respondent 15).

Respondents who worked for FEMA at the time that the DMA 2000 regulations and guidance were formulated reported on their efforts to influence the legislation and were able to review drafts and propose some language changes. As previously mentioned, because using outside groups as participants in the actual drafting of the rule is very challenging for a federal agency, FEMA called together a listening session in order to gather some feedback. This indicates that there were some limitations in place regarding who could be utilized formally to assist and that contractors could more readily be used. The listening session convened individuals from some local communities, representatives of various associations, and academics who had been working in mitigation.

Invitees to the listening session were provided with background information on the three primary topic areas to be covered: mitigation planning under DMA 2000, changes to the HMGP, and PDM with a focus on Project Impact. According to the information shared with participants, FEMA was seeking "views of its stakeholder groups on the new planning criteria, and how best to implement these new provisions" (FEMA Listening Session, 2000). According to the notes, participants expressed concern about a focus on future projects instead of on land use as well as concern about asking local officials to undergo such a technical process (FEMA Listening Session, 2000). Additionally, both NEMA and ASFPM submitted written comments on DMA 2000. Their comments included several concerns about the technical nature of the guidance and the difficulty for small local communities to comply. Additionally, they suggested that the CRS criteria be utilized in order to standardize planning efforts. It is unclear the extent to which the consultants who wrote the final guidance utilized the information from these listening sessions (FEMA, 2001a–g).

The states, on the other hand, have traditionally used in-house reviewers for their oversight role while hiring contractors for the writing of their own plans. One exception is the state of Louisiana, which briefly used contractors for local plan review following Hurricane Katrina. However, this exception stemmed from the significantly increased demand for plan updates driven by the influx of funds. At the local level, many (if not most) communities have elected to use contractors (Respondent 3).

Some states, such as Ohio, took a strong leadership role in early mitigation planning efforts. Ohio initiated a pilot program in which the state provided risk assessment data to fifteen initial communities (Respondent 10). The state of Ohio promoted local mitigation plans when DMA 2000 was just being rolled out and before the availability of the guidance. As a result, the state utilized a grant to do mitigation planning in fifteen recently affected communities and created a mitigation planning guidebook to facilitate that process. To ensure that new plans would be in compliance, the guidance was modified as details regarding the federal guidance were released (Respondent 10). The CRS process was used as a guide, and the state placed a heavy emphasis on public involvement, including requiring grant agreements with the communities. These requirements stipulated that there would be a series of local teams and that mapping would be used in a particular way. Other states have chosen to make similar resources available, in part out of recognition that local governments lack the capacity to undertake these analyses on their own.

Lack of resources severely limits the ability of the public sector to provide sufficient oversight of contractors. Multiple respondents from the private sector reported a lack of involvement in the process by public staff, and one public staff person reported never having the time to actually read the mitigation plan in its entirety: "... I have no idea if they just copied someone else's plan and changed the name" (Respondent 20). Because they lack the technical expertise to accurately review the work submitted, public sector employees have no way of knowing if the plan is truly unique to their community. Instead, they trust that it is.

Respondents indicated that many jurisdictions simply sign contracts and wait to receive a product. This process is one that fails to truly include citizen input, as opposed to a process in which the consultant is used for expertise while the local government manages the process. Although the private sector is often blamed for poor planning processes, the local community itself cannot simply exonerate itself from responsibility (Respondent 17).

Across the country, communities that chose to undertake planning efforts on their own were those that had existing capacity. They saw the opportunity to have a new funding stream for staff. As one example, the Town of Elizabethtown, North Carolina, which was one of the eleven demonstration communities that initially did hazard mitigation plans following Hurricane Fran in 1996, had a strong local champion and developed its own plan. Elizabethtown was able to use the grant funds to build its own capacity and data sources, instead of hiring a contractor (Respondent 3). Communities such as Elizabethtown either had the ability to do GIS or utilized the grant funds to develop it, and if they used consultants, then they did so solely for minimal technical assistance. However, as staff sizes are reduced, or as turnover increases, more communities turn to consultants for the second round of plans. Now the challenge is that the private sector isn't pursuing the work because of reduced grant amounts, while the public sector lacks the capacity (Respondent 5).

Florida is a good example of a state where the lack of public sector capacity has led to greater private sector involvement in the process. During early Local Mitigation Strategies planning in Florida, local governments had strong planning and emergency management staff, and there were only one or two consultants. Local capability included GIS, and they were able to reply upon regional planning agencies for assistance; therefore, the funding stayed with government agencies (Respondent 3). As there have been major cuts in local government services, and as local planners have been laid off, the state has delegated more authority to the local level.

Many respondents cited risk assessment as the reason why FEMA expected that communities would need to hire consultants. Outside of that technical component, there was an assumption that local planning departments could undertake some of the effort within the realm of their normal planning activities. However, local turnover has a significant impact on the ability to retain institutional knowledge and EMAs are particularly fraught with turnover (Respondent 5). Also, FEMA did not make it clear that capacity building was an objective.

The availability of local staff resources also plays a key role. Larger, wealthier communities have greater resources, not just to do the mitigation planning work but also to put together requests for proposals, to submit grant applications, and to implement projects. These communities are able to secure greater funding and are often able to attract more experienced firms when they utilize contractors. Local officials report community frustration at the challenges confronted in the federal grant application process (Respondent 13). Even those officials who value mitigation planning struggle to obtain political support when the program has been sold to communities as a mechanism for accessing grants and not as a means to achieve risk reduction.

Some communities now question whether they should continue updating their plans at all, much less spend money on developing project applications as they "… will have to come out of pocket before we ever get approved for these properties, we are having to spend money to hopefully get money but we may not get that money. It is almost like a gamble" (Respondent 13). The effort required to apply for the grant is not remunerated if the grant is not awarded. Again, this discourages smaller communities that may have a greater need to pursue these resources because their lack of staff and expertise makes their applications more of a resource drain and therefore less likely to produce results. This can be viewed as a failure of implementation in that the stated objectives of the DMA 2000 are not being met. One respondent recommended the use of regional efforts as a means to supplement local capacity (Respondent 21).

Much like the local and state governments and agencies, the federal government also struggles with a lack of sufficient in-house expertise and resources. According to one respondent, the federal government cannot often hire people with highly specialized technical backgrounds because the salaries offered them are not competitive. As a result, the federal government is far more successful in hiring generalists than specialists and turns to the private sector when that expertise is needed intermittently (Respondent 14). The intermittent nature of the need for mitigation work, at least that associated with disaster, also makes it challenging for federal agencies to meet the surge requirements on their own. It is necessary to ask, however, if the higher rates charged by consultants result in a cost savings as opposed to simply hiring more experienced federal staff at higher rates and finding ways to use their expertise on pre-disaster mitigation efforts as well.

The trend is a bit different in post-disaster hazard mitigation and grants administration. The federal government relies on a combination of contractors: full time employees (FTEs), part time employees (PTEs), and DAEs. The states more often utilize contractors to supplement local staff in big events, while local communities are far more limited in their abilities to hire experts. Some private firms will seek contracts with local communities, but most seek the more lucrative contracts at the state level.

The focus on individual projects rather than on more complex solutions, as well as on projects that are more readily funded by federal mitigation programs, also exists in post-disaster mitigation. One local respondent describes a mismatched approach that fails to differentiate between the types of flood risk and that focuses instead on elevation. The respondent describes the limited impact and high cost of structure-by-structure elevation (in which properties that had ceased to flood following significant drainage improvements flooded again as a result of a major hurricane) as opposed to the high-impact action of focusing on mitigating for the more frequent shallow flooding, which can be addressed through area solutions and possibly homeowner funded action (Respondent 18). Although some of the actions could be financed with current grant programs, the state and city have focused completely on financing elevation. The respondent noted that the cost–benefit calculation is a factor because the larger projects do not show the same ratios as those homes that have high claims (Respondent 18).

These types of concerns, which were voiced by many respondents, speak to the need for collaboration and coordination mechanisms that can look at things such as Integrated Water Management (Respondent 18). It is unclear whether these mechanisms should be promoted by the federal initiatives, but Project Impact notwithstanding, these efforts have not been funded.

The private sector, through the various mitigation contractors, has played such a key role that private entities have essentially acted on behalf of the public sector, as can be seen in the Louisiana example cited above. However, it is also worth noting that the private sector encompasses much more than simply those firms that sell services. There is an entire private industry around the manufacture and installation of certain types of mitigation measures such as safe rooms, shutters, and other items. There is also a rapidly growing elevation industry that plays a key role in promoting the use of elevation as a preferred mitigation technique. One respondent described a robust (although much smaller) private industry—composed of home elevators, independent contractors, and engineering firms—that existed as early as the mid-1980s. FEMA actively sought to encourage the growth of expertise among architects in designing structures for flooding. This action was seen as a means to promote safer building and elevation. The effort to educate architects on the NFIP was run by regional, flood insurance staff just before Hurricane Bob. It represented a different model of private sector engagement, one in which the federal government sought to help create a private industry. Interestingly, a similar model was never pursued with hazard mitigation planning, in which federal training often excludes contractor staff (Respondent 25).

The private sector also plays a role as a community or state stakeholder. Despite the earlier private sector role serving as a driver of mitigation, more recently states and communities have struggled to obtain participation from this group. Private industry continues to take steps to protect its infrastructure and investments but it does not necessarily participate in community efforts. For example, most large firms maintain some risk-management staff and focus heavily on the reduction of losses, of business interruption, and of liability concerns.

The lack of emphasis on holistic solutions is also seen in private sector efforts. Many state and local informants reported pushback from both their locally hired contractors and from the contractors used by FEMA (and in one case the state for plan review) (Respondents 13, 18, and 20). One informant even compared the system of contractors to the military industrial complex, describing the sheer amount of money that is made from disasters and the current model of doing business in which grants management has become a lucrative endeavor (Respondent 20). Respondents also reported a lack of understanding regarding the types of mitigation available, stating that the requests they receive from the public are specifically for HMGP and not for mitigation (Respondents 20, 18, and 10). The funds received for grants administration may be greater when there are more isolated projects.

The promotion of DMA 2000 utilized the potential for grant dollars as the primary incentive for developing a plan. "A successful plan is measured by getting grant money; that changes the orientation and what you write the plan for" (Respondent 2). As an unintended consequence, communities care more about the grants than the process (Respondent 11). This gives private sector contractors, who often also focus on the identification of projects, an incentive to streamline their efforts in order to maximize their profits. This can mean that the firms initially utilize more qualified staff to set up a process and later use their lower-level staff to replicate the process in other communities and to fill in the blanks (Respondent 25). As a result, the consultants doing the work may know some projects to identify but do not grasp the concepts and purposes behind them (Respondent 2).

The private sector's role in local planning efforts largely stemmed from a lack of local capacity. Although there was not a high level of capacity available initially within the private sector (and that capacity may be decreasing as indicated by the shift toward template work), private firms quickly grew an industry as federal or state initiatives and grant programs to fund their work. For example, when the LMS was initially rolled out in Florida, the vast majority of communities turned to consultants because the work was unfamiliar (Respondent 21). However, the work was also unfamiliar to the consultants, and the quality of the resulting plans was quite varied. One planner described the first round of LMS plans as a

Christmas list of projects that had no real connection back to the vulnerability assessment. It is unclear if this is a result of the general lack of knowledge and experience within both the private and public sectors or if it is a function of the fact that the LMS was in fact designed to identify projects (Respondent 21).

Another effort that predated DMA 2000 but serves as an excellent example of some of the issues around mitigation plan quality was the initial local hazard mitigation plans in North Carolina following Hurricane Fran in 1996; it also relied heavily on the use of consultants. The demonstration communities worked primarily with local planning firms, which saw the mitigation plans as an opportunity to expand their market beyond land use and coastal area management plans. The processes that they undertook were not collaborative, and interactions between the consultants and the community members were minimal. The plans essentially followed the process laid out in the guidance but were written entirely by consultants.

One state employee at the time recalls receiving some plans that had over a dozen pages of language directly copied from websites and other sources (Respondent 3). However, the state of North Carolina was closely monitoring plan quality and required the consultants to improve the plans drastically. As a result, some consultants who were simply on a learning curve improved tremendously while those who had sought a quick buck realized that "it really wasn't their line of expertise or where they wanted to grow their business" (Respondent 3). This is an example of strong, state involvement driving local quality and potentially pushing low performers out of the market. However, these were demonstration communities; it was a small pilot; and, as evidenced by their early adoption of a mitigation planning requirement, North Carolina clearly saw the value in the process. It is unclear if this same effect has taken place in other states.

The question of plan quality, when plans are completed using contractors, is one that frequently arises. Some private sector respondents complained vehemently about the impacts of bad consultants on the reputation of the industry as a whole. They acknowledged that there are firms that are more focused on the money than the product. They also suggested that communities should seek consultants who are committed to the process. This is not so different from the earlier statement that quality plans require committed communities, regardless of who does the writing. Acknowledging that locals will know the community best, they describe the need for local leaders and for a collaborative process

200

in which the private consultants bring technical expertise to supplement local efforts (Respondent 21).

One of the concerns often cited is a lack of mitigation knowledge among contractor staff, a concern that is tied to the impression that the firms are using less skilled staff (Respondent 2) or staff with other irrelevant expertise. This is significant because it eliminates the key reason for the use of consultants, which is to access expertise not available in the public sector (Respondent 10). In the 1990s, as they pursued hazard mitigation work and tried to break into the industry, the large, private firms would often call upon subject-matter experts (SMEs) to increase their access to expertise. These SMEs were often former public employees (some of whom had headed up the guerilla efforts described in Chapter 4), who had begun working as consultants. However, as funds were made more widely available, in particular following the passage of DMA 2000, which appeared to guarantee funds into the future, the firms developed their own expertise.

This expertise was developed in part by hiring professionals from related fields, such as architecture and engineering, both professions in which a long backlog of work was uncommon. The promise of a steady funding stream was a strong lure for professionals who were used to struggling. The large firms used some of these professionals, despite their lack of exposure to hazard mitigation, as they developed the guidance for the federal programs and later used their experience developing that guidance to secure significant amounts of local work (Respondent 5). The fact that the contracts for the development of the How To Guides and other guidance went to firms that had existing relationships with FEMA but little mitigation planning experience is illustrative of the federal climate and regulations which are very conducive to the use of the private sector. It was more difficult for FEMA to engage local planners who had lead the state efforts, at least beyond Listening Sessions, than it was to expand their existing contract (Respondent 15).

Despite the initial development of in-house expertise among larger private firms, low profit levels associated with mitigation planning, and even with some small-scale hazard mitigation projects, have not been sufficient to induce the private sector to maintain a high level of expertise. Instead, the firms rely on low-level staff to complete the smaller projects with a higher profit margin. Recently, one respondent reported a conversation with staff at one of the large firms who reported that the firm only took on mitigation planning work as a means of showing that the staff had expertise needed to secure the larger federal contracts. As a result, this firm, and quite possibly others like it, was uninterested in improving the quality of its mitigation planning efforts. Instead, this firm and others assume that their staff can do mitigation planning because they have the related engineering and modeling expertise. However, they lack knowledge and expertise in the implementation of projects and have very little understanding of planning practices and local processes. Many firms that have focused primarily on engineering are far more familiar with engineering solutions than land use and zoning. The companies focus on the small amount of money available and see the value solely in the identification of projects that can later be a source of further work. This drives the piecemeal approach and project focus described earlier (Respondent 4).

CREATION AND GROWTH
OF THE MITIGATION INDUSTRY

The growth of the mitigation planning industry, in terms of small, regional, and large firms jumping into the market, peaked in 2005 (Respondent 3). One respondent who worked for one of the larger and more successful firms described an incredibly rapid pace of work with a win rate of 85%, as the firm both secured local mitigation planning contracts and reviewed more than 300 plans for FEMA. He described a market in which there were a few other large firms but not a lot of competition outside of that, with the exception of some local engineering firms in certain communities. "It was actually kind of unusual that as out-of-town consultants we had the advantage over the locals" (Respondent 5). The large firms drew upon their experience as federal contractors to secure local work. These firms hired some former public employees and used SMEs as needed.

Over time, several regional firms became active in the industry, often buying up local firms and becoming large, national firms themselves. These regional firms leveraged local relationships and developed the planning expertise (Respondent 5). As the existence of planning funds, including some large planning grants, drove these additional firms to pursue mitigation planning, the marketplace became very competitive. However, the recent reduction in planning grant awards has reduced the interest among consultants at the same time that local cuts are increasing the need to turn to outside resources (Respondent 4). Large planning efforts, with high budgets (which major cities have), still draw a great deal of competition, but smaller communities do not.

202

One advantage that the larger firms do have is the ability to access a wide range of in-house expertise in technical components such as GIS and engineering. However, the small firms can compensate for this by building partnerships while maintaining lower overhead. Additionally, the smaller firms can work collaboratively with communities who have local resources (Respondent 2).

It is important to continue to recognize the role that the public sector plays as the contracting entity. A local community can look for a firm that will serve as a partner or it can simply seek to purchase a product. As one respondent pointed out, "if you hire somebody for your hazard mitigation plan and that is their entire role with you, you should not be surprised if they do it as quickly and efficiently as they can to get to their bottom line and to move on" (Respondent 1).

Some communities actually utilize their consultants as a neutral party when there is a history of strained relationships among community stakeholders. Under this model, the private firm is an intermediary in support of the local effort. "We wanted to make sure that the community felt like this was a holistic process and that the city was just one vote in the process or one set of votes, because we did have several state personnel on our stakeholders committee" (Respondent 13).

One respondent described the ideal consultant role as that of a facilitator who can assist the community in writing its plan. Under this model, a local champion or agency is the true driver of the process. The respondent added that the alternative, that of very passive participation, does not result in good plans (Respondent 8). This facilitator role essentially involves bringing the benefit of expertise to ask this question: "Have you thought about…" (Respondent 13)?

Communities face some significant challenges when selecting a contractor. Some communities seek smaller companies and individuals with whom they are familiar, and others select large firms in the hope that they will have the needed capacity to provide a robust mitigation plan. Communities also look to see which consultants have worked with neighboring jurisdictions and turn to FEMA for template requests for proposal (RFPs). This eliminates the opportunity to utilize the RFP as a mechanism to ensure that local concerns are addressed. One respondent stated, "I don't think a lot of people know what they are doing when they are doing hiring for this" (Respondent 4). Respondents report seeing greater specificity and differentiation between RFPs for plan updates. This appears to be driven by previous negative experiences (Respondent 5). The communities' initial planning process gives them experience that improves their expertise, provided there is low enough staff turnover to allow for that kind of institutional knowledge.

As one respondent noted,

> Private industry has separate motivations perhaps than government and can do some things extremely well, and can do some things a lot less well, and they need guidance. They need standards, and they need to respond to an end result. The end result is the creation of a plan, and you get paid for it, and that's the end. You will produce a certain plan. If the end result is a partnership for the community to reduce risk, you will get a very different result. (Respondent 1)

The RFPs described above can be a great tool for this.

The current model of private sector involvement in mitigation faces some key challenges as federal funding levels continue to decline (Respondent 5). Larger consulting companies are less willing to take contracts, although this in turn drives demand for the smaller firms that carry lower overhead. In addition, communities that initially saw no value in the process and focused solely on grants see little reason to continue updating plans when no grants are forthcoming (Respondent 5). Many communities have simply not prioritized mitigation planning relative to other needs (Respondent 3). Some consultants are actively working with communities to identify additional funding sources and mechanisms for project implementation, describing this as the only way to keep programs alive (Respondent 5). Some communities, however, have found ways to continue updating their plans using their own staff (Respondent 11).

As the private sector's role in mitigation planning has been reduced, the firms that had done the mitigation planning have expanded into post-disaster state contracts to administer recovery funds and to manage programs. This shift in focus stemmed in part from the realization that the process was quite challenging for local communities to manage. The firms marketed themselves as being able to navigate the rules and as being able to get more federal assistance, not as being able to manage better mitigation outcomes. The ability of firms to fill this space stems in part from the allowance for administrative costs provided in the Stafford Act.

The federal recovery process has become more complicated after years of amendments and interpretations, often leaving states and communities unable to maintain the necessary expertise. Additionally, many states are unable to hire skilled temporary employees when they are under hiring freezes, which makes it easier for them to contract with private sector staff (Respondent 14).

However, private sector firms cannot necessarily keep sufficient staff on hand themselves. Consequently, they either rely on a pool of contractors who jump from firm to firm in each disaster (and could possibly be hired directly by the state) or hire and train individuals following major disasters. There is a very real question of whether another model would be more efficient and effective, particularly if local hiring constraints were lessened following a disaster declaration. As one respondent described it, this current model is just one tool in the toolbox for states that lack emergency management capacity, that have poor leadership, or that are overwhelmed by a major event (Respondent 10).

In general, respondents describe the quality of the contractor staff as decent, but note that local knowledge is lacking (Respondent 24). In other words, the consultant model has not succeeded in fully capturing local needs and information in the planning process. The same challenge is mentioned in reference to mitigation planning.

PRIVATE AS PUBLIC

As the governmental role in hazard mitigation has developed, all levels of government have at times called upon the private sector to manage programs, to expand capabilities, and to administer grants. This has included the tremendous private sector role in assisting FEMA with local and state plan review. This creates a situation in which it is possible for a local plan to be written solely by a contractor and then reviewed by another contractor, with very little public involvement or intervention.*

One respondent observed that the relationship between the state and its contractors seemed inappropriate, with state employees deferring to the contractor. He stated, "… the two were interchangeable. We actually sent our quarterly reports to the contractor" (Respondent 20). This contractor discouraged the city from looking at concerns such as superfund sites, despite that fact that it was a real concern for the community, which was seeking better integration among planning mechanisms. He described similar challenges at the city level where there were more contractor staff involved than city employees. He raised a real question of whether the government was outsourcing its responsibilities. Can that plan really represent the community (Respondent 20)?

---

* It is a FEMA policy that all plans reviewed by contractors must receive an additional cursory review by a FEMA staff person.

The use of contractors in post-disaster recovery and grants administration can also create a situation in which contractor staff members are taking on the role of the state in setting the direction of the recovery efforts and deciding focus areas for mitigation projects.

Academia is another sector that has played a key role. Universities continue as active partners in many communities and work with the federal government on research, on the creation of curriculum, and on other efforts. In California, Cal Poly Corporation operates as a contracting arm of the university and works with the state on its planning efforts. In some cases, however, university efforts were described quite negatively. In one example, an urban planning department made some proposals to beautify levees by putting shops and cafes on top of them (Respondent 4). This recommendation showed a lack of understanding of flood-plain management.

SUMMARY

As the preceding sections have shown, the role of the public and private sectors in hazard mitigation has historically been complex and varied. Although hazard mitigation is not *privatized* in the truest sense of the word (it is not a government service that has been sold to the private sector), it is undoubtedly a service in which the private sector has played a tremendous role. In fact, hazard mitigation is unique in the ways in which the public and private sector roles have changed over time, varied with respect to the type of firm as well as to the type of public entity implementing the hazard mitigation programs or measures, as well as to the incorporation of other actors such as academia (at times in a consultant role). Hazard mitigation, as an activity, did not originate with the public sector; instead, it originated largely with the private sector, which in turn both pushed for a government role and eventually took on the task as a contractor of designing and implementing federal programs. These federal programs were, in turn, largely implemented at the local level by the same (or other) contractors.

The hazard mitigation industry that exists today was largely formed in response to the growing federal role in hazard mitigation, primarily due to requirements for a set amount of mitigation activity and the funding available to purchase it. Also of interest is the role that the private-sector actors play as street-level bureaucrats, administering public programs (Lipsky, 1980). The prevalence of localized solutions, which create a further need for administration, can arguably be connected to the actions of these private sector actors making local policy decisions. Another key theme that contributes to the large role of the private sector is the role of expertise. The reliance on technical risk assessments and on cost–benefit calculations, which are prevalent in various policy realms, also clearly influenced the desire for specialized expertise that was not available within the public sector (Fischer, 2005, 2009; Forester, 1989).

The question of outcomes, such as plan quality and the shortage of holistic solutions, has always been present, from concerns regarding public sector efficiency (frequently voiced by advocates of privatization as a rationale for using the marketplace) to the challenges of maintaining accountability and equity of the public work under private control.

CHAPTER QUESTIONS

1. How were private firms involved in the development of the Disaster Mitigation Act of 2000?
2. Explain the current role of the private sector in local hazard mitigation planning.
3. Describe the creation of a hazard mitigation sector.

REFERENCES

ASFPM (Association of State Flood Plain Managers). (2010). Managing flood risks and floodplain resources. Report of the Third Assembly of the Gilbert F. White National Flood Policy Forum, Washington University, Washington, DC, March 8–9, 2010.

Burby, R.J. (2006). Hurricane Katrina and the paradoxes of government disaster policy: Bringing about wise governmental decision for hazardous areas. *Annals of the American Academy of Political and Social Science, 604,* 171–191.

Chamberlin, J.R. & Jackson, J.E. (1987). Privatization as institutional choice. *Journal of Policy Analysis and Management,* 6(4), 586–604.

Cohen, S. & Eimicke, W. (2008). *The Responsible Contract Manager: Protecting the Public Interest in an Outsourced World.* Georgetown University Press: Washington, DC.

Congressional Record—House. (1999a). H965–H977.

Congressional Record—Senate. (1999b). S11955–S11956.

Colten, C. (2006). *An Unnatural Metropolis: Wresting New Orleans from Nature.* Louisiana State University Press.

CPCU Society Central Illinois Chapter. (2001). Managing flood losses: An international review of mitigation and financing techniques. *CPCU Journal,* 54(2), 75–93.

Disaster Mitigation Act of 2000, Public Law 106-390. (2000). 106th Congress.

Federal Document Clearing House Congressional Testimony. (2000). Testimony Cost of Hazard Mitigation, Capitol Hill Hearing, July 20, 2000.

Federal Emergency Management Agency. (n.d.). *Flood Hazard Mitigation Handbook of Common Procedures*. Interagency Regional Hazard Mitigation Teams.

Federal Emergency Management Agency. (1990). Post-Disaster Hazard Mitigation Planning Guidance for State and Local Governments.

Federal Emergency Management Agency. (2001a). Listening Session Materials: Agenda, March 27–28, 2001.

Federal Emergency Management Agency. (2001b). Listening Session Materials: Detailed Agenda, March 27–28, 2001.

Federal Emergency Management Agency. (2001c). Listening Session Materials: Disaster Mitigation Act of 2000, Summary of Section 322 Mitigation Planning.

Federal Emergency Management Agency. (2001d). Listening Session Materials: Disaster Mitigation Act of 2000, Summary of Section 404(c) State Administration of the Hazard Mitigation Grant Program.

Federal Emergency Management Agency. (2001e). Listening Session Materials: Invitation Letter.

Federal Emergency Management Agency. (2001f). Listening Session Materials: NEMA and ASFPM Comments on the Disaster Mitigation Act of 2000.

Federal Emergency Management Agency. (2001g). Listening Session Materials: Session Notes.

Federal Emergency Management Agency. (2006). Pre-Disaster Mitigation Grant Program. Retrieved July 13, 2015, from https://www.fema.gov/pre-disaster-mitigation-grant-program.

Federal Emergency Management Agency. (2011). Local Mitigation Plan Review Guide.

Federal Emergency Management Agency. (2013). Local Mitigation Planning Handbook.

Federal Interagency Floodplain Management Task Force. (1996). *Protecting Floodplain Resources: A Guidebook for Communities* (2nd ed.). State University of New York: New York.

Fischer, F. (2005). Environmental regulation & risk–benefit analysis: From technical to deliberative policy making. In (eds. Paehlke, R. & Torgerson, D.). *Managing Leviathan: Environmental Politics and the Administrative State*. Broadview Press: Ontario, Canada.

Fischer, F. (2009). *Democracy & Expertise: Reorienting Policy Inquiry*. Oxford University Press: Oxford.

Florida Department of Community Affairs. (1997). *The Local Mitigation Strategy: A Guidebook for Florida Cities and Counties*.

Forester, J. (1989). *Planning in the Face of Power*. University of California Press: Berkeley, CA.

Forrer, J., Kee, J., Newcomer, K.E. & Boyer, E. (2010). Public–private partnerships and the public accountability question. *Public Administration Review, American Society of Public Administration, 70*(30): 475–484.

Frederickson, D.G. & Frederickson H.G. (2007). *Measuring the Performance of the Hollow State*. Georgetown University Press: Washington, DC.

Freudenburg, W.R. (2008). Organizing hazards, engineering disasters? Improving the recognition of political-economic factors in the creation of disasters. *Social Forces, 87*(2), 1015–1038.

Godschalk, D.R., Beatley, T., Berke, P., Brower, D.J. & Kaiser, E.J. (1999). *Natural Hazard Mitigation: Recasting Disaster Policy and Planning*. Island Press: Washington, DC.

Healy, A.J. & Malhotra, N. (2008). Preferring a Pound of Cure to an Ounce of Prevention: Voting, Natural Disaster, and Government Response. Available at http://www.sscnet.ucla.edu/polisci/cpworkshop/papers/Healy.pdf.

Henig, J.R. (1989–1990). Privatization in the United States: Theory and practice. *Political Science Quarterly, 104*(4), 649–670.

Hinshaw, R. (2006). Hurricane Stan Response in Guatemala. Quick Response Report No. QR182 National Hazards Center: Boulder, CO.

Illinois Department of Transportation, Division of Water Resources. (1979). Report on Wilmington's Floodplain Program.

Illinois Department of Transportation, Division of Water Resources. (1983). Hazard Mitigation Plan Illinois River Basin Flooding.

Illinois Department of Transportation, Division of Water Resources. (1985a). Interagency Hazard Mitigation Report.

Illinois Department of Transportation, Division of Water Resources. (1985b). Mitigation Program Review.

Illinois Department of Transportation, Division of Water Resources. (1986). Annual Flood Hazard Mitigation Report.

Illinois Department of Transportation, Division of Water Resources. (1987). Annual Flood Hazard Mitigation Report.

Interagency Floodplain Management Review Committee to the Administration Floodplain Management Task Force. (1994). *Sharing the Challenge: Floodplain Management into the 21st Century*. Administration Floodplain Management Task Force: Washington, DC.

Jerolleman, A. (2013). The Privatization of Hazard Mitigation: A Case Study of the Creation and Implementation of a Federal Program. University of New Orleans. Unpublished.

Kunreuther, H. (2006). Disaster Mitigation and Insurance: Learning from Katrina. *Annals of the American Academy of Political and Social Science, 604*, 209–227.

Laska, S.B. (1991). *Floodproof Retrofitting: Homeowner Self-Protective Behavior*. Program on Environment and Behavior Monograph #49. Institute of Behavioral Science: Boulder, CO.

Lipsky, M. (1980). *Street-Level Bureaucracy: Dilemmas of the Individual in Public Services*. Russell Sage Foundation: New York.

209

Mileti, D. (1999). *Disasters by Design: A Reassessment of Natural Hazards in the United States.* Joseph Henry Press: Washington, DC.

Multihazard Mitigation Council National Institute of Building Science. (2005). *National Hazard Mitigation Saves: An Independent Study to Assess the Future Savings from Mitigation Activities Volume 1—Findings, Conclusions, and Recommendations.* NIBS: Washington, DC.

North Carolina Division of Emergency Management. (1998a). Local Hazard Mitigation Planning Manual.

North Carolina Division of Emergency Management. (1998b). Tools and Techniques: Putting a Hazard Mitigation Plan to Work.

North Carolina Division of Emergency Management. (2000). Keeping Natural Hazards from Becoming Disasters. A Basic Workbook for Local Governments.

North Carolina Division of Emergency Management. (2003). Keeping Natural Hazards from Becoming Disasters. A Mitigation Planning Guidebook for Local Governments.

Pennsylvania Emergency Management Agency (PEMA). (2012). What is Hazard Mitigation? Retrieved July 13, 2015, from http://www.portal.state.pa.us/portal/server.pt/community/programs_and_services/4547/hazard_mitigation/457689.

Schwab, J.C. (ed.) (2010). *Hazard Mitigation: Integrating Best Practices into Planning.* APA Planning Advisory Service Report Number 560.

Turgeson, D. (2005). Obsolescent Leviathan: Problems of order in administrative thought. In (eds. Paehlke, R. & Torgerson, D.) *Managing Leviathan: Environmental Politics and the Administrative State.* Broadview Press: Ontario, Canada.

URS. (2015). History. Retrieved July 13, 2015, from http://www.urs.com/about/history/.

Vale, L.J. & Campanella, T.J. (2005). *The Resilient City: How Modern Cities Recover from Disaster.* Oxford University Press: New York.

Wright, J.M. (2000). *The Nation's Response to Flood Disasters: A Historical Account.* ASFPM: Madison WI.

8

Homeland Security and the Private Sector in Emergency Management Prevention

Lawrence Mason III and Race A. Hodges

Contents

Learning Objectives

- To understand the role of the private sector in disaster prevention
- To understand the growth of the Department of Homeland Security in disaster prevention
- To identify and describe the benefits of public–private partnership in disaster prevention
- To describe the collaborative roles of each level of government in disaster prevention

INTRODUCTION

At the conclusion of this chapter, the reader will have been introduced to the principle of prevention and its role in emergency management. Prevention has become a central concept in the post-9/11 lexicon of emergency management, especially as it relates to terrorism. The private sector's access to resources necessary for achieving prevention-oriented goals, as well as ownership of infrastructure, has provided a prime option for partnership at each level of government. Although these public–private partnerships are an important mechanism for achieving prevention goals, issues with transparency, accountability, and stakeholder disparities still present measurable challenges for emergency managers and policy makers.

PREVENTION IN THE 21ST CENTURY

The rise of new technologies and modern terrorist threats have ushered in a new era of emergency management. The heightened concerns of attacks on U.S. soil, including both minor acts by individuals and actions by hostile governments and other groups, has prompted emergency managers to embrace resources aimed toward the development of preventative measures. The Department of Homeland Security (DHS) defines prevention as "actions taken and measures put in place for the continual assessment and readiness of necessary actions to reduce risk of threats and vulnerabilities, to intervene and stop an occurrence, or to mitigate effects" (DHS, 2007). Prevention is no longer isolated to the idea of physical destruction, as it is now regularly involved with other more contemporary avenues such as cyber, technological, and biological acts of terrorism.

The initial recognized threat of terrorist attacks on U.S. soil was significantly influenced by Pearl Harbor as well as the Cuban missile crisis during the Cold War. While it was an acknowledged threat in times of war, contemporary terrorist threats have changed considerably given that many acts of terrorism can be conducted by single actors or small groups of actors. The added factor of infrastructure access through cyber attacks and biological weapons has increased the abilities of formerly low-level terrorists to cause damage in a wide range of communities, and even to target corporations.

The prevention and protection management objectives, which could be considered a fifth phase in emergency management, underwent considerable development in the post-9/11 era under the direction of the DHS and the *war on terrorism* (Baird, 2010). The antiterrorism goals for a resilient country, community, and government, specifically in regards to prevention, have advanced more collaborative roles for all levels of government and community leadership, and created the need for a vital partnership with the private sector.

HOMELAND SECURITY'S ROLE IN PREVENTION

Actively addressing the threat of terrorism took a noticeable shift following the Oklahoma City bombing in 1996. A series of legislative acts were passed during the Clinton administration in response to this event, the most significant of which was the Antiterrorism and Effective Death Penalty Act of 1996. In addition to legislative action, the federal government required the facility hardening of all federal buildings. Another significant shift regarding terrorism prevention occurred with the creation of the DHS in response to the attacks of 9/11. Leading a new era of emergency management, DHS's mission was to address the new and prominent threat of terrorism. In emergency management, there was a growing understanding of the new influence and need for prevention in the field to engage in modern approaches to disasters and terrorist threats. The evolution of DHS's responsibilities as a central entity managing disasters, both man-made and natural, fast-tracked the principle of emergency management prevention (Sylves, 2008). However, while DHS does play a critical role, the Federal Bureau of Investigation (FBI) is another central agency in counterterrorism investigations. Following 9/11, the FBI shifted away from being characterized as "a reactive law enforcement agency—pursuing suspects after they had allegedly committed crimes..." towards a more proactive agency, especially in regards to counterterrorism efforts (Bjelopera, 2013).

The lessons taken from 9/11 as well as other recent disasters like the Boston Marathon bombing identified a need and opportunity to develop initiatives focused on prevention. Moreover, emergency managers tended to see terrorism as a federal, rather than a state or local, problem. But in the years since 9/11, local emergency managers have been compelled to divide their attention between a new national priority, the *war on terror*, and the "old wars against the more common—and more likely—natural and technological disasters." The National Protection Framework (NPF), an extension of the National Preparedness Goal, is a representation of the new direction of disaster management toward prevention (referred to as protection in this document) and a sustained focus on terrorism. The NPF, as it involves all levels of government, has created an increased need for communication, cooperation, and role awareness at all levels. Specifically, the NPF's wide-ranging capabilities include

- Intelligence and information sharing. Planning and direction: Establish the intelligence and information requirements of the consumer.
- Screening, search, and detection: Locate persons and networks associated with imminent terrorist threats.
- Interdiction and disruption: Disrupt terrorist financing or prevent other material support from reaching its target.
- Forensics and attribution: Preserve the crime scene and conduct site exploitation for intelligence collection.
- Planning: Initiate a time-sensitive, flexible planning process that builds on existing plans and incorporates real-time intelligence.
- Public information and warning: Refine and consider options to release pre-event information publicly, and take action accordingly.
- Operational coordination: Define and communicate clear roles and responsibilities relative to courses of action (Federal Emergency Management Agency [FEMA], 2014).

EVOLVING ROLE OF PRIVATE SECTOR IN PREVENTION

> Because the private sector owns and protects 85% of the nation's infrastructure, while local law enforcement often possess threat information regarding infrastructure, law enforcement–private security partnerships can put vital information into the hands of the people who need it.
>
> U.S. Department of Justice (DOJ)
> *Engaging the Private Sector to Promote Homeland Security:*
> *Law Enforcement–Private Security Partnerships, 2005*

This new threat exemplifies a greater incentive for DHS to engage in partnership in efforts of antiterrorism and disaster prevention.

The history of the private sector's general involvement and partnership in disasters can be traced back to the well-known emergencies like the Great Chicago Fire of 1871 where businesses and charities provided substantial financial assistance to local and state governments (Witham & Bowen, 2007). As DHS has structured the direction of emergency management through continually developing goals of prevention initiatives to combat growing terrorist threats, the need for partnership and collaboration to maintain resiliency has become apparent. The private sector's increasingly integral role in prevention is evident as the development of more modern and radical terrorist threats with the present homeland vulnerabilities become known. Of the many possible reasons for partnership, a few major factors have been outlined to provide a better understanding of what the private sector offers for disaster prevention.

PUBLIC–PRIVATE PARTNERSHIP BENEFITS

Defining the advantages of including the private sector in partnerships for prevention is dependent on the perspective in which the evaluation is directed. For DHS, the partnership is a need and has been for some time as noted above.

> The advent of radical terrorism in the United States has placed great pressure on the law enforcement community. Specifically, agencies have been searching for a way to balance homeland security and traditional crime and disorder responsibilities.
>
> U.S. Department of Justice (DOJ)
> *Engaging the Private Sector to Promote Homeland Security:*
> *Law Enforcement–Private Security Partnerships, 2005, p. 3*

The private sector offers a chance for community leaders and local- and state-level officials to strive toward these goals of a resilient community to prevent terrorism while keeping a relatively balanced level of intervention and independence. For example, the public and private sectors in Boston attributed their resilience in the 2013 Boston bombings to the strong relationships they had developed over the course of almost 20 years. Various public and private organizations worked together to run joint exercises and engaged in efforts to build strong emergency management relationships. Partnership is a useful outlet because the private sector's access to resources is needed to advance a number of terrorist-prevention goals. Specifically, working with the private sector provides an avenue for DHS, local, state, and regional officials to access the following: (1) a large amount of manpower, (2) disaster financing mechanisms, and (3) providing technical support to affected communities. Each of these points is elaborated in the following discussion.

1. *A large amount of manpower.* In the new age of terrorism and its frequency of popping up in unexpected places across the world, accessible manpower is a necessity to successfully implement preventative measures. The private sector is a key factor in providing that manpower. Because the private sector has a heavy presence in security personnel to protect the large percentage of infrastructure it owns, the private security industry is rapidly growing in terms of employment and financial investing, with an estimated market value of $350 million (ASIS International and Institute of Finance Management, 2013).

   In 2013, there were an estimated 2 million private security officers and personnel employed in a variety of roles (more than 1 million employed in security guard roles) (Bureau of Labor Statistics, 2013). In comparison with private security, the public sector's accumulation of security and law enforcement officers may total just fewer than 1 million individuals. Of those, most are local police officers, which totaled 593 full-time officers (DOJ, n.d.). The federal government employs an estimated 120,000 full-time officers (45% employed with the DHS) (Reaves, 2012). As Figure 8.1 indicates, of the federal employees in question, only 5% of this force is actually dedicated to protection and security.

   These statistics suggest that federal and local law enforcement officers are outnumbered and stretched in terms of the officer-to-civilian ratio. The statistics shown in Figure 8.1 and the trending response of local neighborhoods tapping into private security

216

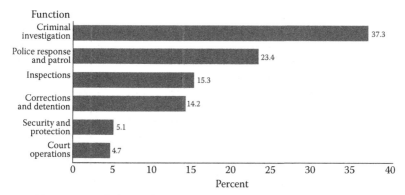

Note: Figure excludes employees based in U.S. territories or foreign countries.

Figure 8.1 Percent of full-time federal officers with arrest and firearm authority, by primary function, September 2008. (From Reaves, B. Bureau of Justice Statistics: Federal Law Enforcement Officers, 2008. U.S. Department of Justice. Accessed on August 19, 2014 from http://www.bjs.gov/content/pub/pdf/fleo08.pdf, June 2012.)

resources present a template for emergency managers on every level that are being faced with similar circumstances.

2. *Disaster financing mechanisms* (Jerolleman, 2013). One common factor exists in every disaster; the recovery will cost considerable amounts of money. Many of the disasters in recent memory have caused millions of dollars in damage, particularly in the case of natural disasters. No greater findings came from the aftermath of Hurricane Katrina than the failure of government to effectively communicate, enact preventive measures before Katrina hit land, and the lack of collaboration on the parts of the local, state, and federal government. However, a silver lining taken from this disaster was the ability for the private sector to step in and provide considerable assistance in providing financial resources.

Beyond New Orleans, Hurricane Katrina had a staggering impact on businesses across much of the Gulf Coast region. For small businesses, the loans that became available following the storm made it possible for the region to get back on its feet with a step toward economic stability (Benefits.gov, n.d.). In 2012, Hurricane Sandy devastated the East Coast and caused millions of dollars of damage, making it the most damaging storm to hit the East Coast in recent memory. Private companies and organizations played a vital role in assisting in the recovery during the aftermath (FEMA, 2013).

217

3. *Providing technical support to affected communities* (Jerolleman, 2013). The rise of the technological era has provided many opportunities for greater resiliency following a disaster through greater accessibility. These new technologies have also opened more doors for potential terrorist threats, both domestic and international, to access a plethora of sensitive documents. If the public sector and DHS are to adequately capitalize on the technological opportunities available, the private sector must have a considerable role in the partnership because of its advanced status of IT security and research. Operational security accounted for more than $200 billion of the total amount, more than homeland security spending and IT security combined (ASIS International and Institute of Finance Management, 2013). For the private sector, IT security has already had significant investment in developing resiliency and protection from technological attacks. As seen in the cyber attacks on a number of large private firms, the private sector has had to remain vigilant and updated in its prevention efforts.

CHALLENGES IN PRIVATE SECTOR PARTNERSHIP

The private sector's main distinction from the public sector is its incentive to protect the investments of the organization and its stakeholders. The 9/11 attacks as well as the recent trend of terrorist attacks have demonstrated terrorist's intention to target facilities and infrastructure that the private sector holds stake in. The private sector's interest in having direct involvement is directly related to business interests. In 1970, Milton Friedman famously noted that:

> the only social responsibility of business is to increase profits for the shareholder.

> C. Ebinger and J. Hayes
> *The Private Sector and the Role of Risk and Responsibility*
> *in Securing the Nation's Infrastructure, 2011*

Although there is a long history of steady partnerships between the emergency management industry and the private sector, the motivations of each side remain different. The need for the private sector's partnership is high, but for the public sector, the challenges of partnership, such as catering to the private sectors profit motive, will have to be taken into account.

In the establishment of these partnerships, the disparity in policies, and cultures regarding transparency and records of accountability has become apparent within the private sector. The public sector and government is structured around the idea of public service and improving upon that principle for the benefit of the public. The option of public–private partnerships in prevention has presented the opportunity to improve the efficiency and overall chances of achieving some of the aforementioned goals and fulfilling the needs of the public. Defining and addressing the risks of accountability present an issue for further compliance.

> If the risks are not addressed properly, the partners may be tempted to avoid any 'relational' interactions in order to minimize the risk of acting outside their prescribed contractual terms.
>
> J. Forrer et al.
> *Public–Private Partnerships and the Public Accountability Question, 2010. p. 480*

The private sector, in most cases, will engage in partnership to achieve its goals. Without an active effort to identify roles, and establish the balance of responsibilities, the public sector leaves itself exposed to potential threats.

Accountability and transparency, mostly because of technology, are a highly demanded addition to the governing process.

> Because public managers are not elected by the people, it is up to elected representatives (such as members of Congress or the president) to ensure that public managers serve the needs of the people.
>
> J. Forrer et al.
> *Public–Private Partnerships and the Public Accountability Question, 2010. p. 475*

Establishing or identifying levels of accountability within the partnership and in the private sector already present a difficult task for managers as outsiders to the organizations. Assuming private sector partners opt not to disclose every detail of respective business operations to governmental partners or the people now being served, the less transparent the partnership and operations become. Since preventing terrorism is heavily involved in information sharing, this can present a considerable obstacle in achieving prevention-oriented goals.

The public and private sectors each have obligations to different groups with possibly conflicting motivations and goals when in a partnership. The responsibility of each sector may be one of the most glaring differences representing the challenge of satisfying the people that the public sector serve and the investments that the private sector seeks to protect. As it is well noted, the private sector's stakeholders are motivated with the goal of increasing profit and protecting assets, which usually are monetary or monetary investments. Moving forward in the partnership, it is imperative for the survival of the partnership on a long-term basis that the stakeholders on both sides are kept informed of their benefit from continued joint endeavors. The proposed benefit of the partnership is based on a quick and timely avenue to access the resources the private sector can provide. Without the support of the stakeholders and their respective desirable goals, the increase of difficulty in the partnership will become apparent.

COLLABORATIVE ROLES

Federal

As the pacesetter, DHS is entrusted with determining the direction and detailing the emphasis of areas of vulnerability. Whether it is evaluated through past precedent, probability, or a privately conducted evaluation, DHS must initiate the process of intelligence sharing abroad and domestically. The challenge that faces DHS and federal enforcement is to not limit the amount of information sharing and the direction it flows. The more fluent the information, the better chance the local law enforcement agencies and first responders have to act and prevent.

> Law enforcement agencies that perceived the risk of a terrorist attack to be higher for their jurisdiction were more likely to undertake steps to improve their preparedness.
>
> L. Davis et al.
> *When Terrorism Hits Home: How Prepared are State and Local Law Enforcement, 2004*

Collaboration across the governmental spectrum is a strenuous task, but it is the central theme in the success of accomplishing emergency prevention goals. State and local law enforcement indicated a need for better intelligence on terrorist threats and terrorist capability; and resourcing of preparedness raises concerns about what public safety trade-offs are being made at the local level to focus on terrorism preparedness (Davis et al., 2004). In an effort to improve the lines of communication, the NPF outlines plans developed with a reliance on intelligence to deter terrorist activities and increase resiliency. Along with that goal is an intended increase in the amount of collaboration and efficiency. Defining the new roles of each level of law enforcement starts with the acknowledgment of needs from each participatory level to benefit those that are expected to carry out increased roles in prevention.

State

Following 9/11, all levels of law enforcement were subject to changing roles to fight the new capabilities of terrorists. State law enforcement have a uniquely positioned role in combating and preventing terrorism because of the overall size of the force, roughly 10% of total police employment, as well as its position between local and federal law enforcement. DHS outlines prevention with a key on intelligence to deter terrorist threats. Specifically, the state has assumed new roles in interaction and intelligence according to a 2005 survey of state police departments, which suggests that states should serve as leaders in terrorism-related information gathering and conduct vulnerability assessments and security planning (Foster & Cordner, 2005).

Local

While every level of law enforcement has a critical role in emergency prevention, the importance of local law enforcement should not be understated. Just as every level has had to adjust to new objectives and goals in the post-9/11 emergency management era, local police departments around the country have had arguably the most drastic adjustment. Overall, the growth of private security was seen through a reduction of police forces across the country. Thus, maintaining a productive and efficient collaborative relationship with private security as first responders to disasters has become one of the most crucial goals for local law enforcement. As such, local law enforcement must remain in collaboration with state law enforcement, as well as stay active and vigilant with its intelligence.

Extending the responsibility of emergency prevention, the inclusion of communities and individuals is an additional benefit to local law enforcement. As seen in the Boston Marathon bombing, the influence of the individual was critical in responding efficiently. Keying in on potentially crucial pieces of information through individual participation is in itself a preventive measure.

221

International Partnerships

On an international level, the need for partnership to combat terrorism through increased intelligence is a necessity. Past attacks such as 9/11, the Boston Bombing, and other attacks abroad have exposed the need for an international alliance to increase resiliency and reduce disaster risks. As seen in the case of the Boston Bombing, the gaps in communication regarding the terrorists between Russia and the United States were critical in possibly preventing the attack. Although Russian officials had initially informed the U.S. government of the bomber's allegiance to radical Islam and his intention to travel to the U.S., information beyond that regarding his activities was not disclosed (Schmidt & Schmitt, 2014). Although the United States is well equipped with resources stationed in many different parts of the world, the Boston Bombing provides an example of how international partnership and intelligence sharing can benefit the United States and the DHS in advancing goals of terrorism prevention.

Advancing the mission of increasing resilience as a nation, useful references of past partnership engagements include the Yokohama Strategy for a Safer World and the Hyogo Framework. These two frameworks both acknowledge and seek to unite countries on the basis of needs and the usefulness of having established preventive measures to reduce the impacts of disasters.

> Disasters, and particularly catastrophic disasters in today's globalized world, can affect not just the areas/regions and countries where they strike. They can also have repercussions on other neighboring communities, areas, and even countries, which serve as receiving areas and host communities for displaced survivors.
>
> A. Sapat and A.-M. Esnard
> *Displacement and Disaster Recovery: Transnational Governance and Socio-Legal Issues Following the 2010 Haiti Earthquake*, 2012

Yokohama Strategy for a Safer World, 1994

In 1994, international partnership was utilized as a tool in the emergency management field to adequately provide a framework for support and cooperation under the Yokohama Strategy for a Safer World (YSSW). This effort gathered international partnerships to address strategies to handle increasingly damaging natural disasters. The YSSW had many findings that brought the issue of disaster management to the forefront internationally;

for prevention and protection aspects, it was also key in detailing that prevention become a prioritized category of countries' disaster planning.

The Yokohama Plan also played a vital role in the introduction of prevention in international partnerships. The outlined principles of how prevention should be involved in the forthcoming partnerships against disasters provided the acknowledgement and stage for emergency managers to incorporate a plan with more emphasis on protection and prevention. For example, the YSSW made the following statements:

> It is recommended that donor countries should increase the priority on disaster prevention, mitigation, and preparedness in their assistance programs and budgets, either on bilateral or multilateral basis.
>
> Disaster prevention and mitigation should become an integrated component of development projects financed by multilateral financial institutions, including regional development tanks.
>
> Yokohama Strategy and Plan of Action for a Safer World, 1994, p. 17

Hyogo Framework, 2005–2015

Drawing and expanding on the findings and strategies of the Yokohama Strategy for a Safer World of 1994, the Hyogo Framework outlines the new strategies for addressing the advanced risks of disasters. Some of the relevant limitations that the Yokohama Strategy recognized included governance, organizational, legal, policy frameworks, risk identification, assessment, monitoring, and early warning (International Strategy for Disaster Reduction, 2005).

Hyogo's key addition to filling the gaps included an invite for the involvement of private sector institutions internationally. Integrating the resources of the private sector was at that time a reflection of the vital role privatization fills in these increasingly challenging times economically.

GROWING TRENDS IN TERRORISM PREVENTION

Cybersecurity

The trends of terrorism prevention are entering a new period of cyber warfare. The term cyber terrorism is now categorized under the *effects-based attacks*, which aim to instill fear and *intent-based attacks*, which are done to further a political or religious objective (Rollins & Wilson, 2007).

In addition, the threat of cyber terrorism is increasingly important to consider as more of the nation's infrastructure (banking, e-mails, etc.) is moved to technological control systems.

Utilizing the National Protection and Program Directorate, which oversees cybersecurity efforts, the DHS can also look to the private sector for preventive measures and increased efficiency in the development of cyber protection. For example, in June 2011, Google publicly disclosed that individuals in China illegally accessed the personal e-mail accounts of several senior U.S. government officials, before this breach even being noticed by the government (Busch & Givens, 2012). The federal government has also launched initiatives aimed at attracting and retaining talented cybersecurity professionals. Since 2010, the federal government has partnered with private sector organizations, such as Monster.com, to establish a verified applicant pool of cybersecurity professionals to fill government positions in this field. Through a variety of competitions and exercises, Monster.com has been able to develop and verify the experience of applicants, with the intention of delivering these applicants to federal hiring authorities through an expedited hiring process (Boyd, 2014). These instance, as well as others, demonstrates the advanced technology resources the private sector offers to government cybersecurity.

Crowdsourcing

The Boston bombing refocused the country's attention on terrorist attacks as domestic terrorism and also reintroduced the possibility of crowdsourcing as a deterrent for terrorism. In response to the attacks, it provided law enforcement with a minute-by-minute timeline that afforded the opportunity to map out the attack and its aftermath. FEMA also has sought to utilize people through crowdsourcing as possible first responders. In addition to the mobile app, FEMA included a *Disaster Report* feature that would allow users to upload photos and incident information (Rockwell, 2013). The trends of crowdsourcing are useful for the point of empowerment and trust placed within the citizens to act instead of wait. That factor of inclusion is critical for creating a resilient community across the nation.

CASE STUDY   Edward Snowden

Edward Snowden, the now former National Security Agency contractor and infamous *whistleblower*, is well known across the world for releasing classified documents revealing copious amounts of U.S espionage activity. While Snowden's actions garnered much attention because of this reason, his actions also exposed the level to which the private sector had gained access to sensitive government documents and as the extent to which private companies were sharing sensitive information with the government.

> Almost 500,000 private employees held top-secret clearances in 2012, giving them access to the most sensitive secrets of the United States, with much of the clearance process itself done by ... the self-same private contractors.
>
> N. Ornstein
> *Edward Snowden and Booz Allen:*
> *How Privatizing Leads to Crony Corruption, 2013*

While the privatization wave has proven beneficial to achieving prevention-oriented goals, it has also increased the number of security risks when contractors are left to police themselves while possessing top-level clearance. Snowden himself was, after all, a private sector employee hired by the technology consulting firm Booz Allen Hamilton. This latter point begs the questions of what adequate safeguards are in place to mitigate to potential risk of allowing the private sector to take greater control in governmental affairs. In Snowden's case, the decision to contract out services to achieve prevention-oriented goals may have resulted in a significant back step in the government's pursuit of prevention-oriented goals. Even beyond American borders, the ability to track and implement terrorist prevention has been affected. An anonymous official working with the British Intelligence Agency's Government Communication Headquarters stated that, "Snowden has been very damaging to our work. We have specific evidence of where key targets have changed their communication behavior as a direct result of what they have read" (Leyden, 2014). By extension, the government will either have to contract out additional services to the private sector to address this newfound problem, or address the problem internally, which may require resources that the government simply does not have.

Therefore, the risk moving forward centers around whether the U.S. government will develop a higher level of resiliency within these high-security clearance sections of government and intelligence organizations. Snowden's impact went far beyond the leak of classified information; his actions have called into question whether there is too much privatization in certain areas of government. As theorized during the aforementioned discussion of accountability and transparency, the risk with privatization lay within the process of instituting and identifying accountability.

CASE STUDY   Privatization of Military Forces

The private sector's involvement in military operations can be seen well throughout history. However, the issue has garnered renewed attention based on the size, scope, and authority to which private sector military contractors (PSMCs) are engaged in military operations in the modern era. The well-publicized war on terrorism following the attacks of 9/11 led to many military initiatives throughout the Middle East intended to thwart suspected terror cells. It also opened the door to what became a gradual privatization of military forces. In 2011, for example, there were well over 150,000 private military personal contracted by the United States to wage war in both Iraq and Afghanistan, whereas only 145,000 uniformed personnel were present (Swartz & Swain, 2011). As seen in Iraq, there were a number of reports claiming American soldiers used unnecessary and deadly force. Most notably, the risk of using private security contractors was made starkly evident during the shooting involving Blackwater security contractors that killed seventeen Iraqi civilians and injured twenty more (Johnston & Broder, 2007). This event, which occurred in September 2007, provided additional strain on an already tiring relationship between Iraq and the United States.

Soon after this event, Robert Griffin, the assistant secretary of state, resigned from his position citing his lack of performance in providing proper oversight of private military contractors. While this incident highlighted the inability of the American government to hold the private sector accountable to rules and regulations designed to protect people in times of war, subsequent legislation has now made it easier for the government to prosecute the private sector when they step beyond these bounds. Despite these changes, the four men employed by Blackwater responsible for the shooting were only finally sentenced seven years later in 2014.

There are a litany of other instances in which PSMCs have violated international humanitarian law (IHL). While IHL was initially developed to impose rules of conduct during war on nation states, the ability of governments to prosecute PSMCs for violation of IHL remains difficult. Additionally, it is unclear whether and when states can be held

226

responsible for IHL violation committed by private contractors, which may provide a disincentive to actively monitor and regulate their actions.

Considering the many benefits of having access to additional forces in certain circumstances, including Iraq and past missions going back to the 1980s, the need for clearer processes of accountability and transparency are necessary as the government looks to more partnerships with the private sector (Thurner, 2008).

CASE STUDY   2014 Sony Entertainment Pictures Hacking

Toward the end of 2014, Sony Pictures Entertainment SPE, a subsidiary of the larger Japanese-based Sony Entertainment Corporation, experienced a massive security breach in which more than 47,000 of its employee Social Security Numbers and medical histories were stolen, as well as a litany of internal e-mails written by top-level executives. Shortly after the breach was made public, the group *Guardians for Peace* came forward taking responsibility for the attack. In doing so, the group demanded that SPE not release the upcoming film entitled *The Interview* (2014), a comedic piece whose central plot involved assassinating the North Korean Leader Kim Jong-un (Stirling, 2014). While not much is known of the Guardians for Peace group, the U.S. government has moved forward with the conviction that the North Korean government was either sponsoring the group or intimately involved with their actions.

As of July 2015, the culprits behind the attack have still not been indubitably verified. A number of cybersecurity experts have come forward expressing their doubts about whether the North Korean government could even mount such an attack, citing a lack of sufficient cyber infrastructure. Other critics maintain that such a massive security breach must have involved insiders within the organization. Nevertheless, the U.S. government quickly moved forward with retaliatory efforts. On January 1, 2015, President Obama signed an Executive Order issuing economic sections on North Korea. Additionally, the North Korean government experienced a cyber attack on their own infrastructure in December 2014, during which the entire county lost Internet connectivity for almost nine hours. While the North Korean government was quick to blame the United States government for this, the culprit remains at large.

The incident involving the cyber attack of SPE highlighted how cyber attacks on private companies can quickly escalate into nation-state conflict. While the tensions between the U.S. government and

227

the North Korean government have been contentious for a number of years, this tension has been initiated almost entirely by governmental actors. The SPE incident introduced a new element into this dynamic, in which the private sector became directly involved in what some have called *state sponsored vandalism.*

CONCLUSION

This chapter has provided an introduction to the principle of prevention and its role in emergency management. Prevention has become a central concept in the post-9/11 lexicon of emergency management, especially as it relates to terrorism. The private sector's access to resources necessary for achieving prevention-oriented goals, as well as ownership of infrastructure, has provided a prime option for partnership at each level of government. Although these public–private partnerships are an important mechanism for achieving the goals of prevention, this chapter highlighted important issues with transparency, accountability, and stakeholder disparities that present measurable challenges for emergency managers and policy makers.

CHAPTER QUESTIONS

1. How are private firms involved in prevention?
2. Explain the value of public–private partnerships in support of prevention.
3. Describe a recent event that highlights the challenges of prevention.

REFERENCES

ASIS International and Institute of Finance Management. (2013). Groundbreaking study finds U.S. security industry to be $350 billion market. Accessed from: https://www.asisonline.org/News/Press-Room/Press-Releases/2013/Pages/Groundbreaking-Study-Finds-U.S.-Security-Industry-to-be-$350-Billion-Market.aspx (accessed July 12, 2015).

Baird, M.E. (2010). The "phases" of emergency management. Intermodal Freight Transportation Institute, p. 9. Accessed from: http://www.vanderbilt.edu/vector/research/emmgtphases.pdf on August 13, 2014.

Benefits.gov. (n.d.). Disaster relief: Business physical disaster loans. U.S. Small Business Agency. Accessed from: http://www.benefits.gov/benefits/browse-by-category/category/DIR on August 19, 2014.

Bjelopera, J. (2013). *The Federal Bureau of Investigation and Terrorism Investigations.* (CRS Report No. R41780). Washington, DC: Congressional Research Service.

Boyd, A. (2014). New site to bolster cybersecurity community, workforce. *Federal Times.* Retrieved from: http://www.federaltimes.com/story/government /cybersecurity/2014/12/22/new%20-site-cybersecurity-community-workforce /20774373/ (accessed July 12, 2015).

Bureau of Labor Statistics. (2013). Occupational employment and wages. 33-9032 Security guards. Accessed from: http://www.bls.gov/oes/current/oes339032.htm.

Busch, N. & Givens, A. (2012). Public–private partnerships in Homeland Security: Opportunities and challenges. *The Journal of Naval Postgraduate School Center for Homeland Defense and Security,* 7. Accessed from: http://www.hsaj .org/?fullarticle=8.1.18.

Davis, L., Riley, J., Ridgeway, G., Pace, J., Cotton, S., Steinberg, P., Damphousse, K. & Smith, B. (2004). When terrorism hits home: How prepared are state and local law enforcement. RAND Corporation. Accessed from: http://www .rand.org/pubs/monographs/MG104.html on August 18, 2014.

Department of Homeland Security (DHS). (2007). *DHS Lexicon: Terms and Definitions.* Washington, DC: DHS, 28 pages. Accessed from: https://dhsonline.dhs .gov/portal/jhtml/dc/sf.jhtml?doid=52981.

Ebinger, C. & Hayes, J. (2011). The private sector and the role of risk and responsibility in securing the nation's infrastructure. *Journal of Homeland Security and Emergency Management, 8*(1), 5.

Federal Emergency Management Agency (FEMA). (2013). One year later: New Jersey private sector gets down to business with Sandy recovery. Accessed from: http://www.fema.gov/news-release/2013/10/28/one-year-later-new -jersey-private-sector-gets-down-business-sandy-recovery.

Federal Emergency Management Agency (FEMA). (2014). National Prevention Framework: Prevention core capabilities. Washington, DC: Department of Homeland Security. Retrieved from: http://www.fema.gov/media-library -data/20130726-1913-25045-6071/final_national_prevention_framework _20130501.pdf.

Forrer, J., Kee, J.E., Newcomer, K.E. & Boyer, E. (2010). Public–private partnerships and the public accountability question. *Public Administration Review, 70*(3), 475–484. ProQuest Central.

Foster, C. & Cordner, G. (2005). The Impact of Terrorism on State Law Enforcement. Washington, DC: The Council of State Governments and Eastern Kentucky University. Retrieved from: http://www.csg.org/knowledgecenter/docs /misc0504terrorism.pdf (accessed July 12, 2015).

International Strategy for Disaster Reduction. (2005). Hyogo Framework for Action 2005–2015: Building the resilience of nations and communities to disasters. *World Conference on Disaster Reduction,* p. 2, Hyogo Japan.

The Interview, directed by Evan Goldberg and Seth Rogen, (2014; Culver City, CA; Sony Pictures Home Entertainment, 2015), DVD.

Jerolleman, A. (2013). The privatization of hazard mitigation: A case study of the creation and implementation of a federal program. University of New Orleans Theses and Dissertations, Paper 1692.

Johnston, D. & Broder, J. (2007). F.B.I. says guards killed 14 Iraqis without cause. *New York Times*.

Leyden, J. (2014). GCHQ: We can't track crims any more thanks to Snowden. Retrieved from: http://www.theregister.co.uk/2014/12/23/gchq_criminal _tracking_post_snowden (accessed July 12, 2015).

Ornstein, N. (2013). Edward Snowden and Booz Allen: How privatizing leads to crony corruption. *The Atlantic*. Accessed from: http://www.theatlan tic.com/politics/archive/2013/06/edward-snowden-and-booz-allen -how-privatizing-leads-to-crony-corruption/277052/.

Reaves, B. (2012). Bureau of justice statistics: Federal law enforcement officers, 2008. U.S. Department of Justice. Accessed from: http://www.bjs.gov/con tent/pub/pdf/fleo08.pdf on August 19, 2014.

Rockwell, M. (2013). FEMA expands disaster crowdsourcing. *Federal Computer Week*.

Rollins, J. & Wilson, C. (2007). Terrorist capabilities for cyberattack: Overview and policy issues. *CRS Report for Congress*, p. 3.

Sapat, A. & Esnard, A.-M. (2012). *Displacement and Disaster Recovery: Transnational Governance and Socio-Legal Issues Following the 2010 Haiti Earthquake*. Risk, Hazards and Crisis in Public Policy, Hoboken, NJ: Policy Studies Organization, (3)1–24. doi: 10.1515/1944-4079.1095.

Schmidt, M. & Schmitt, E. (2014). Russia didn't share all details on Boston bombing suspect, report says. *New York Times*.

Stirling, D. (2014). The Interview. Directed by Seth Rogen and Evan Goldberg. Los Angeles, 2014. Film.

Swartz, M. & Swain, J. (2011). Department of Defense contractors in Afghanistan and Iraq. Background and analysis. Congressional Research Service. Accessed from: http://fas.org/sgp/crs/natsec/R40764.pdf.

Sylves, R. (2008). *Disaster Policy and Politic: Emergency Management and Homeland Security*. Washington, DC: CQ Press.

Thurner, J. (2008). Drowning in Blackwater: How weak accountability over private security contractors significantly undermines counterinsurgency efforts. *The Army Lawyer*.

U.S. Department of Justice. (2005). Engaging the private sector to promote home-land security: Law enforcement–private security partnerships. Bureau of Justice (Exec. Summary), p. vii.

U.S. Department of Justice. (n.d.). Bureau of Justice Statistics. Law enforcement: Local police. Accessed from: http://www.bjs.gov/index.cfm?ty=tp&tid=71 on August 20, 2014.

Witham, E. & Bowen, S. (2007). *Financing Recovery from Catastrophic Events: Final Report*. Washington, DC: Homeland Security Institute. Accessed from: http://www.homelandsecurity.org/hsireports/Financing_Recovery_HSI _final_report.pdf on August 10, 2014.

Yokohama Strategy and Plan of Action for a Safer World. (1994). p. 17.

9

Nonprofits, Academic Institutions, and Their Role in the Disaster Management Cycle

Tara Lambeth, Monica Farris, Susan Lenore Garner,
Sabrina Freeman, and Maggie Louise Olivier

Contents

Learning Objectives

- To understand the four phases of the Disaster Management Cycle: Preparedness, Response, Recovery and Mitigation.
- To understand the role of nonprofits in the Disaster Management Cycle.
- To understand the role of academic institutions in the Disaster Management Cycle.
- To understand the combined roles of nonprofits and academic institutions in the Disaster Management Cycle.

INTRODUCTION

Disaster management, also referred to as emergency management, is a process rather than a single activity. The whole community is a part of this process, including academic institutions and nonprofits (Federal Emergency Management Agency [FEMA], 2014b). This process is best explained as a cycle consisting of four phases: preparedness, response, recovery, and mitigation. Preparedness involves the plans made by organizations to be ready for an event; response is the actions taken by organizations in reaction to a disaster; recovery is the methods used by organizations to recuperate over the long term; and mitigation includes the processes used by organizations to reduce the effects of disaster. Although many organizations play a part in this process, academic institutions and nonprofits specifically perform important roles in each stage. This chapter will examine the responsibilities and expectations of academic institutions and nonprofits within each phase, as well as their relationship to one another.

PREPAREDNESS

Definition of Preparedness

Preparedness is the first step in disaster management. It is an ongoing process of planning, organizing, training, equipping, exercising, evaluating, and taking affective action (FEMA, 2013c). Preparedness ensures that communities, organizations, and individuals have taken the necessary steps to cooperatively respond to a disaster in a manner that minimizes loss and maximizes sustainability.

Both nonprofits and academic institutions participate in disaster preparedness. Like all stages of disaster management, preparedness is a cross-sector collaboration, meaning it is a partnership between government, the private sector, nonprofits, and the community toward a common objective (Simo & Bies, 2007). To this point, nonprofits and academic institutions often work conjointly, with each other or with government or private sector entities, to help with community preparedness.

Responsibilities/Expectations of Community during Disaster Preparedness

The community is often not aware of what hazards to prepare for, or the methods that need to be taken to prepare for these hazards. Nonprofits and universities are often given the task of educating the community about preparedness, and providing resources and training to help the community better prepare for any hazards it may face.

Comparison of Roles—Response of Nonprofits and Academic Institutions

Preparedness and Nonprofits

Nonprofit organizations are typically organized around a mission, as opposed to a strategy. Nonprofit missions include causes like fighting homelessness or ending hunger. Working from a mission standpoint allows the nonprofit to support a variety of programs with the same goal, but often neglects a clear, long-term plan of efficacy (Rangan, 2004). Adherence to a specific mission is the same reason many nonprofits do not participate in disaster management work until after the preparedness phase (Gazley, 2012) unless disaster management is the explicit mission of the organization (Kinzie, 2012).

The Red Cross also offers preparedness in the form of training. This training is provided through targeted programs for individuals and families, businesses, schools, and organizations, and school-aged children. Red Cross training focuses on preparation skills such as assembling a disaster kit (Figure 9.1), developing and updating a plan based on knowledge of

Figure 9.1   Supply kit. (Courtesy of UNO-CHART.)

Figure 9.2 American Red Cross, staging mobilization kits for deployment. (Courtesy of FEMA/Greg Henshall.)

a hazard, as well as implementing drills and exercises to test the plan (American Red Cross, 2014b).

Preparedness training provided to groups and organizations, such as through the Red Cross, is an asset for the aforementioned mission-oriented nonprofits that may be lacking a preparedness strategy of their own (Figure 9.2). This need has created a niche for nonprofits that are direct service providers for other community agencies. These organizations, such as Collaborating Agencies Responding to Disasters (CARD), provide preparedness resources for nonprofits, as well as working to coordinate the preparedness efforts of nonprofits and local government agencies (CARD, 2012).

Similarly, some nonprofits partner with the private sector to encourage preparedness. In Washington, DC, the Nonprofit Roundtable of Greater Washington, the Center for Nonprofit Advancement, the Community Foundation for the National Capital Region, the United Way of the National Capital Region, and several other nonprofits partnered with corporate sponsor Deloitte to create a preparedness website, preparedonline.org. This collaboration is an effort to bolster preparedness for nonprofits as well as comprehensive communication among nonprofits in instances of disaster (Kinzie, 2012).

Preparedness and Academic Institutions

The National Center for Disaster Preparedness is an academic research center housed at Columbia University (Figure 9.3). The center focuses on expanding knowledge to affect policy and practice in disaster preparedness for government and nongovernment systems. They also have training available and serve as a source of reliable information for the media and the public in time of emergency (National Center for Disaster Preparedness [NCDP], 2014).

Figure 9.3 Establishment of the National Disaster Preparedness Training Center at the University of Hawaii. (Courtesy of FEMA/Tomas Kaselionis.)

Columbia University is not the only academic institution with a center specializing in preparedness. The University of Hawaii is home to the National Disaster Preparedness Training Center (NDPTC) (Figure 9.3). The center participates in preparedness by offering FEMA-certified training courses that raise awareness of disasters and innovate response and recovery through the use of tools such as social media (NDPTC, n.d.).

There are many more research and planning centers housed in academic institutions that work in preparedness (Figure 9.4). Other

Figure 9.4 UNO-CHART staff photo. (Courtesy of UNO-CHART.)

examples include Arkansas State University's Regional Center for Disaster Preparedness Education; George Washington University's Institute for Crisis, Disaster, and Risk Management; University of Wisconsin's Disaster Management Center; University of Delaware's Disaster Research Center; the Natural Hazards Center at the University of Colorado; and the Center for Hazards Assessment, Response, and Technology at the University of New Orleans (UNO-CHART) (Figure 9.4).

Research centers housed within institutions are an effective way for educational institutions to do preparedness work. Through the work of the centers, universities are also able to help the larger community. Moreover, the research and training work the centers provide creates opportunities for cross-sector collaboration.

Advantages/Challenges to Adequate Response

It can be difficult to obtain funding and community support during the disaster preparedness phase, as the support for preparation most often happens during or after a disaster. When a hazard or disaster has not occurred, or has not occurred in a long time, communities often forget about the importance of preparation, and feel that the hazard or disaster will not affect them. However, universities and nonprofits can pool their resources to better help communities prepare for disaster.

Collaborative Partnerships during Preparedness

Nonprofits, such as the Red Cross, work in conjunction with academic institutions to provide training to faculty, staff, and students. In fact, the Red Cross has programs directly targeted to schools (American Red Cross, 2014c) (Figure 9.5). Also, Red Cross trainers may use an institution's campus location to provide local training in order to reach individuals in the community. Conversely, academic institutions may also offer training for nonprofits, like the training program available through the University of Hawaii. This training can provide disaster preparedness skills for non-profits who otherwise would not have them available.

In addition to cooperatively providing training, nonprofits and academic institutions can also work together to further the preparedness of the community. This preparedness can be accomplished through any number of programs or activities. One example of a preparedness activity is UNO-CHART's Risk Literacy project (Figures 9.5 and 9.6).

Figure 9.5 UNO-CHART presenting at the Adult Learning Institute Conference, 2014. (Courtesy of UNO-CHART.)

CASE STUDY   Preparedness

Though UNO-CHART's specific focus is hazard and disaster work, Louisiana Language Access Coalition's (LLAC's) is not (Figure 9.6). LLAC was formed as result of a need outlined by the Latino Forum. The group's primary objective is to promote inclusion, services, and access for limited English proficient people (LLAC, n.d.). Working collectively, along with community stakeholder groups, UNO-CHART and LLAC have been able to integrate their missions to provide disaster preparedness information and resources to limited English proficient and nonreader audiences.

Risk Literacy is an effective example of successful partnering between nonprofit organizations and academic institutions (Figure 9.7). The partnering of these two groups allows for a level of community outreach that an academic institution does not have on its own. Also, the resources and expertise of an academic institution are valuable assets for nonprofits that do not typically work in preparedness. Through this type of cross-sector collaboration, preparedness becomes a possibility for even the most vulnerable populations.

Conclusion

Both nonprofits and universities engage in preparedness activities to help the community better prepare for disasters. However, nonprofits may not

Figure 9.6 UNO-CHART flashcards, in English and Spanish, for preparing for storms in Louisiana. (Courtesy of UNO-CHART.)

have the resources that universities do, and universities may not have the community contacts that nonprofits have. When nonprofits and universities collaborate, they provide effective emergency preparedness for the entire community.

RESPONSE

Definition of Response

Response is the third aspect of the disaster management cycle. It follows preparedness in the cycle, and involves "putting your preparedness plans into

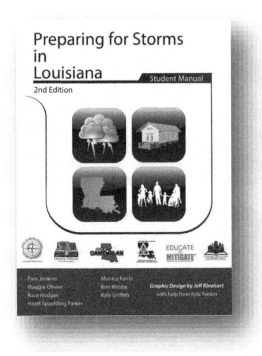

Figure 9.7 UNO-CHART preparing for storms in Louisiana Student Manual. (Courtesy of UNO-CHART.)

action" (FEMA, 2014a, p. A-3-4). FEMA defines response as the "actions taken to save lives and prevent further damage in an emergency situation" (2014a, p. A-3-4). In other words, disaster response is an effort to protect lives and property in an extreme event. And, FEMA points out that "response activities take place during an emergency" (2014a, p. A-3-4). Therefore, the response to a disaster occurs while the disaster is happening, rather than before or after.

Responsibilities/Expectations of Community during Disaster Response

Many members of the community take part in responding to disasters (Figure 9.8). These can include nonprofits, businesses, universities, trained responders, and volunteers from the local area. These organizations have responsibilities to respond to the community's needs.

Figure 9.8 Salvation Army responding in New Orleans after Hurricane Katrina. (Courtesy of FEMA/Win Henderson.)

Nonprofits have many responsibilities when responding to disaster, which often encompass much more than their usual workload. Nonprofits frequently expand to provide many more services than they originally did, in order to help the community. After Katrina, the issues most nonprofit groups were dealing with were "housing, health and human services, and development" (Simo & Bies, 2007, p. 130). The responsibilities of nonprofits can span much more than food and shelter, however. Nonprofits offer their communities a range of services after disaster, including information, communication, resources, food, medicine, and mental health resources, as well as aid to children, seniors, people with disabilities, and the homeless (UNC Center for Law, Environment, Adaptation and Resources, 2011).

The affected communities have responsibilities when responding to the disaster as well. Kapucu (2009) underlines the need for communities to engage in disaster response. Communities can often respond to disasters better than governmental agencies, as they know what they need and are able to act quickly to fix their situation (Patterson, Weil, & Patel, 2010). In other words, communities have local knowledge and access to local resources, which outside agencies may not have. This was the case for the community of Village de l'Est in New Orleans East, a Vietnamese community that responded to Hurricane Katrina on its own, without outside assistance (Patterson et al., 2010).

Universities also support response after a disaster. One of the main responses to disaster is evacuation. There was a mandatory evacuation issued for Hurricane Katrina in New Orleans. After Hurricane Katrina, UNO-CHART administered surveys to city residents who made use of the City Assisted Evacuation Program (CAEP) during the storm. The CAEP is an evacuation program available to those who do not have personal transportation. While most of the users of the evacuation system were satisfied, they did have some recommendations to improve it (Kiefer, Jenkins, & Laska, 2009, p. 1). Specifically, the report recommends that more organizations be involved in the CAEP process, including nonprofits and universities, as they have the local knowledge and means to communicate that would make evacuation more successful (Kiefer et al., 2009, p. 2).

Because there were difficulties evacuating the city during the storm, a group of volunteers formed the nonprofit Evacuteer after Hurricane Katrina (Figure 9.9). The group set up *evacuspots* around the city for residents without access to vehicles. These evacuspots are in place for whenever an emergency occurs, and a network of volunteers has been trained to help get residents out of the city. Evacuteer holds drills and recruits volunteers in order to prepare for the event of evacuation. The group also puts on events throughout hurricane season to promote preparedness (Thier, 2012).

Nonprofits often take over for the private sector and government after a disaster, particularly when those organizations are unable to fulfill their roles (Simo & Bies, 2007) (Figure 9.10). This was the case for Hurricane Katrina. Eikenberry et al. point out that nonprofits and nongovernmental organizations were "compelled to respond in Katrina's aftermath because of perceived and real failures of the U.S. government administration" (2007, p. 167). Part of this is due to the catastrophic nature of the event, and part of it was FEMA's focus on man-made disasters over natural ones (Kapucu, 2009). This can occur in other disasters and catastrophes as well. The

Figure 9.9 City residents boarding a bus in New Orleans. (Courtesy of the University of New Orleans Transportation Institute.)

Figure 9.10 Astrodome in Houston, Texas, after Hurricane Katrina. (Courtesy of FEMA/Andrea Booher.)

government often does not have enough resources to adequately respond to disasters on its own, particularly at the local level (Kapucu, 2009).

The government does not always have access to local knowledge, and nonprofits have local knowledge that the federal government may not have. According to the CLEAR Report, "nonprofits are the most local of all response and recovery organizations, and thus their role is critical to effective disaster relief" (UNC Center for Law, Environment, Adaptation and Resources, 2011, p. 1). And, after Hurricane Katrina, much of the immediate response came from nonprofits and nongovernmental agencies (Eikenberry, Arroyave, & Cooper, 2007). This was due to the large magnitude of the disaster. The disaster was so catastrophic that the government and other agencies were unable to adequately respond (McCurry, 2009, p. 1). Therefore, nonprofit agencies stepped in to respond, as is customary in many disaster situations. This nonprofit-led response often lasts for a prolonged period of time. According to McCurry, "the government depends on nonprofits to provide shelter and care for the survivors in the days and weeks following the event" (2009, p. 2).

However, nonprofits do not just provide for immediate needs when responding to disaster. And, they may end up working in a different capacity than they were before the disaster occurred. The roles of nonprofits often change after a disaster, as they adapt to what their clients and communities need. In fact, "local faith-based, volunteer, nongovernmental organizations have been much more flexible and adaptive in the work of recovery" (Patterson et al., 2010). Nonprofits are not only flexible and

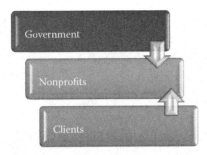

Figure 9.11 Advantages/challenges to adequate response. (Courtesy of Tara Lambeth.)

adaptive; they also exist to work for the good of the community (Patterson et al., 2010). And, they have resources within the community, as well as the knowledge of what the community needs, in order to respond quickly to disastrous events (Figure 9.11).

Advantages/Challenges to Adequate Response

Universities and nonprofits have many challenges to overcome when responding to disasters. They must coordinate with their community and their clients, as well as the local, state, and federal governments. And, they are obligated to help, while simultaneously working through the disorganization and absence of management that comes with a post-disaster environment (Eikenberry et al., 2007). Furthermore, they have limited resources and must garner donations to respond adequately (McCurry, 2009). This often results in anger and distrust from their clients, as they may not have the resources necessary to help everyone all at once (McCurry, 2009).

While nonprofits are helpful when responding to disaster, there are recommendations for nonprofits to more successfully respond. Simo and Bies recommend that the private sector should fund the public sector when responding to disaster, and that there should be more collaboration across sectors when planning for emergencies (2007, p. 140). And, the CLEAR Report recommends more coordination and communication during disaster response, as well as collaboration with a central emergency response organization (UNC Center for Law, Environment, Adaptation and Resources, 2011). Eikenberry et al. recommend that the response be well coordinated, while also providing space for organizations to adapt and make changes as they respond. McCurry (2009) recommends that the government aid nonprofits in obtaining resources, and help with funding during disaster. Busch and Givens (2013), on the other hand, claim that public–private partnerships are the best way to respond to disasters, and lead to more resilient communities. Kapucu calls for a network of public, private, and nonprofit organizations to aid in disaster response efforts (2009, p. 911). In fact, the updated National Response Framework "places a strong emphasis on coordination and integration of capabilities at all levels of government, private organizations, nonprofit organizations, and individual citizens" (Kapucu, 2009, p. 911). And, all of these organizations should be properly managed during the event, as a disorganized disaster response network is not as effective as a well-managed one (Kapucu, 2009, p. 913).

Collaborative Partnerships during Response

According to Simo and Bies (2007), "cross-sector collaborative efforts in disaster response create and enhance public value" (p. 139). However, over half of the nonprofit agencies in Louisiana closed after Katrina (Simo & Bies, 2007, p. 130). Still, the closing of some agencies allowed for the opening of new ones. After Katrina, there was an opportunity for new agencies to open and new collaborations to occur. Often, collaborations were made with local and national universities who contributed to the response.

In fact, universities are not just involved in disaster response, as "the role of the university spans all phases of the disaster cycle" (Ahmad, 2007, p. 1). Universities have access to the resources and knowledge needed to manage disaster, and they are able to facilitate coordination and collaboration among community members (Azad, Anzari, Azad, & Qadri, 2013). Particularly, universities contribute to the response phase of the disaster cycle, as they are able to acquire volunteers and resources (Ahmad, 2007) (Figure 9.12). And, volunteers are essential to the disaster response effort (Simo & Bies, 2007). Local universities are able to train these volunteers in order to help the community with basic needs after a disaster has occurred (Ahmad, 2007).

Furthermore, access to knowledge is essential during disaster response, as "cooperation without information is not sufficient to increase response effectiveness" (Comfort, Ko, & Zagorecki, 2004, p. 3014). Having the necessary information to respond helps community members and emergency managers respond more effectively (Comfort et al., 2004). In addition, communication and networks are also important when responding to a disaster (Comfort et al., 2004). Universities offer the information, communication, and networks that can help communities successfully respond after an event.

Figure 9.12 Volunteers in New Orleans after Hurricane Katrina. (Courtesy of FEMA/Marvin Nauman.)

There are three factors that contribute to resilience after a disaster: grassroots organizations partnering with other groups, education and training, and collaboration between sectors (Simo & Bies, 2007, p. 127). Universities, both public and private, provide education and training for their communities (Figure 9.13). And, they have access to multiple members of their surrounding community, including businesses, nonprofits, community organizations, and other members of the academic

Figure 9.13 Disaster Resistant University Workshop, 2013. (Courtesy of UNO-CHART.)

community. The Disaster Resistant University Workshop, held annually by UNO-CHART, is an example of training and collaboration among university communities. The Disaster Resistant University is a FEMA concept, and a series of workshops that provide a platform for members of the higher-education community and practitioners to come together and learn best practices of mitigation and resilience.

Other than training, universities sometimes act as evacuation centers during an emergency (Hirunsalee, Denpaiboon, & Kanegae, 2013) (Figure 9.14). They have the personnel and infrastructure available to provide help and shelter to the community. According to Fulmer et al., the response of a university "during a catastrophe can supplement, support, and improve the efficacy of the local and citywide response" (2007, p. 76). And, universities often have available volunteers that are willing to help in the event of a disaster (Fulmer et al., 2007, p. 80). Southern University acted as an American Red Cross shelter for evacuees during Hurricane Katrina, and Louisiana State University (LSU) acted as a hospital and morgue during the emergency (Dyer & Chew, 2005).

After Hurricane Katrina, members of universities throughout New Orleans coordinated and lead response efforts (Rubin, 2009). Because they were local, the students and faculty members of New Orleans' universities were able to offer information about the situation in the city, "providing local knowledge and perspective on housing, neighborhood history, public health, civil engineering, and environmental policy, and explaining how these were shaped by the city's distinct politics and culture"

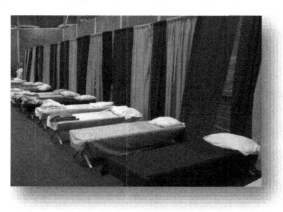

Figure 9.14 LSU Field House Shelter in Baton Rouge after Hurricane Katrina. (Courtesy of FEMA/Liz Roll.)

(Rubin, 2009). In addition, Cornell, Illinois, Columbia Universities, and the Association of Community Organizations for Reform Now (ACORN) worked together to respond in the Lower Ninth Ward neighborhood. This partnership worked with local people in the community, in order to help the community bounce back after the storm (Rubin, 2009).

Conclusion

Responding to a disaster requires volunteers, resources, and infrastructure from the community. Nonprofits and universities, as members of their communities, respond at the local level. Using local knowledge, manpower, and resources allows these agencies to respond to emergencies in an efficient, knowledgeable, and effective way. And, collaboration among these community groups provides an even more effective response to disaster. More funding for these groups and collaboration among them will allow for even more successful response in the future.

RECOVERY

Definition of Recovery

According to FEMA (2011), the goal of recovery is to return an affected community's activities and systems activities to normal. Recovery begins right after a disaster occurs. Some recovery activities may occur during response efforts, and should include mitigation activities during repairs and rebuilding (FEMA, 2011).

Comparison of Roles—Nonprofits and Academic Institutions during Recovery

As previously discussed, universities and nonprofits play vital roles in preparation and response. Because the outcome of the recovery process is largely dependent on what happens in other phases (FEMA, 2011), universities and nonprofits play a role in the recovery process often before it even begins.

While nonprofits are less involved in recovery, they facilitate recovery by operating in other phases (Kusz, 2014). Nonprofits are essential to response and recovery efforts, but are often criticized for leaving too soon after a disaster occurs (Simo & Bies, 2007). During Katrina, for instance,

Figure 9.15 Students from the Missouri University of Science and Technology assisted in tornado recovery in Arkansas. (Courtesy of FEMA/Christopher Mardorf.)

nonprofits were very present for immediate response efforts, but were largely absent for recovery (Kusz, 2014).

Universities are more likely to participate in the recovery process by working with the community to ensure the public and important decision makers have the necessary information to make decisions in such a way that the community can fully recover while incorporating new ideas and policies that lessen the impact of future disasters (Ahmad, 2007) (Figure 9.15).

It is during the recovery phase of a disaster that universities begin researching and reporting what went wrong during each phase of the disaster (Ahmad, 2007). This research is reported and frequently published in academic journals to form best practices for future events, often influencing policy decisions. Universities often lead efforts to educate community stakeholders, to make community disaster plans, and to train and educate the community about preparedness. Many of these efforts originate and take place during the recovery phase (2007).

Benefits and Challenges for Nonprofits during Recovery

A number of new nonprofits emerge in the aftermath of a disaster, their missions ranging from providing laundry services to residents to helping people to rebuild their homes (Kusz, 2014). Although some of these new entities are innovative and fill important gaps, other nonprofits and private actors are often wary of the new agencies and suspicious of their motives. New nonprofits are sometimes thought to be ignorant of the existing nonprofit landscape, believing themselves to be the only entity that can fill important gaps, while ignoring nonprofits that function in neighborhoods on a daily basis. The emergence of fraudulent nonprofit organizations that has become commonplace in the recovery period has increased suspicion of newer nonprofit agencies for government agencies as well as other nonprofits (Simo & Bies, 2007).

The recovery process often leads to long-term coalition building between nonprofits and other public and private actors in an effort to fill in gaps in response, which are usually discovered through research conducted in the recovery phase (Simo & Bies, 2007). Nonprofits play a large role in initiating, organizing, and maintaining cross-sector collaboration efforts (Alesch, Holly, Mittler, & Nagy, 2001). Collaboration can lead to improvements in response and recovery; however, collaboration efforts are not always successful (2001).

Nonprofits that are normally involved in response efforts are often affected by disaster on multiple levels (Alesch et al., 2001). They can be directly affected, incurring damage to buildings, property, and physical resources, and also indirectly affected, using up many of their resources in the response phase. It is during the recovery phase that nonprofits must collect new resources and rebuild their response capacity in order to ensure they can meet the expectations of the community should another disaster strike (2001).

Larger nonprofits, such as the American Red Cross, are often operating in conflict with smaller nonprofits that already exist within a

Figure 9.16 Red Cross and the North Carolina Baptist Men Convention work together to hand out food after Hurricane Ike. (Courtesy of FEMA/Mike Moore.)

community (Kusz, 2014) (Figure 9.16). Smaller nonprofits provide many of the same services as larger organizations, but on a much smaller scale. They are often less known to the public at large, and as a result, are much less often the recipients of large donations. In fact, after Katrina, many smaller, community-based nonprofits found themselves in the position of having to join with larger nonprofit organizations just to stay in business (2014, p. 159). This becomes a problem as smaller nonprofits that know the community are swallowed up by larger nonprofits that may not understand the intricacies of the smaller nonprofits' community networks.

Benefits and Challenges for Academic Institutions during Recovery

Universities play a vital role in information gathering and distribution during the recovery phase. This role is particularly important in initiating the planning process for future disasters. Successes, failures, weak points, and strong points must be well understood in order to plan for future events (Ahmad, 2007).

Universities often work alone or in collaborative efforts with nonprofit and government agencies in order to develop a curriculum to educate the public, including future academic researchers as well as government and community leaders and citizens, about disasters (Ahmad, 2007) (Figure 9.17). In addition, universities often develop disaster research

Figure 9.17 UNO-CHART facilitates a community rating system user group in Louisiana, to help communities better recover. (Courtesy of UNO-CHART.)

centers that specialize in researching the effects of disaster and determining best practices, such as the UNO-CHART and the LSU Agricultural Center. Such research centers provide a place for interdisciplinary research to occur, and provide an outlet for collaboration with other organizations and government agencies in information gathering and dissemination and planning and preparation efforts (Frankel, 2010). These research centers are often funded wholly or in part by grants received from government entities as well as from nonprofit agencies and private actors.

Universities assist in recovery mainly by providing information to those who will then act the information to produce tangible results (Ahmad, 2007). Often, however, this information is not properly utilized, and advice from researchers is ignored in favor of immediate action that might not produce the best results and that is not based on best practices and scientific knowledge. For instance, following the Gulf Coast BP oil spill in 2010, academics from the Massachusetts Institute of Technology (MIT) produced multiple reports containing response guidance, which were provided to government agencies and also to the Senate (Frankel, 2010). Despite MIT's advice to let experts lead the response and recovery effort, BP was allowed to take the wheel, and dangerous dispersants were used to dissolve the oil to save time and money, despite warnings from academic researchers. This resulted in the devastating loss of flora and fauna sensitive to chemicals, which ultimately slowed recovery (Frankel, 2010).

Collaborative Partnerships during Recovery

Hurricane Katrina brought devastation to the entire Gulf Coast region. Universities were no exception (Rubin, 2009). New Orleans Universities, including Tulane University, Southern University of New Orleans, and the University of New Orleans, found that the hurricane and subsequent flooding had resulted in a loss of records and information-sharing networks, destruction of buildings and resources for faculty and students, and even a lack of housing for faculty and students. As a result, universities relied on each other, and formed partnerships that allowed them to share resources in order to facilitate recovery for everyone. Outside universities from Mississippi and elsewhere in the country also contributed resources and volunteers (2009).

Urban planning programs were common among local universities and outside contributors. Cornell and Columbia formed a partnership with ACORN and the ACORN Housing Corporation to work in New Orleans's Lower Ninth Ward (Reardon, Green, Bates, & Kiely, 2009). Though many of the faculty leading this effort had prior experience building coalitions with grassroots organizations in difficult situations, New Orleans after Katrina represented an entirely new and more complex set of challenges.

Statements of faculty and students indicate that they learned a great deal and were able to gather information and make plans for recovery that were vital in the continuing effort to restore the Ninth Ward, a community whose prospects for recovery had been questioned by experts and the media, to normalcy (Reardon et al., 2009). In this situation, academics were able to provide technical expertise to an organization in order to help low-income residents of color defend their neighborhood that was threatened with extinction (2009).

Conclusion

Universities and nonprofit organizations contribute meaningfully to disaster recovery, offering resources, information, and labor to disaster recovery efforts. When universities and nonprofits collaborate, they provide an even more meaningful recovery effort, combining information with community networks to help communities recover from hazardous and disastrous events more effectively.

MITIGATION
Definition of Mitigation

Mitigation is another phase within the cycle of disaster management and is defined as "any sustained action taken to reduce or eliminate long-term risk to life and property from a hazard event" (FEMA, 2013a). Such actions may include demolishing or elevating an at-risk structure, floodproofing, the construction of a safe room, code enforcement, development of a mitigation plan, installation of warning systems, the purchase of generators, hazard mapping, and education activities focused on hazards and mitigation.

Responsibilities/Expectations of Community during Disaster Mitigation

The mitigation of disaster can be accomplished in various ways. The FEMA highlights examples of mitigation successes for various hazards across the country. A portfolio of these success stories can be accessed on their website and queried by hazard and region (Department of Homeland Security, n.d.). In 2005, the Multihazard Mitigation Council of the National Institute of Building Sciences published the results of a study examining expected benefits and future savings related to three FEMA hazard mitigation programs. A key finding of the research was a 4.0 benefit–cost ratio when examining total benefits of certain FEMA mitigation grants between mid-1993 and mid-2003. In other words, for every $1 spent on mitigation activities, there is an average savings of $4 (Multihazard Mitigation Council, 2005).

Comparison of Roles—Mitigation Efforts of Nonprofits and Academic Institutions

Universities play an important role in mitigation-related education and outreach activities. Vulnerable residents need information on hazards and hazard reduction methods to make better decisions about building and rebuilding, potential mitigation projects, insurance, mitigation funding mechanisms, etc. (Ahmad, 2007).

Since 2001, UNO-CHART has provided such education and outreach throughout the state of Louisiana. Through its applied research projects, UNO-CHART assists residents, local and state officials, and communities in better understanding and reducing risk to hazards. Education and outreach efforts have targeted various stakeholders, including owners of repetitive flood loss properties, universities, small businesses, faith-based organizations, adult literacy programs, and locally appointed/elected government officials (UNO-CHART, 2014) (Figure 9.18).

In addition, staff at the LSU AgCenter developed an online mapping tool to communicate risk (Figure 9.18). Residents and local officials use this tool to examine potential flood and wind conditions at a specific location. The site also provides important information such as the meaning of concepts such as base flood elevation (LSU AgCenter, 2014). Such information can help a homeowner and/or builder to determine the height at which to build or elevate a particular structure.

Universities also play a role in mitigation planning. The work of the Institute for Hazard Mitigation Planning and Research at the University of Washington focuses on mitigation and planning. The institute partners with government entities, universities, and the private sector to develop mitigation plans for Washington area communities, conduct hazard identification and vulnerability assessments, and offer courses on hazard

Figure 9.18 UNO-CHART executive workshop on risk management in Livingston Parish, Louisiana. (Courtesy of UNO-CHART.)

mitigation and floodplain management (Institute for Hazards Mitigation Planning and Research, 2014). In addition, UNO-CHART has facilitated the development of FEMA-approved hazard mitigation plans for its main campus as well as its off-campus, university-owned buildings. These plans include risk assessments, community capability assessments, mitigation strategies, and outreach strategies (FEMA, 2013a).

Another role for universities in the mitigation process is conducting research to develop and/or improve upon methods of mitigation. For instance, there are several universities conducting research that focuses on mitigating the effects of wind on buildings and people. Researchers at the Wind Engineering and Fluids Laboratory (WEFL) at Colorado State University conduct research and service projects related to the mitigation of wind effects on buildings and pedestrians (WEFL, 2008). Additionally, the National Wind Institute (NWI) at Texas Tech University focuses on research, commercialization and education related to wind science, wind energy, wind engineering, and wind hazard mitigation (NWI, 2014). Researchers at this institute developed the first above-ground storm shelters to protect people from tornadoes and hurricanes (NWI, 2014). Their efforts in storm shelter research also led to the formation of the National Storm Shelter Association (NSSA), which exists to "ensure the highest quality of manufactured and constructed storm shelters for protecting people from injury or loss of life from the effects of tornadoes, hurricanes, and other devastating natural disasters" (NSSA, 2013). Furthermore, Florida International University (FIU) is making significant contributions to wind research and the mitigation of wind impacts with its Wall of Wind (WoW). This WoW, capable of generating wind speeds of category

5 hurricanes, has allowed FIU to produce state-of-the-art mitigation methods and products (FIU, 2014).

The role of nonprofits in mitigation is similar to that of universities. The Natural Hazard Mitigation Association (NHMA) is made up of hazard mitigation professionals from across the United States. Among its many projects, members of NHMA assist various communities with mitigation planning, training, outreach, and implementation of mitigation projects (NHMA, 2014). NHMA also holds an annual symposium where mitigation professionals share information related to planning, mitigation funding, current community mitigation projects, and related policies (NHMA, 2014).

Another nonprofit with significant disaster-related expertise is the American Red Cross. Red Cross chapters across our nation implement education and outreach programs that increase awareness with the goal of reducing potential impacts to various disasters (American Red Cross, 2014). One such program, Ready Rating, provides resources to businesses, schools, and other organizations. These resources include tools and information that are designed to improve one's ability to prepare for, respond to, recover from, and mitigate the impacts of a disaster (American Red Cross Ready Rating, 2014).

The National Fire Protection Association (NFPA) is an international nonprofit whose mission is to reduce the impacts of fire hazards. The NFPA works toward its mission through advocacy, research, training, and education. Training and education includes a focus on mitigation of potential impacts of wildfire (NFPA, 2014).

There are also various examples of nonprofits established at the local level to address hazard mitigation. In 2005, the city of Deerfield Beach, Florida, created a nonprofit organization with the mission to educate residents on mitigation focused on hurricane risks (U.S. Government Accountability Office [GAO], 2007).

Advantages/Challenges to Adequate Mitigation

While the benefits of mitigation have been demonstrated in various ways, challenges still exist for all groups whose goals include mitigation. The cost of mitigation projects is a significant challenge for communities to overcome. Although funding is available, delays in receiving the funds as well as required cost sharing often prohibits communities from taking advantage of such programs. Despite outreach efforts, much of the public does not have a full understanding of their risks and the importance of mitigation. Universities and nonprofits can play a significant role in education and outreach efforts, but these groups also need funding to implement such efforts as they require a "long-term and sustained effort" (GAO, 2007, p. 47).

Collaborative Partnerships during Mitigation

Considering these challenges, it is recommended that universities and nonprofits seek partnerships in order to extend their reach and provide a more coordinated effort to achieve their mitigation goals.

The Natural Hazards Center at the University of Colorado at Boulder is a leader in coordinating mitigation efforts among hazard mitigation experts. The center's mission is "to advance and communicate knowledge on hazards mitigation and disaster preparedness, response, and recovery" (Natural Hazards Center, 2014). The center supports the sharing of mitigation-related information through such activities as the publishing of a bimonthly newsletter, maintaining free resources such as their website and library, and holding its annual workshop that allows for the sharing and integration of activities among researchers, practitioners, and policy makers from around the world, supports and conducts research, and provides educational opportunities for the next generation of hazards scholars and professionals. The Natural Hazards Center also conducts hazards research as well as provides research funding to others.

Another example of nonprofit and university collaboration in mitigation activities is the Oregon Partnership for Disaster Resilience (OPDR). OPDR is an association of public, private, and professional organizations that partners with the University of Oregon. With the mission to develop a "disaster resilient and sustainable state," OPDR provides planning assistance to Oregon communities (OPDR, 2014).

Conclusion

Although it can be difficult to obtain funding and support for mitigation efforts, it is one of the most important steps of the disaster management cycle, as it reduces communities' risk to hazards and disasters. Effective mitigation efforts often involve nonprofits and universities, and the collaboration of these organizations results in even more effective mitigation.

As the whole community experiences the disaster management cycle, preparing for, responding to, recovering from, and mitigating disaster, nonprofits and academic institutions play an important role in assisting the community throughout that cycle. Academic institutions often provide information and training during this cycle, while nonprofits provide resources and community networks. Academic institutions and nonprofits experience many challenges when assisting communities throughout the disaster management cycle, but there are benefits as well. The community can be doubly helped by the collaboration partnerships of academic institutions and nonprofits, as they pool their knowledge and resources to better help the community manage disaster. Continued collaboration between these entities will result in communities that are more able to successfully get through the disaster management cycle.

CHAPTER QUESTIONS

1. How is the involvement of nonprofits and academic institutions similar to that of the private sector? How is it different?
2. Explain the advantages of collaboration between communities and other entities.
3. Describe the ways in which nonprofits assist in recovery.

REFERENCES

Ahmad, R. (2007). Roles of the university in disaster management. *The Malaysian Journal of Medical Sciences MJMS*, 14(2), 1.

Alesch, D.J., Holly, J.N., Mittler, E. & Nagy, R. (2001). Organizations at risk: What happens when small businesses and not-for-profits encounter natural disasters. Public Entity Risk Institute PERI.

American Red Cross. (2014a). Emergency preparedness. Retrieved May 23, 2014, from http://www.redcross.org/prepare.

American Red Cross. (2014b). Preparedness programs. Retrieved May 23, 2014, from http://www.redcross.org/take-a-class/program-highlights/preparedness -programs.

American Red Cross. (2014c). Programs & services. Retrieved December 19, 2014, from http://www.redcross.org/la/new-orleans/programs.

American Red Cross Ready Rating. (2014). Retrieved December 19, 2014, from http://www.readyrating.org/.

Azad, A.P., Ansari, B., Azad, M.H.B. & Qadri, N. (2013). Role of public sector universities in disaster management using stage-wise resource capability management model. *Interdisciplinary Journal of Contemporary Research in Business*, 4(12), 142–152.

Busch, N.E. & Givens, A.D. (2013). Achieving resilience in disaster management: The role of public–private partnerships. *Journal of Strategic Security*, 6(2), 1.

Collaborating Agencies Responding to Disaster (CARD). (2012). More about CARD. Retrieved May 23, 2014, from http://cardcanhelp.org/about-us/more -about-card.

Comfort, L.K., Ko, K. & Zagorecki, A. (2004). Coordination in rapidly evolving disaster response systems the role of information. *American Behavioral Scientist*, 48(3), 295–313.

Department of Homeland Security. (n.d.). Best Practices List. Retrieved December 19, 2014, from https://www.llis.dhs.gov/bestpracticeslist.

Dyer, S. & Chew, C. (2005). Hurricane puts Louisiana higher ed leadership to the test. *Diverse: Issues in Higher Education*, 22(17), 24–25.

Eikenberry, A.M., Arroyave, V. & Cooper, T. (2007). Administrative failure and the international NGO response to Hurricane Katrina. *Public Administration Review*, 67(s1), 160–170.

FEMA (Federal Emergency Management Agency). (2011). Fundamentals of emergency management. Retrieved May 18, 2014, from http://www.fema.gov.

FEMA (Federal Emergency Management Agency). (2013a). Local mitigation planning handbook. Retrieved December 19, 2014, from https://www.fema.gov /media-library/assets/documents/31598.

FEMA (Federal Emergency Management Agency). (2013b). 508 Final Guidance. Guidance, FU2013 Hazard Mitigation Assistance Unified.

FEMA (Federal Emergency Management Agency). (2013c). Preparedness. Retrieved May 16, 2014, from http://www.fema.gov/preparedness-0.

FEMA (Federal Emergency Management Agency). (2014a). Animals in disasters: The four phases of emergency management. Retrieved May 20, 2014, from http:// www.training.fema.gov/emiweb/downloads/is10_unit3.doc.

FEMA (Federal Emergency Management Agency). (2014b). Whole Community. Retrieved December 19, 2014, from https://www.fema.gov/whole-community.

Florida International University Engineering and Computing. (2014). Wall of wind takes national stage in disaster mitigation. Retrieved December 19, 2014, from https://cec.fiu.edu/2014/05/wall-of-wind-takes-national-stage-in-disaster -mitigation/.

Frankel, E.G. (2010). The Role of American Universities in Large Disaster Management. MIT Faculty Newsletter, Vol. XXIII No. 1. Retrieved January 21, 2014 from http://web.mit.edu/fnl/volume/231/frankel.html.

Fulmer, T., Portelli, I., Foltin, G.L., Zimmerman, R., Chachkes, E. & Goldfrank, L.R. (2007). Organization-based incident management: Developing a disaster volunteer role on a university campus. *Disaster Management & Response*, 5(3), 74–81.

GAO (US Government Accountability Office). 2007. Various mitigation efforts exist, but federal efforts do not provide a comprehensive strategic framework. GAO-07-403. Government Accountability Office, Washington, DC.

Gazley, B. (Director) (2012). Nonprofits and COADs in disaster planning: Are we building collaborative capacity? University of Central Florida Conference. Lecture conducted from University of Central Florida.

Hirunsalee, S., Denpaiboon, C. & Kanegae, H. (2013). Public attitudes toward the additional roles of university in disaster management: Case study of Thammasat University in 2011 Thailand floods. *Procedia Environmental Sciences*, 17, 899–908.

Institute for Hazards Mitigation Planning and Research. (2014). University of Washington. Retrieved December 19, 2014, from http://depts.washington.edu/mitigate/mission/.

Kapucu, N. (2009). Public administrators and cross-sector governance in response to and recovery from disasters. *Administration & Society*, 41(7), 910–914.

Kiefer, J., Jenkins, P. & Laska, S. (2009). City-assisted evacuation plan participant survey report.

Kinzie, S. (2012). Nonprofits launch effort to improve emergency preparedness. *Washington Post*. Retrieved January 21, 2014, from http://www.washingtonpost.com/wp-dyn/content/article/2010/01/11/AR2010011103260.html.

Kusz, K.W. (2014). Markets of sorrow, labors of faith: New Orleans in the wake of Katrina. *Ethnic and Racial Studies*, (ahead-of-print), 1–3.

LLAC (Louisiana Language Access Coalition). (n.d.). About us. Retrieved June 5, 2014, from http://louisianalac.org/AboutUs.html.

LSU AgCenter. (2014). Louisiana FloodMaps Portal. Retrieved December 19, 2014, from http://www.lsuagcenter.com/en/family_home/home/design_construction/Laws+Licenses+Permits/Getting+a+Permit/Your+Flood+Zone/flood_maps/.

McCurry, R.A. (2009). Dependence on non-profits during major disaster relief: A risky dilemma. *The George Washington University Homeland Security Policy Institute*.

Multihazard Mitigation Council. (2005). *Natural Hazard Mitigation Saves: An Independent Study to Assess the Future Savings from Mitigation Activities—Volume I*. Washington, DC: Multihazard Mitigation Council.

National Center for Disaster Preparedness (NCDP). (2014). What we do. National Center for Disaster Preparedness NCDP. Retrieved May 27, 2014, from http://ncdp.columbia.edu/about-us/what-we-do/.

National Disaster Preparedness Training Center at the University of Hawaii. (n.d.). NDPTC. Retrieved May 30, 2014, from https://ndptc.hawaii.edu/training.

National Fire Protection Association (NFPA). (2014). Retrieved December 19, 2014, from http://www.nfpa.org/about-nfpa.

National Storm Shelter Association (NSSA). (2013). Retrieved December 19, 2014, from http://www.nssa.cc/pages/objectives.

National Wildlife Institute (NWI). (2014). Texas Tech University. Retrieved December 19, 2014, from http://www.depts.ttu.edu/nwi/about/nwi_intro.php.

Natural Hazard Mitigation Association (NHMA). (2014). Retrieved December 19, 2014, from http://nhma.info/about/.

Natural Hazards Center. (2014). University of Colorado at Boulder. Retrieved December 19, 2014, from http://www.colorado.edu/hazards/.

Oregon Partnership for Disaster Resilience (OPDR). (2014). University of Oregon. Retrieved December 19, 2014, from http://csc.uoregon.edu/opdr/about.

Patterson, O., Weil, F. & Patel, K. (2010). The role of community in disaster response: Conceptual models. *Population Research and Policy Review*, 29(2), 127–141.

Rangan, V.K. (2004). Lofty missions, down-to-earth plans. *Harvard Business Review*, 82(3), 112–119.

Reardon, K.M., Green, R., Bates, L.K. & Kiely, R.C. (2009). Commentary: Overcoming the challenges of post-disaster planning in New Orleans. Lessons from the ACORN Housing/University Collaborative. *Journal of Planning Education and Research*, 28(3), 391–400.

Rubin, V. (2009). Response to "Post-disaster planning in New Orleans" necessary conditions for community partnerships. *Journal of Planning Education and Research*, 28(3), 401–402.

Simo, G. & Bies, A.L. (2007). The role of nonprofits in disaster response: An expanded model of cross-sector collaboration. *Public Administration Review*, 67(s1), 125–142.

Thier, D. (2012). New Orleans group promotes hurricane awareness. *New York Times*. Retrieved January 21, 2014, from http://www.nytimes.com/2012/03/07/us/new -orleans-evacuteers-promote-hurricane-awareness.html?_r=0.

UNO-CHART (Center for Hazards Assessment, Response, and Technology). (2014). Retrieved December 19, 2014, from http://www.uno.edu/chart/.

UNC Center for Law, Environment, Adaptation and Resources (2011). CLEAR Report recognizes the importance of non-profits in disaster relief and calls for improved coordination in disaster response and recovery. Retrieved January 21, 2014, from http://www.learningace.com/doc/645466 /fdbe73ca4a9118a8eee787d9e71d336b/clearreportnonprofit.

Wind Engineering and Fluids Laboratory (WEFL) at Colorado State University. (2008). Retrieved December 19, 2014, from http://www.windlab.colostate .edu/index.htm.

10

Continuity of Operations and Business Continuity

Sarah Wild

Contents

Learning Objectives

- The reader will gain an understanding of the concept of Continuity of Government (COG), including terminology, key agency players, and core plan components.
- The reader will gain an understanding of the regulatory framework surrounding continuity on a local, state, and federal level, including an increased emphasis on the private sector.
- The reader will gain an awareness of the intersection of between continuity efforts in public and private sectors.
- The reader will gain practical understanding of continuity efforts through case studies that highlight best practices.

CONTINUITY OF OPERATIONS (OBJECTIVE: INTRODUCE CONTINUITY)

The Federal Emergency Management Agency (FEMA, 2015a) defines *continuity* as an organization's ability to perform its essential functions continuously. In the event of man-made, technological or natural disaster, the objective of continuity is to identify essential functions and ensure that those functions can be continued throughout, or resumed rapidly after, a disruption of normal activities. Continuity of operations is critical throughout the public and private sectors, at all levels of government and business. A disaster or emergency situation can disrupt normal operations, leave office or business facilities damaged or inaccessible, and disrupt business supply chains for extended periods of time. For example, a lapse in basic services or disruption of normal business practice can quickly become a public health issue that jeopardizes lives. Consider the importance of trash collection and effective wastewater systems in an urban setting. The average American disposes of nearly seven pounds of trash per day (Humes, 2012); in a matter of days, trash can pose a public health threat by attracting rodents, mosquitoes, and other disease vectors. The elimination of waste in all forms is crucial and depends on the provision of normal public service and normal business operation. The private sector plays an important role in assisting people after a disaster. For example, the prolonged closure of businesses such as pharmacies and grocery stores can threaten lives, especially vulnerable populations who are often dependent on medications and medical equipment.

Since the Cold War, continuity has been of increasing importance to planners. During the Cold War, the concern centered on ensuring continued operation of government in the event of a nuclear war. In recent decades, specifically since Hurricane Andrew in 1992, a shift has taken place in the way emergency management agencies consider business needs. In the aftermath of Hurricane Andrew, small businesses led the charge by pushing the notion of business continuity forward.

On federal, state, and local levels, the focus on an *all-hazards* approach has elevated the role of business in continuity planning and preparedness. FEMA lists nine implications that relate to disasters: threat to the survival of the business, concern for the physical safety of employees, decentralization of business operations, expanding regional impacts where disasters across the country influence local business continuity, concern for the human relationships that a business depends on for its survival, recovery time of zero, renewed importance of critical data backup system, and the inclusion of physical security concerns. From this list, the reader can imagine the far-reaching consequences that disaster can have on businesses of all sizes and all levels of government.

This chapter explores the concept of *continuity* in the field of disaster planning and management. The text identifies recurring issues, underscores the importance of public–private partnerships, and discusses the regulatory framework within which all disaster response occurs. As we will see, continuity lies in the interface—the cooperation between public and private sectors and purposeful interjurisdictional communication and planning. This chapter traces the trend toward the privatization of disaster preparation and response over the last two decades and highlights best practices that save lives, livelihoods, and property.

Modern emergency management recognizes that, since most hazards cannot be prevented, resources must be allocated to reducing vulnerability, as a proactive means to mitigate the impacts of emergencies (McEntire, 2005). In recent decades, the body of principles, rules, and continuity standards in the United States has been influenced by disastrous hurricanes, floods, earthquakes, epidemiological threats, and terrorism. Hurricane Andrew in 1992, the terrorist attacks of September 11, 2001, Hurricane Katrina in 2005, and Hurricane Sandy in 2012 have all done their part to force policy makers' hand in preparedness and future planning for the next unthinkable catastrophe.

To delve into the idea of continuity, some basic terminology is necessary. Table 10.1 provides a description for basic terminology used in this chapter and throughout texts and directives in the field of disaster policy, response, preparation, and mitigation.

LOSS OF GOVERNMENT WITHOUT DECAPITATION—THE CASE OF NEW ORLEANS

In August 2005, Hurricane Katrina, which peaked as a category five, and made its final landfall as a category 3 hurricane (CNN.com, 2014), with sustained winds 100–140 miles per hour (NOVA, 2005). The storm first made landfall in the United States in Miami/Dade County, Florida, continuing to batter the Gulf Coast, and making landfall for the second time at Buras, Louisiana. As the storm lumbered toward New Orleans, many residents remained in the city despite mandatory evacuation orders, in part because 100,000–130,000 (Wolshon, 2002) of the city's nearly 500,000 inhabitants did not have a means of transportation. More than 1000 people in New Orleans died during the storm (Jenkins, Kiefer, & Laska, 2010) and the immediate aftermath of Hurricane Katrina.

The highly televised storm brought unparalleled levels of destruction to Orleans Parish and neighboring Plaquemines and St. Bernard parishes. During Hurricane Katrina, the City of New Orleans experienced the initial 14–17 ft storm surge (NOVA). Compounding the effect, the Mississippi River–Gulf Outlet canal, a tidewater canal that connected the Mississippi River to Lake Borgne, acted as a funnel that intensified the powerful seawater surge. As a result, the back flooding breeched the Industrial Canal, the 17th Street Canal and the London Avenue Canal, (Kiefer & Leavitt, 2008) and caused flooding in the 9th Ward into St. Bernard Parish. The floodwaters went on to sweep a million-gallon Murphy Oil crude oil tank off its foundation, which contaminated much of St. Bernard Parish (Allen, 2011). These compounded events landed a devastating blow to infrastructure of all types in New Orleans, inundating 80% (Jenkins et al., 2010) of the city and forcing 62,000 people (Quigley, 2006) to the rooftops to eventually be rescued by the Coast Guard, National

Table 10.1 The Following Acronyms and Terminology Appear Throughout Disaster Policy, Continuity of Operations and Business Continuity Texts, Reports and Legislation

Acronym	Name	Description
BC	Business Continuity (Disaster Recovery Journal, 2015)	The strategic and tactical capability of the organization to plan for and respond to incidents and business disruptions in order to continue business operations at an acceptable predefined level.
BCM	Business Continuity Management (TechTarget, 2013)	A framework for identifying an organization's risk of exposure to internal and external threats.
BIA	Business Impact Analysis (Disaster Recovery Journal, 2015)	A process designed to assess the potential quantitative (financial) and qualitative (nonfinancial) impacts that might result if an organization were to experience a business disruption.
CAT	Continuity Assessment Tool	Self-assistance guide for nonfederal entities to identify continuity strengths and areas for improvement.
CBRNE	Chemical, Biological, Radiological, Nuclear, or Explosive	Reliable chemical, biological, radiological, nuclear, and explosive countermeasures equipment.
CET	Continuity Evaluation Tool	Facilitates assessments of all federal, state, territorial, tribal, and local government jurisdictions continuity plans and programs.
CI	Critical Infrastructure (FEMA, 2013)	The assets, systems, and networks, whether physical or virtual, so vital to the United States that their incapacitation or destruction would have a debilitating effect on security, national economic security, national public health or safety, or any combination thereof.

(Continued)

Table 10.1 (Continued) The Following Acronyms and Terminology Appear Throughout Disaster Policy, Continuity of Operations and Business Continuity Texts, Reports and Legislation

Acronym	Name	Description
COG	Continuity of Government	The principle of establishing defined procedures that allow a government to continue its essential operations in case of catastrophic event.
COOP	Continuity of Operations Plan (FEMA, 2015a)	The overarching strategy, policies, and procedures required to support the continuity of operations program.
DHS	Department of Homeland Security	Mission: to secure the nation from the many threats we face.
DR	Disaster Recovery	Disaster recovery is the area of security planning that deals with protecting an organization from the effects of significant negative events.
EOC	Emergency Operations Center	A central command and control facility responsible for carrying out the principles of emergency preparedness and emergency management.
EOP	Emergency Operations Plan	The plan that each jurisdiction has and maintains for responding to appropriate hazards.
HSPD	Homeland Security Presidential Directive	Directive governing homeland security policy.
ICS	Incident Command System	Standardized on-scene incident management concept designed specifically to allow responders to adopt an integrated organizational structure equal to the complexity and demands of any single incident or multiple incidents without being hindered by jurisdictional boundaries.
MAA	Mutual Aid Agreement	An agreement among emergency responders to lend assistance across jurisdictional boundaries.

(Continued)

268

Table 10.1 (Continued) The Following Acronyms and Terminology Appear Throughout Disaster Policy, Continuity of Operations and Business Continuity Texts, Reports and Legislation

Acronym	Name	Description
MOA	Memorandum of Agreement	A written document describing a cooperative relationship between two parties wishing to work together on a project or to meet an agreed upon objective.
MOU	Memorandum of Understanding	A legal document outlining the terms and details of an agreement between parties, including each party's requirements and responsibilities.
NIMS	National Incident Management System	A systematic, proactive approach to guide departments and agencies at all levels of government, nongovernmental organizations, and the private sector to work together seamlessly and manage incidents involving all threats and hazards.
SLG	State and Local Guide	Provides emergency managers and other emergency services personnel with information on FEMA's concept for developing risk-based, all-hazard emergency operations plans.
SOP	Standard Operating Procedure	A detailed explanation of how a policy is to be implemented.

Guard, and volunteers in boats. More than 95,000 jobs were lost in the first ten months after the storm, roughly accounting for 2.9 billion dollars in lost wages,* 2.2 billion of which was associated with the private sector to include tourism, port operations, professional services, construction, educational services, health care, manufacturing, mining, finance, and many others (Dolfman, Fortier Wasser, & Berger, 2007).

As the catastrophe unfolded, leadership in Southeast Louisiana were out of reach and out of touch due to various breakdowns in communication; storm-related technological failures, lack of information, and lines of communication. All disaster responses must begin at a local level, from local- and state-level leadership. The federal government does not have the power to dictate local response to states and communities, without the explicit request of local leadership. The situation in New Orleans was such that continuity of government had disintegrated, not only preventing important decisions from being made but also slowing the response from outside of the region. Five key elements were lacking in the initial response to Hurricane Katrina (FEMA, 2006):

1. Communications and interoperability—In the aftermath of Hurricane Katrina, the physical and social infrastructure was compromised, leading to organizational and management problems, greatly exacerbating hardware problems. Interoperability describes the ability of systems or organizations to work together.
2. Unified command—The Department of Homeland Security (DHS)/FEMA agencies involved in the response showed little adherence to the precepts of Unified Command, which calls for incident commander position to be shared by two or more individuals in different responding agencies.
3. Logistics and staging—Adequate prepositioning of supplies and personnel in preparation for Hurricane Katrina were severely lacking, despite forewarning.
4. Staffing—A mass, mandatory evacuation took place in New Orleans in preparation for the storm, causing human resources to be stretched particularly thin.
5. Lack of operating procedures—Due in one part to the scale of the storm, to outdated procedures, and also to response teams with no procedures at all, many procedures were not modern or coordinated enough to meet an event of such magnitude.

---

* During the first ten months after the storm.

In the week following the landfall of the hurricane, there was active discussion in the Pentagon, in the White House, and elsewhere of invoking the Insurrection Act,* which allows martial law to be declared (Allen, 2011). The local authorities such as the mayor and governor were still alive, so there was not a case for federal preemption, even though the mayor and governor were unable to exercise their legal authorities with the resources provided. The situation exemplified the absence of continuity of government as natural and man-made disasters compounded in Southeast Louisiana while the world looked on in disbelief.

In his 2011 Los Angeles World Affairs Council Speech, retired U.S. Coast Guard Admiral Thad Allen described,

> We had not lost the leadership in the government. We had a standing mayor; we had a standing governor... we did not have decapitation,† but we lost continuity of government... we had forces flowing into New Orleans for eight days. Urban search and rescue teams, state 6 policeman there under mutual-assistant pacts, Coast Guard—we saved 33,000 people in seven days in New Orleans. But they were all self-deployed. They didn't report to anybody other than their chain of command back to their original agencies, because New Orleans and the state did not have the infrastructure to accept those resources and apply them to mission effect.

T. Allen
Managing the unexpected: Leadership in times of crisis, 2011

Formidable and deadly problems in the aftermath of hurricane Katrina included levee breaches; flooding; tens of thousands of people stranded on rooftops with no access to food, water, or sanitation; stranded adult and minor prisoners, hospital patients, elderly in nursing homes; sweltering summer heat; and shootings and looting and race-related violence. In the absence of continuity of government and unified command structure, more than 1000 people in New Orleans, mostly elderly, died in their attics or their rooftops waiting to be rescued. Hurricane Katrina

---

* Federal laws reinforce the concept that the federal government should respect state sovereignty. For example, section 331 of the Insurrection Act requires the state legislature or, in its absence, the state governor, to make a formal request of the federal government before the president may send in federal troops to assist state efforts to restore order (White House Report).
† Decapitation: disrupting or defeating an enemy by eliminating its military and political leadership (Brough).

destroyed several large hospitals, rendered many others inoperable, and forced the closure of nearly all other health-care facilities (White House Report). People died in hospitals as backup generators gradually used the remainder of their fuel and life support systems stopped. At St. Rita's Nursing Home, in St. Bernard Parish, Louisiana, thirty-four nursing home residents drowned (White House Report). In 2005, these events unfolded in New Orleans as the world watched their televisions, dumbfounded at the slow response and seeming ineptitude of local officials to provide adequate relief efforts. The problems were brought by the hurricane and levee breaches, but much of the disaster continued to unfold as a *Problem of Government Continuity*.

ALL RESPONSES BEGIN AT A LOCAL LEVEL

When a disaster occurs, response and recovery resources will be deployed at a federal level, but first, operational measures to address emergencies and their immediate aftermath must be implemented locally. This *bottom–up* approach is a product of the American federalist system, which functions under the premise that governments exist to do things that individuals, alone or in free and voluntary association, are not best positioned to do for themselves such as ensuring public safety and providing law enforcement (Townsend, 2006). Certain measures have been put in place to ensure that the federal government continues to respect states' sovereignty even during times of disaster. Section 331 of the Insurrection Act requires the state legislature or, in its absence, the state governor, to first make a formal request of the federal government before the president may send in federal troops to assist state efforts to restore order (Townsend, 2006). In the absence of *decapitation*, as described by Admiral Allen, local and state officials are the first responders to emergencies. Only when the community response capability is exceeded *and* they request specific assistance, are they supported by higher-level governments. For this reason, municipal governments must have plans and resources in place to not only respond effectively to emergencies within their jurisdiction, but to provide for continuity of government and clear lines of communication that enable local and state officials to request the necessary aid in a timely and organized manner. As President Bush acknowledged from Jackson Square in New Orleans in the aftermath of Hurricane Katrina in 2005, "the system, at every level of government, was not well-coordinated, and was overwhelmed in the first few days" (Townsend, 2006).

272

Disruption of Community Critical Infrastructure

Critical infrastructure refers to "systems, facilities, and assets so vital that if destroyed or incapacitated would disrupt the security, economy, health, safety, or welfare of the public" (Kiefer & Leavitt, 2008). These types of infrastructure can include transportation, commerce, utilities (water, gas, and electricity), public safety, communications, information systems, and many more. Often, *interdependency* occurs, which means that two or more infrastructures depend on one another (Kiefer & Leavitt, 2008). Approximately 85% (Government Accountability Office [GAO], 2006) of the nation's critical infrastructure is owned by the private sector, making continuity between public and private sectors more important than ever. One of many examples of interdependency during Hurricane Katrina was that many of the pumping stations, critical to removing water from the city resulting from the topped levees and floodwall breeches, stopped working due to power outages and the consecutive flooding of the pumping equipment itself (Townsend, 2006).

Findings: Eighty-five percent of critical infrastructure is privately owned, placing a premium on effective private sector responses and continuity in the event of natural, man-made, technological, terrorist, or epidemiological emergency.

Natural disasters are not the only hazards that require continuity planning on a local level and rely heavily on private sector responses. The threat or occurrence of terrorist attack, biohazard events, epidemiological events, technological disasters, and nuclear disasters are all events that have the potential to quickly overwhelm local authorities. The risk of pandemic influenza outbreak has long troubled planners, especially in geographies where the occurrence of concurrent natural disasters are likely, such as Louisiana. According to the East Baton Rouge Parish Emergency Operations Plan

> The Center for Disease Control (CDC) has estimated that a major influenza pandemic may reduce the available workforce by 40% for up to 2–3 months, in the most severe cases. This includes 30% of the population anticipated to be ill and 10% additional population who are not ill but will remain home to care for those who are ill, to self-isolate with a household that is ill, or to reduce risk by social distancing. Absenteeism attributable to illness, the need to care for ill family members, and fear of infection may reach 40% during the peak weeks of a community outbreak, with lower rates during the weeks before and after the peak. The

potential for a 40% reduction in the labor force will require East Baton Rouge Parish to adjust essential services and staffing patterns to support these services. A pandemic may increase demand on governmental or non-governmental social services and decrease available social service workforce, thus the availability of social services may be impacted

City of Baton Rouge Parish of East Baton Rouge
East Baton Rouge Parish emergency operations plan, 2005,
Annex O: Appendix 14

Most recently, the deadly West African Ebola virus outbreak has killed 11,164 people with suspected and confirmed case counts upward of 27,225 people in nine countries (CDC, 2014). Viewing the outbreak through the lens of continuity, any epidemiological risk such as the Ebola virus challenges current continuity plans by introducing exponentially more risks and complexity to preparation and response on the public side, but supply chain and food security concerns in the private sector.

"It's a health crisis, but it has impacted food security," WFP spokeswoman Fabienne Pompey said. The U.N. food agency has already provided aid for months to several thousand people, including those in isolation wards and their families. While none of the regulations restricts the movement of basic necessities, fear and inconvenience are disrupting supplies. In West Africa, some one million people in isolated areas might need food assistance in the coming months, according to the U.N. World Food Program, which is preparing a regional emergency operation to bring food by convoy to the needy. The three-month operation can be extended.

Associated Press
Ebola outbreak disrupting flow of goods, driving prices up, 2014

Key Agency Players

Local emergency support framework includes a robust spectrum of public agencies that, in turn, partner with private sector entities and nonprofit groups that provide services and support. In many cases, public agencies depend on services that have been outsources to the private business or not-for-profit sector. Synergy is created when public agencies partner with nonpublic entities to ensure that essential services are accessible to the citizenry. The entities in Table 10.2 are interdependent in various ways, with healthy partnerships often resulting in improved outcomes.

Table 10.2 This Table Shows the Interdependency of the Private and Public Sectors in Disaster Preparation and Response

Privatization Continuity Matrix	Nonprofits, NGOs	Local Media	Academia	IT Companies (Apple, Google, Amazon)	Logistics Companies (UPS, FedEx)
Office of Emergency Preparedness—ideally coordinates all involved groups	Education and social services	Evacuation information	Informed research, current data	Tech infrastructure to facilitate communication	Supply chain and relief effort support
Police department	Building trust, disseminating important information to diverse communities	Evacuation information	Informed research, current data	Tech infrastructure that allows two-way conversation between law enforcement and citizenry	Relief effort support
Fire department	Community outreach, education programs	Information dissemination	Informed research, current data	Tech infrastructure that allows two-way conversation between fire department and citizenry	Relief effort support

(Continued)

Table 10.2 (Continued) This Table Shows the Interdependency of the Private and Public Sectors in Disaster Preparation and Response

Privatization Continuity Matrix	Nonprofits, NGOs	Local Media	Academia	IT Companies (Apple, Google, Amazon)	Logistics Companies (UPS, FedEx)
State National Guard	Building trust, disseminating important information to diverse communities	Information dissemination, evacuation information	Informed research, current data	Responsive systems to track supplies and personnel	Relief effort support
Emergency medical services	Assisting vulnerable groups		Informed research, current data	Responsive systems to track supplies and personnel	Relief effort support
Sheriff's department	Building trust, disseminating important information to diverse communities	Evacuation information	Informed research, current data	Responsive systems to track supplies and personnel	Relief effort support
Health department	Disseminating information, education	Health and safety information	Informed research, current data	Responsive systems to analyze risks and dangers to citizens	Relief effort support

(Continued)

Table 10.2 (Continued) This Table Shows the Interdependency of the Private and Public Sectors in Disaster Preparation and Response

Privatization Continuity Matrix	Nonprofits, NGOs	Local Media	Academia	IT Companies (Apple, Google, Amazon)	Logistics Companies (UPS, FedEx)
New Orleans—U.S. Army Corp of Engineers	Disseminating education	Public information and information	Informed research, current data	Tech infrastructure that allows two-way conversation between Corps and civil society	Relief effort support
Sewer and Water Board	Preparedness education	Health and safety information	Informed research, current data	Responsive, interactive systems to analyze risks and dangers to citizens	Relief effort support
Department of Public Works	Preparedness education	Public information	Informed research, current data	Responsive, interactive systems to analyze risks and dangers to citizens	Relief effort support
Regional Transit Authority	Evacuation, such as CAEP	Contra flow information for evacuations, road closures	Informed research, current data	Responsive systems to track transit, routes, and personnel during evacuation and disaster	Relief effort support

(Continued)

277

Table 10.2 (Continued) This Table Shows the Interdependency of the Private and Public Sectors in Disaster Preparation and Response

Privatization Continuity Matrix	Nonprofits, NGOs	Local Media	Academia	IT Companies (Apple, Google, Amazon)	Logistics Companies (UPS, FedEx)
Airports	Evacuation, such as CAEP	Evacuation information	Informed research, current data	Apps to communicate flight and travel updates in real time	Relief effort support
Mayor's office (economic development)	Disseminating information, continuity education	Raise awareness about programs	Informed research, current data	Connect business owners to resources at all stage of the process, responsive apps that facilitate communication	Relief effort support
Homeless services	Reaching vulnerable populations	Reaching vulnerable populations	Informed research, current data	Monitoring the safety of homeless citizens	Relief effort support
Local FEMA	Preparedness education, building trust	Preparedness information and education	Informed research, current data	Responsive systems	Relief effort support

(Continued)

Table 10.2 (Continued) This Table Shows the Interdependency of the Private and Public Sectors in Disaster Preparation and Response

Privatization Continuity Matrix	Nonprofits, NGOs	Local Media	Academia	IT Companies (Apple, Google, Amazon)	Logistics Companies (UPS, FedEx)
Oil and hazardous materials response—EPA and DHS	Education, preparation, reaching vulnerable populations	Health and safety information, evacuation information	Informed research, current data	Interactive apps, maps and emergency information	Relief effort support
Urban Search and Rescue—DHS (FEMA)	Education, preparation, reaching vulnerable populations		Informed research, current data	Interactive apps, maps and emergency information	Relief effort support
Firefighting—USDA (Forest Service)	Education, preparation, reaching vulnerable populations	Fire evacuation information, road closures, risk levels	Informed research, current data	Interactive apps, maps and emergency information	Relief effort support

Core Components of Business Continuity Plan for Local Governments

The previous section detailed ways that synergy has been created as public agencies partner with the private and not-for-profit sectors. In addition to finding ways to improve services by leveraging partnerships throughout the community, local governments must also focus on internal (local governmental) continuity planning. This includes resilience, recovery, and contingency planning. In Louisiana, the Governor's Office of Homeland Security and Emergency Preparedness (GOHSEP) suggests ten core components that each business continuity plan for local governments must contain (GOHSEP, 2014)

1. Essential functions
2. Orders of succession
3. Delegations of authority
4. Continuity facilities
5. Continuity communications
6. Vital records management
7. Human capital
8. Test, training, and exercise program
9. Reconstitution operations
10. Devolution of control and direction

Additionally, Cashen (2006) suggests the following elements to be included in the development of a continuity of operations plan: classification of emergencies and COOP responses; incident command system; identification of essential functions and critical services; alternate operating locations and facilities, to include drive-away kits; staff/dependent care plans to include personal preparedness transportation, lodging, and food; photographs, charts, roster, and maps; tests, training, and exercise; and plan management/maintenance to include after-action reports.

DISASTER SPECIFIC REGULATORY FRAMEWORK FOR FEDERAL LEGISLATION

The *centerpiece legislation* for providing federal aid in disaster relief is the Robert T. Stafford Disaster Relief and Emergency Assistance Act (Stafford Act), which underscores the role of state and local resources.

The Act establishes the process by which state governors request assistance from the federal government when local resources become overwhelmed due to an incident or disaster (Stafford Act, 2013). Since 1974, the Stafford Act has been invoked in disaster and emergency response, with an average of thirty-eight major disasters declared annually (Townsend, 2006). The Stafford Act ensures that the process is initiated locally, and requires that responses begin at a local level. The Stafford Act, in part, provides for education and training to policy makers with regard to responses to incidents or crises involving critical infrastructures, including the continuity of government and private sector activities through and after such incidents or crises (Stafford Act: 62).

The National Response Framework and the Disaster Mitigation Act of 2000, both discussed in Chapters 1 and 3, provide a context within which government works with the whole community on issues of national preparedness.

National Fire Protection Association (NFPA 1600)

Recognized as the national preparedness standard,* NFPA 1600 sets forth standards on disaster and emergency management and business continuity programs. The document is used by public, not-for-profit, nongovernmental, and private entities on a local, regional, national, international, and global basis. Additionally, NFPA 1600 has been adopted by the DHS as a voluntary consensus standard for emergency preparedness (FEMA).

Homeland Security Presidential Directive 5 (HSPD-5)

Presidential Directives establish national policies, priorities, and guidelines. Launched in 2003, HSPD-5 directed the creation of a comprehensive National Incident Management System, called NIMS, to improve continuity of government by providing structure and mechanisms to support state and local incident managers. NIMS is "a systematic, proactive approach to guide departments and agencies at all levels of government, nongovernmental organizations, and the private sector to work together seamlessly and manage incidents involving all threats

---

* By the National Commission on Terrorist Attacks Upon the United States (the 9/11 Commission).

and hazards—regardless of cause, size, location, or complexity—in order to reduce loss of life, property and harm to the environment" (FEMA). The intent of the NIMS system is to standardize communities approach to resource management in an effort to increase continuity across governmental agencies, law enforcement, and key private sector entities.

Presidential Policy Directive/PPD-8: National Preparedness

In some ways, PPD-8 has replaced the Homeland Security Presidential Directive 5 (HSPD-5). Launched in 2011, the PPD-8 directs "the development of a national preparedness goal that identifies the core capabilities necessary for preparedness and a national preparedness system that will allow the Nation to track the progress of our ability to build and improve the capabilities necessary to prevent, protect against, mitigate the effects of, respond to, and recover from those threats that pose the greatest risk to the security of the Nation" (DHS, 2011). The PPD-8 includes six key elements (FEMA, 2015a):

1. National Preparedness Goal: "A secure and resilient nation with the capabilities required across the whole community to prevent, protect against, mitigate, respond to and recover from the threats and hazards that pose the greatest risk."
2. National Preparedness System—Outlines the approach, resources, and tools for achieving the National Preparedness Goal.
3. National Preparedness Report—Identifies progress toward achieving the National Preparedness Goal and is used to inform the president's budget. Key findings include that the nation has increased its collective preparedness from external threats, natural disasters, and technological hazards.
4. National Planning Frameworks—A collection of frameworks focused on each of the mission areas (prevention, protection, mitigation, response, and recovery).
5. Federal Interagency Operational Plans—Identify the federal government's activities to deliver the core capabilities outlined in the frameworks mentioned above. Plans are intended to demonstrate how federal efforts can work together to support state and local plans.
6. Build and Sustain Preparedness—Four key elements: A comprehensive campaign, including public outreach and community-based

and private sector programs; federal preparedness efforts; grants, technical assistance, and other federal preparedness support; and research and development.

Additional Continuity Regulations That Define Minimum Requirements for Emergency Management and Business Continuity

Through the Health Insurance Portability and Accountability Act of 1996, known as HIPAA, the health-care sector requires disaster recovery plans including data backup plans. The Food and Drug Administration (FDA) Code of Federal Regulations includes requirements for the backup of electronic records, in part to ensure continuity in case of a disaster. The Federal Information Security Act, FISMA, addresses the need for data security in the effort to keep government running during a crisis. The FEMA issues Continuity of Government Planning and Continuity Guidance Circulars to states, territories, tribal and local government jurisdictions, and private sector organizations (FEMA, 2013).

The finance sector adheres to the Federal Financial Institutions Examination Council (FFIEC) Handbook, which makes directors and managers accountable for contingency planning and timely resumption of operations after a disaster event (Noakes-Fry, Baum, & Runyon, 2005). The utilities sector mandates recovery plans though the North American Electric Reliability Council (NERC), not-for-profit international regulatory authority whose mission is to ensure the reliability of the bulk power system in North America (NERC, 2014) and the Federal Energy Regulatory Commission (FERC, 2014). Rural Utility Services (RUS) administered by the U.S. Department of Agriculture (USDA) require rural utility managers to maintain an emergency restoration plan as a condition of borrowing (Noakes-Fry, Baum, & Runyon, 2005).

Each state passed disaster legislation to provide continuity framework in the event of a disaster; Louisiana passed the Louisiana Homeland Security and Emergency Assistance and Disaster Act (2003) and California passed the California Emergency Services Act (Updated 2006). Governors Offices in each state include such elements as continuity of government, the emergency services of governmental agencies, mobilization of resources, mutual aid, and public information (California Emergency Services Act, 2006). As previously discussed, all responses begin at a local level, which includes land use planning and reviews and audits.

CONTINUITY OF OPERATIONS IN A SHARED PUBLIC–PRIVATE LANDSCAPE (OBJECTIVE: UNDERSCORE PRIVATIZATION TRENDS AND IMPORTANCE OF CONTINUITY BETWEEN PUBLIC AND PRIVATE SECTORS)

Growth of Privatization

Over the last two decades, the privatization of government services has increased, with a great deal of federal services being contracted out to the private sector. Since the *reinventing movement* (Osborne & Gaebler, 1993) in the 1990s, which shifted the emphasis of government performance from efficiency to effectiveness, the practice of privatization has grown. This transition had happened in part to address serious budgetary shortfalls on state and local levels through contracting the provision of some public services to the private sector (Carroll, 2014).

Public–private partnerships have become essential in preparation and rapid response when disaster threatens or strikes a community. These partnerships have been successful in the areas of food, temporary shelter, logistics, communications, and many more. To address the issue of food and temporary shelter during Hurricane Irene in 2011, the Maryland Emergency Management Agency exemplified one of many innovative and successful disaster response scenarios that have leveraged public–private partnerships to benefit those affected by disasters (Snyder, Donoho, Menzies, & Davidson, 2012).

> Drawing on prior relationships, Maryland Emergency Management Agency (MEMA) contacted the Maryland Retailers Association (MRA) to arrange meals for an emergency shelter housing 2500 evacuees from Ocean City. "This relationship allowed MEMA to reach hundreds of retailers with one phone call," said Patrick Donoho, president of MRA. A single point of contact for MEMA and the private sector is vital to quick response and coordinated efforts between the public and private sectors. MRA was able to reach out to all its grocers directly and quickly identify a company that was willing and able to respond to the request.
>
> K. Snyder
> *Maryland businesses get their stake in emergency response, 2012*

Logistics represents another important field where privatization and public–private partnerships have transformed the landscape of disaster planning and response. Ken Sternad, president of the UPS Foundation, highlighted partnerships with the Red Cross and other nonprofit organizations such as St. Bernard Project in New Orleans (Sternad, 2012). In St. Bernard Parish, UPS helps nonprofit organizations with planning and logistics. During a crisis event, UPS logisticians help with inventory management, commodity tracking, warehousing, and transportation (Sternad, 2012), which help supplies and resources to be quickly deployed to areas in the greatest need.

The Internet giant Google was in a position to respond to the Haiti earthquake in 2010 after noting multiple sites across the web with siloed, independent missing persons' databases, which required victims, family members, and friends to find and search on each separate missing person database. In response, Google engineers created the Person Finder application within seventy-two hours of the disaster, which has been adopted by CNN, the *New York Times*, and National Public Radio (NPR) (Snoad, 2012).

The success stories of the businesses mentioned above highlight large corporations. Often, corporations with a national presence are more successful at continuity efforts than smaller ones, in part due to the total percentage of assets affected in an emergency event. As mentioned earlier in this text, approximately 85% of critical infrastructure is managed by the private sector in the United States (GAO), and much of that is comprised of small, local businesses. In light of the trend toward privatization of disaster services in recent years, federal government and state agencies have worked to improve continuity planning for small businesses by providing guides and resources dedicated to business continuity. Ready.gov, a division of the FEMA, provides a business continuity planning suite designed to aid in program management, implementation, and improvement though information, testing, exercises, and business testimonials designed especially to raise awareness and help small businesses make continuity planning a priority (FEMA, 2015b).

Additionally, governors' and mayors' offices work to coordinate with and provide resources such as training to the business community through information sessions and workshops designed to bring groups together, foster collaboration, and provide necessary tools.

For example, Tulsa, Oklahoma, annually hosts a symposium called *A Day Without Business*, which is a collaborative effort between local government and the business community. The symposium has shown the successful implementation of public–private partnerships that strengthen preparedness throughout the business community.

CONTINUITY CONCERNS IN THE AGE OF SOCIAL (OBJECTIVE: EXPLORE EMERGING USES FOR TECHNOLOGY AND SOCIAL MEDIA IN LOCAL BUSINESS CONTINUITY PROCESSES)

In recent decades, continuity professionals from government and business have embraced social media as a tool to effectively respond to localized and widespread events such that the adoption of information and communications technologies has

> **Findings:** Social media has facilitated instantaneous two-way communication between responders and citizenry in times of emergencies and disaster.

been perceived as a *game changer* (Mergel & Bretschneider, 2013: 390). For emergency management, the growth of social media technologies has provided opportunity by increasing the speed of information dissemination, encouraging public participation and enhancing collaboration among government agencies, private enterprises, and individuals when disasters occur. Social media is changing the way people experience, react to, and recover from a range of disaster situations (Hondula & Krishnamurthy, 2013: 274) For example, during the Virginia earthquake of 2011, more than 5000 messages per second were sent by Twitter users, and many residents along the East Coast received notifications via social media warning them of the danger of the earthquake's shock waves (Crowe, 2013: 74). During the Boston Marathon bombings of 2013, Twitter emerged as a critical element in providing evacuation instructions and as a reflexive tool to create two-way communication between responders and citizenry:

> Police immediately began requesting via Twitter that people evacuate the finish line area, that there were injured people who needed assistance and that if there were video and photos taken in the area to please send them in. When the bombs went off, the police Twitter account had 55,000 followers. Three hours later, that number had grown to 100,000. At the end of the ordeal, the total was close to 300,000.

> J. McKay
> *Boston's experience with social media is key during emergencies, 2014*

Social media such as Twitter, Facebook, and Instagram has become an everyday example of disaster management privatization and the reflexive and interconnected relationships that emerge between public responders, the private sector, and citizenry.

CASE STUDIES Objective: Compare Best Practices
and Innovative Solutions in Various Cities

Disaster events often cannot be prevented but many communities have developed innovative methods and strategies to respond to large-scale natural and man-made emergencies. The following *best-practice* scenarios are drawn from throughout the nation and highlight cases where robust public–private partnerships have been created over time. In each case study, a high degree of continuity is present; in each case, the citizens have benefitted from the privatization of many aspects of the response and preparation, making the difference between life and death for some, and for others helping the local business community to get back on its feet and lead recovery efforts.

TULSA, OKLAHOMA

By 1987, Tulsa had faced nine presidential-declared disasters dealing with floods and tornadoes within 15 years. By the 1990s, the community was determined to strengthen its preparation and response efforts. In 1998, the city was chosen as a location for Project Impact, a FEMA initiative designed to enhance mitigation efforts (Jerolleman & Kiefer, 2013). In recent decades, Project Impact was replaced with Tulsa Partners, putting Tulsa back on the map for exemplary public–private partnerships. Tulsa Partners have worked with the Homebuilders Association to popularize the Saferoom program (Jerolleman & Kiefer, 2013) and Millennium houses, which were designed to be energy efficient, disaster resistant, have healthy indoor air quality, be handicapped accessible, and affordable (Tulsa Partners, Inc., 2015). These measures, combined with ongoing education programs, downloadable disaster and emergency kits, workshops, and symposiums have helped to reduce the risk of injury or fatality caused by tornadoes. In the process, Tulsa Partners have strengthened the community for the unfortunate event of any other type of emergency scenario.

SAN DIEGO COUNTY

In 2003, San Diego County endured an 11-day siege in which local authorities were quickly overwhelmed by a series of fires that originated in the backcountry but threatened millions of urban coastal residents in San Diego within the course of hours. County Supervisor Dianne Jacob said, "The Cedar fire was the first time in the history of our county that a fire that started in the backcountry actually went into the cities. It was at that point that people realized that what happens in the backcountry doesn't stay in the backcountry and that this is a regional issue" (Jones, 2013).

The largest fire was the Cedar fire, which was ignited by a lost hiker in San Marcos, northeast of San Diego, to alert rescuers (Jones, 2013). While it did alert rescuers, it also claimed sixteen lives (USDA, 2003), consumed 376,237 acres in San Diego County, and destroyed more than 2000 homes (USDA, 2003). Fueled by hot, gusting Santa Ana winds, 15,000 fire personnel (Cal Fire, 2012) in Southern California battled 50-ft-high walls of flames (Cal Fire, 2012) that were burning an average of two acres per second (Jones, 2013). The Cedar fire, Paradise fire, and Otay fire were three of the fourteen fires that raged for eleven days in San Diego County. When finally extinguished, more than 750,000 acres in Southern California had been scorched, causing more than $3 billion in property damage. In San Diego County, suppression costs totaled $43,230,826 (Cal Fire, 2012). Three hundred thousand people were evacuated (USDA, 2003), and tens of thousands remained sheltered at Qualcomm Stadium. The response was disorganized due to a lack of formal operational agreements and interagency coordination (USDA, 2003).

The 2003 fires exposed the region's continuity weaknesses and gaps in preparation. By the time the 2007 fire season arrived, bringing another round of record-setting destruction, San Diego County agencies and organizations had worked tirelessly to make improvements to prevent a repeat of the 2003 fire season. Between 2003 and 2007, San Diego County agencies has improved preparedness, information sharing between responders, instituted mutual aid agreements, and implemented a reverse 911 system (Scanlon, 2008). These changes were aided by the San Diego Association of Governments (SANDAG, n.d.), formed in 1980, an entity highly instrumental in improving the continuity of municipal and tribal governments in San Diego County. SANDAG, especially in the years between 2003 and 2007, worked to develop and enhance regionalism in San Diego County and to create a consolidated, efficient, and effective response to common problems and disasters that do not fit neatly into ascribed jurisdictional lines.

Success in San Diego County was due to an exhaustive list of strategic improvements made to continuity of government, communication with citizens, and cooperation with nongovernmental groups in the region. The 2007 San Diego County Fire Storm After Action Report published by the Office of Emergency Services in San Diego County details the following areas of improvement that led to the much more effective response in 2007: advance preparation, public awareness campaign, updated Geographic Information Systems (GIS), animal services, construction and engineering, logistics, mutual aid agreements, technology and automation, volunteer and donations management, medical examiner, liaison operations, environmental health issues (air pollution control district, department of environmental health), communications, shelter operations, coordination with the military, hospital evacuations, special needs populations, reverse 911, and general evacuations.

In conclusion, San Diego County was able to drastically improve their response to cyclic wildfire events in the region by making public–private partnerships and continuity of government throughout the region a priority. In the course of four years, San Diego County agencies used the tragedies and embarrassments of the 2003 wildfire season to dramatically improve preparation and response in the region. During the fire season of 2007, these improvements withstood a major test and emerged as a success.

MIAMI-DADE COUNTY (HURRICANE ANDREW)

In 1992, Hurricane Andrew proved to be one of the most expensive natural disasters in U.S. history, causing an estimated $26 billion damage in the United States (NOAA, 2012). The storm left 250,000 people homeless and interrupted the operations of some 8000 businesses employing about 123,000 people (Sanchez, Korbin, & Viscarra, 1995). In the aftermath of the hurricanes, the business community worked alongside first responders to mobilize resources for their workforce, including transportation, financial assistance, housing, cleanup, and reconstruction materials in an effort to help employees rebuild their lives and communities.

Since Hurricane Andrew, Miami-Dade County has emerged as a leader in local continuity efforts. Launched in 2007, the Miami-Dade Business Recovery Program is a county-led public–private collaboration with close support from Florida International University

289

with the purpose of ensuring private sector emergency preparedness, response, recovery, and mitigation (Business Recovery, 2014).
The Business Recovery Program has grown to include an expanding list of organizations inclusive of solid waste management, public
safety, human services, utilities, National Weather Service, and more.
Business Recovery Program goals have been to

- Develop symbiotic relationships where businesses benefit from
  being able to open their doors quickly after a disaster
- Build a disaster-resilient private sector
- Create and maintain a perpetual network of private and public
  sector participants (FEMA, 2014)

By working together in this way, information can be quickly
shared between the private and public sectors, which facilitates
emergency management response and enables businesses to make
necessary decisions that ensure continuity of operations during and
following any type of hazard.

Additionally, Miami-Dade County utilizes GIS through ESRI (ESRI,
2015) applications to identify risks, a particularly helpful feature considering the danger of flooding in Miami-Dade County. If a GIS map
shows that a specific area is particularly prone to flooding, the county
might consider constructing a new canal. In an interview with Soheila
Ajabshir, GIS manager for the Miami-Dade County Department of
Emergency Management, "We've learned that if we spend a few million (dollars) in advance, we can save the insurers and the county millions" (Geospatial, 2014). Additionally, Miami-Dade County uses GIS
maps to track *repetitive loss* claims, in this case properties marked as red
flag for insurance fraud. In conclusion, after Hurricane Andrew, Miami-
Dade County was able to improve disaster preparedness in the region
through creative and reflexive public–private partnerships to improve
continuity among stakeholders in the community.

SUMMARY

Over the last two decades, the privatization of government services
has increased, with a great deal of federal services being contracted
out to the private sector. This trend continues to make public–private

partnerships essential in preparation and rapid response when disaster threatens or strikes a community. As discussed in the case of New Orleans, an effective preparedness system should ensure that all levels of government interface effectively to keep people safe and secure through purposeful interjurisdictional communication and planning. The threat or occurrence of terrorist attack, biohazard events, epidemiological events, technological disasters, and nuclear disasters are all events that have the potential to quickly overwhelm local authorities, making partnerships between public entities and the private sector vital. When a disaster occurs, response and recovery resources will be deployed at a federal level, but first, operational measures to address emergencies must be implemented locally.

CHAPTER QUESTIONS

1. Explain the difference(s) between continuity of government and business continuity.
2. Describe two roles of the private sector in disaster preparation and response.
3. What are three advantages to communities forming public–private partnerships to prepare for disasters?
4. List five of the ten necessary components for local government business continuity plans and provide a local example for each.
5. How does the American federalist system affect disaster response on a local level?
6. How does the private ownership of the majority of critical infrastructure affect disaster preparation?
7. Describe three key pieces of disaster policy legislation and any impact they may have on continuity between the public and private sectors.
8. Chapter 10 lists various case studies that list best practices for continuity in disaster response. Provide a best-practice case study for your locality or state that illustrates continuity through public–private partnerships (one to two paragraphs).
9. Provide three emerging uses for technology and social media in addressing continuity processes during disasters.
10. Over the past two decades, has the privatization of government services increased or decreased? Please explain any important implications.

REFERENCES

Allen, T. (Director). (2011). Managing the unexpected: Leadership in times of crisis. Los Angeles World Affairs Council. Lecture conducted from Los Angeles World Affairs Council, Los Angeles.

Associated Press. (2014). Ebola outbreak disrupting flow of goods, driving prices up. *Continuity Insights*. Retrieved August 23, 2014, from http://www.continuityinsights.com/news/2014/08/ebola-outbreak-disrupting-flow-goods-driving-prices.

Business Recovery—Miami-Dade County. (2014). Retrieved September 14, 2014, from http://www.miamidade.gov/fire/business-recovery.asp.

Cal Fire. (2012). Fire Protection. Retrieved July 13, 2015 from http://www.fire.ca.gov/fire_protection/fire_protection_2003_siege_video.php.

California Emergency Services Act. (Updated 2006). Office of Emergency Services California. Retrieved August 19, 2014, from http://hazardmitigation.calema.ca.gov/docs/ESA-all8-06-final.pdf.

Carroll, J. (2014). Private delivery of public services, 20 years on. *PA TIMES Online*. Retrieved July 26, 2014, from http://patimes.org/private-delivery-public-services-20-years/.

Cashen, K. (2006). *A Compilation of Necessary Elements for a Local Government Continuity of Operations Plan.* Monterrey, CA: Navy Postgraduate School.

Centers for Disease Control and Prevention. (2014). 2014 Ebola outbreak in West Africa. Retrieved August 23, 2014, from http://www.cdc.gov/vhf/ebola/outbreaks/2014-west-africa/index.html.

City of Baton Rouge Parish of East Baton Rouge. (2005). East Baton Rouge Parish emergency operations plan. Retrieved August 23, 2014, from http://brgov.com/dept/oep/plan.asp#Table of Contents.

CNN.com. (2014). Hurricane Katrina statistics fast facts. Retrieved January 13, 2015, from http://www.cnn.com/2013/08/23/us/hurricane-katrina-statistics-fast-facts/.

Crowe, A. (2013). *Leadership in the Open a New Paradigm in Emergency Management.* Hoboken, NJ: CRC Press.

Department of Homeland Security (DHS). (2011). Presidential Policy Directive/PPD-8: National Preparedness. Retrieved July 13, 2015 from http://www.dhs.gov/presidential-policy-directive-8-national-preparedness.

Disaster Recovery Journal. (2015). Retrieved July 12, 2015 from http://www.drj.com/resources/tools/glossary-2.html.

Dolfman, M., Fortier Wasser, S. & Berger, B. (2007). The effects of Hurricane Katrina on the New Orleans economy. Retrieved January 13, 2015, from http://www.bls.gov/opub/mlr/2007/06/art1full.pdf.

ESRI. (2015). Retrieved July 13, 2015 from http://www.esri.com.

Federal Emergency Management Agency. (2006). Proceedings of the DHS/FEMA Initial Response Hotwash. Retrieved Aug 11, 2015 from https://www.hsdl.org/?view&did=467679.

Federal Emergency Management Agency (FEMA). (2007). Big City Partnership–Miami-Dade County. Retrieved September 14, 2014, from http://www.fema .gov/pdf/privatesector/miami_dade_p.pdf.

Federal Emergency Management Agency (FEMA). (2009). Continuity Guidance Circular 1 States, Territories, Tribal, and Local Government Jurisdictions and Private Sector Organizations. Retrieved July 26, 2014, from http:// www.fema.gov/pdf/about/org/ncp/coop/continuity_guidance_circular .pdf.

Federal Emergency Management Agency (FEMA). (2013). What is Critical Infrastructure? Retrieved July 12, 2015 from http://www.dhs.gov/what -critical-infrastructure.

Federal Emergency Management Agency (FEMA). (2014). What is continuity of operations? Information brochure. Retrieved July 26, 2014, from http://www .fema.gov/media-library/assets/document/98748.

Federal Emergency Management Agency (FEMA). (2015a). Continuity of Operations. Retrieved July 12, 2015 from http://www.fema.gov/continuity-operations.

Federal Emergency Management Agency (FEMA). (2015b). Ready.gov. Retrieved July 13, 2015 from http://www.ready.gov.

Federal Energy Regulatory Commission (FERC). (2014). Retrieved August 11, 2014, from http://www.ferc.gov/.

Geospatial. (2014). Miami-Dade County harnesses GIS data. *Government Technology*. Retrieved September 14, 2014, from http://www.govtech.com /geospatial/Miami-Dade-County-Harnesses-GIS.html.

Government Accountability Office (GAO). (2006). Critical infrastructure protection—Progress coordinating government and private sector efforts varies by sectors' characteristics. Retrieved August 16, 2014, from http://www.gao.gov/ assets/260/252603.pdf.

Governor's Office of Homeland Security & Emergency Preparedness (GOHSEP), State of Louisiana. (2014). Retrieved August 23, 2014, from http://www .getagameplan.org/planBusiness.htm.

Hondula, D.M. & Krishnamurthy, R. (2014). Emergency management in the era of social media. *Public Administration Review*, 74(2), 274–277.

Humes, E. (2012). Grappling with a Garbage Glut. Retrieved January 13, 2015, from http://www.wsj.com/articles/SB10001424052702304444604577337702024537204.

Jenkins, P., Kiefer, J.J. & Laska, S. (2010). "Attending to the Forgotten: The Elderly, Collaborative Practice, and Evacuation." Strategic Collaboration in Public and Nonprofit Administration: A Practice-Based Approach to Solving Shared Problems. Ed. Dorothy Norris-Tirell. Washington, DC: Taylor & Francis.

Jerolleman, A. & Kiefer, J.J. (2013). *Mitigation and Emergency Management. Natural Hazard Mitigation*. Boca Raton, FL: CRC Press, 25.

Jones, H. (2013). Cedar fire's lessons, 10 years later. U-T San Diego. Retrieved August 22, 2014, from http://www.utsandiego.com/news/2013/Oct/24/wild fire-cedar-anniversary-fire/.

293

Kiefer, J.J. & Leavitt, W.M. (2008). Infrastructure Interdependency and the Creation of a Normal Disaster the Case of Hurricane Katrina, and the City of New Orleans. *Public Works Management and Policy*, 38, 286–306.

Louisiana Homeland Security and Emergency Assistance and Disaster Act. (2003). Governors Office of Homeland Security and Emergency Preparedness. Retrieved August 20, 2014, from http://www.gohsep.la.gov/legal/lhsaea.pdf.

McEntire, D.A. (2005). Why vulnerability matters: Exploring the merit of an inclusive disaster reduction concept. *Disaster Prevention and Management*, 14(2), 206–222.

McKay, J. (2014). Boston's experience with social media is key during emergencies. Retrieved August 23, 2014, from http://www.emergencymgmt.com/training/Bostons-Experience-Social-Media.html.

Mergel, I. & Bretschneider, S.I. (2013). A three-stage adoption process for social media use in government. *Public Administration Review*, 73(3), 390–400.

National Oceanic and Atmospheric Administration (NOAA). (2012). Hurricane Andrew. Retrieved July 13, 2015 from http://www.srh.noaa.gov/mfl/?n=andrew.

Noakes-Fry, K., Baum, C. & Runyon, B. (2005). Laws influence business continuity and disaster recovery planning among industries. Retrieved August 16, 2014, from https://www.gartner.com/doc/483265/laws-influence-business-continuity-disaster.

North American Electric Reliability Council (NERC). (2014). North American Electric Reliability Corporation. Retrieved August 24, 2014, from http://www.nerc.com/Pages/default.aspx.

NOVA. (2005). Storm That Drowned a City. Retrieved July 12, 2015 from http://www.pbs.org/wgbh/nova/earth/storm-that-drowned-city.html.

Office of Emergency Services County of San Diego. (2007). 2007 San Diego County fire storm after action report. Retrieved August 20, 2014, from http://www.sandiegocounty.gov/oes/docs/2007_SanDiego_Fire_AAR_Main_Document_FINAL.pdf.

Osborne, D. & Gaebler, T. (1993). Reinventing government: How the entrepreneurial spirit is transforming the public sector. New York: Plume.

Quigley, B. (2006). Six Months after Katrina: Who Was Left Behind. Retrieved June 6, 2015.

Ready business mentoring guide—Preparing small businesses for emergencies (2011). *Ready.gov*. Retrieved August 22, 2014, from http://www.ready.gov/document/ready-business-mentoring-guide-working-small-businesses-prepare-emergencies.

Robert T. Stafford Disaster Relief and Emergency Assistance Act, as Amended. (2013). Retrieved August 18, 2014, from https://www.fema.gov/media-library/assets/documents/15271?fromSearch=fromsearch&id=3564.

Sanchez, J.I., Korbin, W.P. & Viscarra D.M. (1995). Corporate support in the aftermath of a natural disaster: Effects on employee strains. *Academy of Management Journal*, 38(2), 504–521.

SANDAG. (n.d.). History. San Diego's Regional Planning Agency. Retrieved August 22, 2014, from http://www.sandag.org/index.asp?fuseaction=about .history.

Scanlon, P. (2008). Information sharing during the San Diego Wildfires of 2007. *Police Chief Magazine.* Retrieved August 22, 2014, from http://www .policechiefmagazine.org/magazine/index.cfm?fuseaction=display _arch&article_id=1468&issue_id=42008.

Snoad, N. (2012). Google's crisis response initiative. The role of business in disaster response. Retrieved August 22, 2014, from http://www.uschamberfoundation .org/sites/default/files/publication/ccc/Role%20of%20Business%20in%20 Disaster%20Response.pdf. 34 p.

Snyder, K., Donoho, P., Menzies, J. & Davidson, O. (2012). Maryland businesses get their stake in emergency response. The role of business in disaster response. Retrieved August 22, 2014, from https://www.uschamber.com/sites/default/fil.

Sternad, K. (2012). We love the logistics of disaster response. The role of business in disaster response. Retrieved August 22, 2014, from hhttp://www .uschamberfoundation.org/sites/default/files/publication/ccc/Role%20 of%20Business%20in%20Disaster%20Response.pdf. 20 p.

TechTarget. (2013). Retrieved July 12, 2015 from http://searchcio.techtarget.com /definition/business-continuity-management-BCM.

Townsend, F. (2006). The federal response to Hurricane Katrina. Lessons learned. The White House. Retrieved August 17, 2014, from http://www.floods.org/PDF /Katrina_Lessons_Learned_0206.pdf.

Tulsa Partners, Inc. (2015). Retrieved July 13, 2015 from http://tulsapartners.org/tpi/.

Wolshon, B. (2002). Planning for the evacuation of New Orleans. *ITE Journal, 72*(2), 44–46.

U.S. Department of Agriculture (USDA). (2003). The 2003 San Diego County Fire Siege Fire Safety Review. United States Department of Agriculture, 1. Retrieved August 20, 2014, from http://www.fs.usda.gov/Internet/FSE _DOCUMENTS/stelprdb5297020.pdf.

INDEX

Page numbers followed by f denote figures; t denote tables; n denote notes.

309

Printed in the United States
by Baker & Taylor Publisher Services